The Post–Cold War Trading System

Who's on First?

Sylvia Ostry

A Twentieth Century Fund Book

The University of Chicago Press • Chicago and London

SYLVIA OSTRY is chancellor of the University of Waterloo and chair of the Centre for International Studies at the University of Toronto. She is the former Canadian ambassador to the Uruguay Round of the General Agreement on Tariffs and Trade.

The University of Chicago Press, Chicago 60637
The University of Chicago Press, Ltd., London
© 1997 by The Twentieth Century Fund
All rights reserved. Published 1997
Printed in the United States of America
06 05 04 03 02 01 00 99 98 97   1 2 3 4 5

ISBN: 0-226-63789-1 (cloth)
ISBN: 0-226-63790-5 (paper)

Library of Congress Cataloging-in-Publication Data

Ostry, Sylvia.
    The post–cold war trading system : who's on first / Sylvia Ostry.
        p. cm.
    "Twentieth Century Fund book."
    Includes bibliographical references and index.
    ISBN 0-226-63789-1 (cloth : alk. paper).—ISBN 0-226-63790-5
(pbk. : alk. paper)
    1. International trade.   2. United States—Commercial policy.
3. Commercial policy.   4. International economic integration.
I. Title.   1005568011
HF1379.085   1997
382—dC20   96-42495
                                                          CIP

To Bernard, for his endless patience and boundless support

Contents

While the debates of international economists and diplomats seem distant and abstract to most Americans, the impact of surging trade over the past several decades has become a pervasive reality for most citizens. Trade touches consumers' lives almost every day. Our trading partners make our televisions and many of our cars; they may pay our wages or cost us our jobs. Trade issues are real in a way that, short of war itself, world politics is not. When American statesmen consider what is politically possible, they would do well to remember this fact: for the average citizen, the consequences of international trading decisions, even those by supranational institutions, are increasingly vivid and real. Most of the other changes in the world are merely things that happen on the nightly news.

So it is not surprising that the negotiations under the General Agreement on Tariffs and Trade (GATT) should have stimulated ever wider debate among Americans about domestic policy, including investment in the workforce and the social safety net. Indeed, international trade has become the favorite scapegoat of those—Pat Buchanan and Ross Perot are respectively the noisiest and wealthiest, if not the most thoughtful, examples—who need something to blame for income stagnation and wealth inequality. Unless there is a miraculous turnabout on these matters, trade is likely to be swept into the "sound bite" category of public discourse: your sky-is-falling simplification versus mine.

One thing that may help combat this tendency is a greater understanding of the evolving world trade system.

In the years since World War II, a series of international agreements under GATT auspices (the Dillon Round, Kennedy Round, the Tokyo Round, and most recently, the Uruguay Round) slashed barriers among participating countries. While the Uruguay agreements left significant portions of the American business community dissatisfied, advocates of free trade recognize that, in key areas, that round moved the evolving world commercial order to a different level. Now, with the launch of the World Trade Organization (WTO), the global trading system has reached a level that requires supranational oversight and adjudication. Indeed, the role anticipated for the WTO will raise, as never before, questions about where national sovereignty ends and the authority of international trading regimes begins.

Given the incendiary potential of the politics of trade and the growing importance of trade agreements, the Twentieth Century Fund welcomed the opportunity to support the efforts of Sylvia Ostry, chairman of the Centre for International Studies at the University of Toronto, to analyze and explain the major developments in world trade politics. Ostry brings a wealth of experience and knowledge to her task, the exposition of the emerging new architecture of trade in the post–Uruguay Round era. Her focus on the WTO and the role of international organizations in general is only proper, for the future prospects for free trade will be greatly affected by the performance of such bodies.

In thinking about these issues, it is important to remember that debates about trade agreements often sound like simple choices between free markets and government intervention. But, more typically, successful implementation of new trade arrangements depends on follow-up activities by governments. Regional pacts such as the European Common Market and the North American Free Trade Agreement (NAFTA) are underpinned by significant new public institutions. And the emergence of the WTO makes clear that the dawn of a new global architecture for governing the international economy is imminent.

The list of items that must be addressed in order to have worldwide coordination of trade seems to expand each year, encompassing such issues as capital requirements, disclosure, safety nets, tax matters, antitrust measures, environmental regulation, as well as trade negotiations themselves. In fact, in the long run, we probably will need several new international institutions to monitor global trade and the competitive environment. Perhaps the continuing effort to build such bodies within the European Union (EU) offers the most valuable lessons about what lies ahead for global commerce.

The EU and its member states also offer lessons about how to cope with the worker displacement that inevitably accompanies free trade. To some extent, the economic integration of Europe is politically possible and individually tolerable because of the existence of worker retraining and readjustment programs, specific economic-development commitments to affected areas, and strong social support for families. Compared to Western Europe, however, America virtually ignores the consequences to workers of job displacement, whether they are losers because of technology or competition, domestic or foreign. This passivity is especially striking because the United States also offers a substantially more limited social safety net than is the norm in Western Europe.

International trade does threaten some people. They are those who own capital, land, and skills that are not very productive in international comparisons. But while unskilled workers are likely to suffer from increased trade, many skilled workers should benefit. National efforts to block trade can mitigate these redistributions. But the price is high; some individuals will gain, but the country may lose.

America led the postwar movement toward free trade but never really dealt with its consequences for workers. Europe, on the other hand, established what has been called the social democratic compromise. Now that the playing field has leveled between us and our once-impoverished trading partners, we must resolve not to stop progress toward free trade, but rather to catch up in the area of sustaining those Americans who are hurt by economic forces beyond their control.

In recognition of this imperative, in recent years the Fund has sponsored several major studies of trade issues. Patrick Low examined the events leading up to and during the Uruguay Round in *Trading Free: The GATT and U.S. Trade Policy;* Robert A. Pastor, in *Integration with Mexico: Options for U.S. Policy,* explored U.S.-Mexico relations under NAFTA; in *American Trade Politics* (now in its third edition), I. M. Destler analyzed the U.S. trade policymaking system; and *The Free Trade Debate: Reports of the Twentieth Century Fund Task Force on the Future of American Trade Policy* investigated the benefits and drawbacks of both free trade and managed trade. In an effort to find solutions to the problems global trade precipitates in the workforce, the Fund is currently sponsoring a study by James K. Galbraith on the causes and cures of the inequality crisis, as well as a study by Jonas Pontusson on workforces, economic inequality, and public policy in economically advanced nations. In each case, the Fund hopes that solid analysis and sound reasoning can help offset the sloganeering of both sides on trade issues.

We are grateful to Sylvia Ostry for her contribution to our understanding of current developments in the area of international trade organizations; it will serve as a strong foundation for further exploration of this complex set of issues.

Richard C. Leone, *President*
The Twentieth Century Fund
April 1996

During the 1980s a spate of articles and books about the emergence of Japan as a "technological superpower" generated widespread debate and concern in the United States about America's economic status. There was also, in part for the same reason, a renewed interest among economists in the economics of growth and whether or not overall standards of living among different countries converge over time, as neoclassical theory predicts. This "convergence controversy" highlighted the remarkable performance of the industrialized countries after World War II; indeed, by the early 1970s Europe and Japan had attained a standard of living roughly equivalent to that of the United States. From the ashes of war, the European and Japanese economies had achieved rough convergence in technological capabilities, capital per worker, education levels, and managerial capacity with the U.S. economy.

What were the forces behind the birth of the Organization for Economic Cooperation and Development (OECD) "convergence club"? What explained this virtually unique historical event? While no simple answer will suffice, clearly a major factor was American postwar policy, which included the Marshall Plan and the creation of the multilateral economic institutions. In effect, the United States was the master builder who constructed the convergence club.

Its role in building the postwar architecture of international economic cooperation was largely a product of the Cold War. It was a magnificent achievement that created unprecedented prosperity and stability for the Western world, and, indeed, greatly benefited the United States. But it had some unexpected consequences, one of which was the creation of the convergence club. The United States, the undisputed economic and technological superpower in 1950, never really considered the possibility that several decades later Europe and Japan would catch up with or even challenge its predominance in some respects. And there was another surprise. While the OECD countries all chose capitalism and rejected communism, it became clearer over time that capitalism came in a variety of brands. There weren't just two systems—capitalism and communism—but a range of market system variants with structural differences that affected openness to trade, investment, and technology.

These two "surprise" outcomes shaped the evolution of U.S. trade policy. First of all, from an exclusive focus on multilateralism and the GATT in the three decades following the end of the war, by the onset of the 1990s U.S. policy had become multitrack: multilateral, regional; and unilateral. Further, because of structural differences of access and other system differences, the focus of U.S. trade policy increasingly shifted to what were once considered domestic policies and practices, and also expanded beyond trade to include investment and technology. Moreover, and perhaps most importantly, the end of the Cold War has greatly lessened the "high policy" constraints on American trade policy. The glue that bound the Western powers within a broad and consensual policy template has dissolved.

Another powerful ongoing trend is also transforming the trade policy agenda in a fashion that could not have been imagined in the postwar period, the globalization of the international economy. The ever tightening and more complex linkages among nation states, first by trade, then by financial flows, and more recently by a surge of foreign direct investment have greatly enhanced the power and ubiquitousness of the multinational enterprise in the international arena. This deepening integration of the world economy, fed or even led by the continuing revolution in information and communication technology, has reinforced the shift of trade policy inside the border and the latent push to system harmonization.

This book begins by exploring the origins of the convergence club of the advanced countries and, in particular, the main engine of growth, the diffusion of technology. The erosion of the wide U.S. economic lead, which had existed after the war, began a gradual process of erosion of American commitment to the rules-based GATT system it had built. Changes in that system over the 1970s and the high-tech trade wars of the 1980s reflected not only this shift in American policy but the accelerating globalization and deeper integration of the international economy. U.S.-Japanese tensions exemplified a new form of protectionist pressure, competition between different market models or *system friction*. In the coming years, East Asia, the most dynamic region in the global economy, will be a major arena for system competition in part because of spillover from U.S.-Japanese conflict but also because of the unique nature of the region itself.

These are the issues that will be explored in the following chapters. An account of the construction of the postwar trading system will be followed by an analysis of its transformation over the 1970s and 1980s. The concluding chapter will present some policy options to strengthen and sustain the new multilateral system created by the Uruguay Round. The World Trade Organization faces a formidable challenge of adaptation to a world of deeper economic integration in which the domain of trade policy has moved inside the border and barriers to access are often deeply embedded in the formal and informal institutions that govern behavior. The policy proposals to entrench and extend the Uruguay Round gains are of a modest and incremental nature: But the need for urgent action is underlined. It is not difficult to outline a grand vision of the global trading system of the twenty-first century. But the trouble with grand visions is that they require visionary political leadership for implementation and sustainability. However, as the subtitle of this book—*Who's on First?*—suggests (by way of an American baseball metaphor) the leadership and coordination role of the United States in a multipolar world can no longer be taken for granted. The EU, and even less Japan, cannot simply be "assumed" to fill the void. With the end of the Cold War, the foreign policy of the great powers can be described, at best, as "groping along" in a search for a new international order. One can hardly expect this miasma to exempt trade policy. The trading system of the twenty-first century is shrouded in a fog of uncertainty. Until the fog clears, the first priority must be to reinforce the foundation for constructing that system seems and to build a global partnership to guide its course.

Acknowledgments

This book rests on many years of experience in the Government of Canada and international institutions. Experience is not what happened but what one learns from what happened, and learning comes from the exchange of knowledge among colleagues. I can't list the scores of names of my colleagues in the Department of Foreign Affairs in Ottawa, the OECD, and the GATT, but I can and do acknowledge my enormous debt to all of them.

Since I left government service I've learned so much from Jagdish Bhagwati, a giant among trade policy scholars today. My warmest thanks also go to the staff of the Centre for International Studies at the University of Toronto for their invaluable assistance in the preparation of this book. Finally, I could not have completed this work without the financial assistance of the Twentieth Century Fund, to which I express my most sincere gratitude.

One

The Sources of Convergence

The burgeoning theoretical and empirical literature on economic growth in recent years has stressed the absence of any automatic or in-built mechanism for a narrowing of differences in real per capita output or productivity among countries.[1] Yet, as figure 1.1 shows, the very large gaps between the United States, on the one hand, and the major European countries and Japan on the other, which characterized the early postwar years, had dramatically narrowed by the early 1970s, and the convergence club was born. Admittedly war damage had widened the gap with the United States, so part of the convergence was due to reconstruction. Nonetheless, in the longer sweep of history, this development was unique.

The United States was, and still is, in the lead; indeed, there is some evidence of a recent widening of the U.S. preeminence, as we will discuss later. This convergence, however—especially in the case of Japan, where the ascent was most rapid—began to generate a debate about the future. Would the United States, like Britain before it, be overtaken by a Japanese "technological superpower"?[2] This concern, in turn, regenerated interest among many economists in growth theory and economic history, long neglected as subjects of "mainstream" analysis. The postwar resurgence of the seriously damaged European and Japanese economies, which had captured the early agenda of the OECD[3] and then faded into oblivion, once more became a focus of interest. If convergence is not endogenous to the process of economic growth, what accounts for the postwar record? Was the standard explanation offered in the earlier OECD discussions—

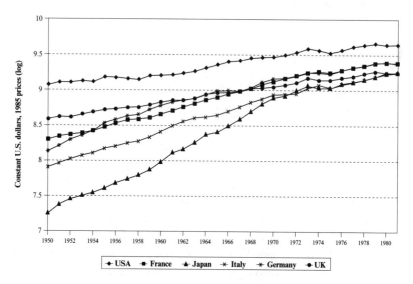

Figure 1.1 Real per Capita GDP, 1950–1981

Source: Data from Robert Summers and Alan Heston, *Penn World Table 5.6*, 1995.

technological catch-up—the whole story? What were the mechanisms of catch-up? In this chapter we will review the convergence process, which is more complex than the term *catch-up* implies. In the next two chapters the role of the United States as the motor and driver of convergence will be analyzed.

The Nature of U.S. Technological Leadership

American technological leadership after World War II was across-the-board dominance—that is, the American lead was apparent in all industries and not simply in "high tech."[4] The lead in capital intensive, mass production sectors was long-standing, having emerged at the end of the nineteenth century when the United States overtook the

Table 1.1 **Comparative Levels of Productivity, 1870–1979 Means of Fifteen Countries Compared with the United States (U.S. GDP per man-hour = 100)**

	PRODUCTIVITY LEVEL RELATIVE TO THE U.S.
1870	77 (66)[a]
1890	68 (68)[a]
1913	61
1929	57
1938	61
1950	46
1960	52
1973	69
1979	75

Source: Moses Abramovitz, "Catching Up, Forging Ahead, and Falling Behind," *Journal of Economic History* 46, no. 2 (June 1986): 391.

[a]Figures in parentheses are based on relatives with the United Kingdom = 100. List of countries: Australia, Austria, Belgium, Canada, Denmark, Finland, France, Germany, Italy, Japan, Netherlands, Norway, Sweden, Switzerland, United Kingdom, and United States.

United Kingdom. No convergence by Europe or Japan was apparent over the first half of the twentieth century: indeed, as is shown in table 1.1, the gap in productivity levels between the United States and other present-day advanced countries widened, especially after World War I.

But there was no similar early lead in American high-tech preeminence. The U.S. dominance in sectors such as pharmaceuticals, aerospace and electronics was a new phenomenon. So catch-up after World War II involved a multitrack process or, put another way, multiple avenues for the diffusion of technology as well as other conditions to ensure that technology was effectively applied.

The American lead in mass production stemmed from several sources. The higher productivity partly reflected economies of scale based on production for a large, protected domestic market, the largest and richest in the world. In a world where exporting was costly, and competitive advantage stemmed from economies of scale, smaller domestic markets provided less opportunity to move ahead. Abundance of natural resources such as coal and iron as well as much higher real wages also favored these capital- and resource-intensive sectors. An American invention, scientific management (or Fordism, as it came to be termed), was an essential ingredient in superior performance. Technology alone, if narrowly viewed as codified knowledge, is not a sufficient condition for high productivity if, for example, the organization of the work process does not facilitate its effective implementation. Finally, the higher productivity of American firms made them dominant exporters and encouraged them to establish subsidiaries abroad, thereby reinforcing and extending their world primacy.

The sources of American preeminence in high tech were very different and only emerged after World War II. For example, for much of the first half of the century, German industry, especially in the chemicals group, was more advanced in industrial research and universities in Germany and the United Kingdom led in science fields such as physics and chemistry.[5] Nobel Prizes in Germany, the United Kingdom, France, and the United States illustrate the marked contrast between the pre– and post–World War II periods (figure 1.2). The leap forward in American high tech is explained largely by enormous investment in research and development (R&D) by industry, academic institutions, and government as well as a significant increase in the number of students in higher education. A large proportion of both government and industrial R&D flowed from the Department of Defense and so, in a very significant sense, was a consequence of the U.S. wartime role.

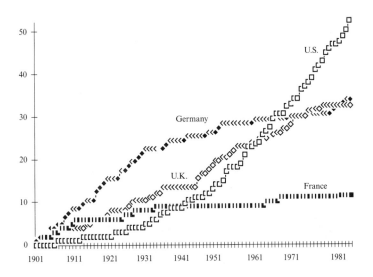

Figure 1.2 Cumulative Nobel Prizes in Physics and Chemistry, 1901–1990

Source: Sylvia Ostry and Richard Nelson, *Technonationalism and Technoglobalism: Conflict and Cooperation* (Washington, D.C.: Brookings Institution, 1995), 4. Reprinted with permission of the Centre for International Studies, University of Toronto.

Thus, U.S. R&D expenditure per person employed in 1960 was two or three times that in Europe (table 1.2). The gap with Japan was far greater, underlining how wartime devastation had affected a country that had built a technologically advanced prewar industrial structure that was, however, geared almost exclusively to military objectives. The American lead in higher education was not quite as massive but nonetheless significant. In 1950 the average years of postsecondary education of an American worker was well over twice that of a counterpart in Western Europe and Japan.[6]

Given the dual nature of U.S. technological leadership, it's obvious that the process of postwar convergence was

Table 1.2 Research and Development Expenditure per Person Employed, 1960–1973 (dollars in 1985 U.S. relative prices)

	1960	1973
France	207	448
Germany	179	475
Japan	89	342
Netherlands	291	514
United Kingdom	343	480
United States	809	814

Source: Angus Maddison, *Dynamic Forces of Capitalist Development* (New York: Oxford University Press, 1991), 152.

bound to be complex and multifaceted. To better understand the role of U.S. leadership in this process, it's useful to review the notion of catch-up in more detail.

Technology Catch-Up

Recent studies of postwar convergence have stressed the importance of technology as an explanatory factor. This confirms the idea of catch-up based on the "technology gap" with the United States, first enunciated by the Organization for European Economic Cooperation (OEEC)[7] established under the Marshall Plan and further elaborated by the OECD, its successor. Thus, a recent comprehensive analysis of convergence has estimated that technology, as measured by total factor productivity (TFP) or the output produced by given amounts of capital and labor, accounted for two-thirds of the convergence in real output per man-hour in the period up to the early 1970s. The remaining one-third was due to increasing capital intensity,[8] reflecting rates of growth of domestic investment in both Europe and Japan during the 1950s and 1960s two to three times greater than prewar performance. Increased investment of course also involves transfer of embodied technology in leading-edge equipment. Roughly similar results, with some variation by individual countries, have been estimated in a number of other recent analyses.[9] These results are estimates of *overall* convergence for the *whole economy*. When manufacturing is considered separately, the gap in productivity performance narrows more rapidly, pointing to the role of this sector as a driving force in the convergence process.[10]

One major diffusion route for catch-up in both mass production and high tech industries was trade. Another was American foreign direct investment (FDI) in Europe. The more rapid convergence in manufacturing reflects the fact that few services were traded in this period and the U.S. investment in Europe was predominantly confined to capital intensive, manufacturing industries. The reduction of trade barriers by successive GATT negotiations and through the creation of the European Economic Community (EEC; now the European Union, or EU), as well as a decline in transport costs, eroded the comparative advantage provided by the large U.S. market. Hence both trade and investment increased competition and efficiency in the smaller protected markets of Europe as trade barriers were reduced. To a lesser extent, the same thing happened in Japan. Trade also served as a mechanism for acquiring the benefits of U.S. technology in capital equipment and intermediate goods. For small open economies, these indirect benefits or spillovers of foreign (U.S.) R&D by trade are estimated to have a larger effect on domestic productivity than did investment in domestic R&D.[11]

U.S. foreign investment in Europe was also an important source of technology flows. The stock of American FDI increased nearly fivefold between 1950 and 1966, an unprecedented development. Almost all of the increased stock

Table 1.3 Stocks of United States Direct Investments Abroad by Sectors and by Countries, 1950 and 1966 (in millions of U.S. dollars)

	1950			1966		
	TOTAL	MANUFACTURING	MANUFACTURING TOTAL (%)	TOTAL	MANUFACTURING	MANUFACTURING TOTAL (%)
Total	11,788	3,831	32.5	54,562	22,050	40.4
Europe	1,733	932	53.8	16,200	8,879	54.8
Canada	3,579	1,897	53.0	16,840	7,674	45.6
Latin America	4,445	781	17.5	9,854	3,077	31.2
Africa	287	55	19.2	2,078	331	15.9
Asia	1,001	60	5.6	3,891	794	20.4
of which: Japan	(19)			(756)	(333)	44.0
Oceanic	256	107	41.8	2,064	1,060	51.3
of which: Australia	(201)			(1,918)	(999)	52.1

Source: OECD, *International Economic Exchanges*, vol. 4 of *Gaps in Technology* (Paris: OECD, 1970), 285.

Table 1.4 Indices of Growth of U.S. Technological Receipts by Area Compared with Other Economic Indices, 1965

	(1957 = 100)	
	UNITED KINGDOM	OECD EUROPE
United States technological receipts	373	369
GNP (current prices)	160	167
Gross investment machinery and equipment	165	179
Industrial production	129	153

Source: OECD, *International Economic Exchanges*, vol. 4 of *Gaps in Technology* (Paris: OECD, 1970), 262.

in Europe was in manufacturing (table 1.3). The share of manufacturing in total U.S. foreign capital stocks rose from 32.5 percent in 1950 to 40.4 percent in 1966 despite high investments in oil. The main motive for this postwar internationalization of U.S. manufacturing firms was to exploit their technological advantage. But one major consequence of the investment was to speed the flow of technology to the host country. Technology payments to the United States grew more rapidly than output or investment over the 1957–65 period (table 1.4). An increasing proportion of the flow was intrafirm, except for Japan, which relied on licensing rather than investment for access (table 1.5). One consequence of these different routes to access, as we shall see in the next chapter, was that Fordism was "imported" to Europe by American investment but not to Japan, where investment was blocked during the postwar years.

While investment provided a direct route to technology access, just as in the case of trade, spillovers were also important. The statistics on royalties and licensing fees capture only a portion of the intrafirm knowledge flows. Education and training, exchange visits by technical personnel as well

Table 1.5 Proportion of U.S. Receipts for Licenses, Patents, Royalties, and Management Fees Derived from Transactions between Parent Companies and Subsidiaries

	UNITED KINGDOM	OECD EUROPE	JAPAN
1957	44.4	43.1	15.4
1965	72.3	70.8	24.5

Source: OECD, *International Economic Exchanges,* vol. 4 of *Gaps in Technology* (Paris: OECD, 1970), 262.

as more complex and tacit forms of knowledge involved in managing an operation cannot be measured yet are essential aspects of intrafirm technology transfer with significant effects on productivity. We shall return to this point in our discussion of the Marshall Plan program of technical assistance.

In addition to these varying types of intrafirm transfers, foreign subsidiaries may also provide spillovers to other firms within the same industry and to firms in other industries when trained managers and technicians move to competing firms or set up their own firms. Furthermore, local firms, either in the same industry or in the supplier industry, are stimulated to seek newer forms of technology, which they may not have known about before the establishment of the foreign subsidiary. Thus the rate of technology diffusion is speeded up.

But neither the intra- nor interindustry spillovers are "automatic." All the case studies and more aggregated statistical analyses demonstrate that the extent and nature of spillover, by trade or investment, is contingent on certain conditions in the host country.[12] As Abramovitz stressed in his seminal article on the convergence club, catch-up was conditional on what he termed the "social capabilities" of the laggard countries.[13] But he provided no rigorous defini-

Table 1.6 Expenditures for R&D as Percentage of GDP

	U.S.	U.K.	JAPAN	GERMANY	FRANCE
1964[a]	2.9	2.3	1.5	1.6	1.8
1971	2.4	N/A	1.9	2.2	1.9
1978	2.2	2.1	2.0	2.3	1.7
1981	2.4	2.4	2.3	2.4	2.0

Source: U.S. National Science Board, *Science and Engineering Indicators, 1993* (Washington, D.C.: GPO, 1993), appendix table 4-35.

[a]1964 figure is percentage of GNP.

tion of that term, and as we shall see in the next chapter, the notion is indeed very complex.

Given the inherited social capabilities of Europe and Japan, the pace of postwar convergence was enhanced by a number of other factors. Among the basic conditions necessary to maximize diffusion is a competitive environment, and one of the benefits of foreign investment, as pointed out above, is that it increases competition. In the postwar years, this competitive thrust was especially effective since American firms with a lead in product and process innovation were established in oligopolistic sectors with high entry barriers.

Another important condition for potential convergence is the technological capacity of host-country firms. Acquiring knowledge requires investment in knowledge. Especially in the high-tech sectors, for which the scientific underpinnings of industrial technologies are very strong, convergence demanded heavy investment in R&D and higher education to narrow the gap between the United States and the others. The convergence club countries well understood this need, and massive efforts were undertaken (tables 1.6 and 1.7).

The growing employment of scientific personnel in the OECD countries ensured a transnational flow of informa-

Table 1.7 Scientists and Engineers Engaged in R&D per 10,000 Workers

	U.S.	U.K.	JAPAN	GERMANY	FRANCE
1965	64.7	19.6	24.6	22.6	20.9
1972	58.0	30.3	38.1	35.4	28.1
1981	61.9	35.7	55.6	44.0	36.3

Source: U.S. National Science Board, *Science and Engineering Indicators, 1993* (Washington, D.C.: GPO, 1993), appendix table 3-22.

tion through scientific and engineering books and journals, academic exchanges, international meetings, and the like. This flow of knowledge across borders made it difficult for a firm to capture or appropriate the full benefit from its investment in R&D: much scientific and engineering took on the character of a public good. The magnitude of these R&D spillovers can be significant as measured by social rates of return to capital and R&D that are considerably higher than private rates.[14]

In conclusion, it is apparent from this brief survey of the sources of convergence that technological catch-up was the basic and dominant factor. But while necessary, it was by no means sufficient. The domestic policies of Europe and Japan and embedded social capabilities were also essential if *potential* convergence was to become *actual* convergence. Furthermore, the two major conduits for international technology flows—investment and trade—didn't just "happen" after the war. Both entailed policy initiatives both domestic and international. The construction of the postwar convergence club required a master architect and builder: the United States.

Two

Building the Convergence Club: Technology and Investment

The remarkable growth in Europe and Japan of the postwar years was achieved by a combination of technology transfer, high rates of investment, and a range of growth-friendly domestic policies. While, of course, this growth depended on the efforts of the countries themselves, those efforts alone could not have produced the "golden age" of postwar growth. What was essential was the role of the master-builder (i.e., the United States) in fostering high rates of domestic investment and technology diffusion in the countries devastated by the Second World War.

Far and away the most important policy initiative in the rebuilding of Europe was the Marshall Plan. What is most remembered about the Marshall Plan is the aid provided by the United States that helped finance infrastructure reconstruction and alleviate resource shortages. Less well known but much more relevant in the context of the convergence club story was the Marshall Plan program on promoting technology diffusion by a variety of measures, including investment in new plant and equipment (embodied technology), direct technology assistance, and foreign (i.e., American) investment. There was, however, no Marshall Plan for Japan, and the mechanisms for technology transfer were very different than was the case for Europe. Thus, this chapter will deal first with the U.S. role in Europe and then with the reconstruction of Japan. In the following chapter the role of the United States in the formation of the GATT will be examined since the liberalization of trade was an essential building block in the construction of the convergence club.

The Marshall Plan

> *The most unsordid act in history.*
> WINSTON CHURCHILL

Was Winston Churchill right? Was the Marshall Plan, which contributed more than $13 billion to European recovery, the most noble example of Wilsonian vision? Was this generosity a selfless effort to create free markets and democracy by instilling in the war-weary Europeans the basic American values of true liberalism centered on market rationality and the rights of the individual? Was it, in other words, the act of the world's first benign hegemon?

Or was the Marshall Plan—so strongly supported by American business, labor, and elected officials—an immensely successful diplomatic maneuver to outwit the Soviet Union and score a triumphant preemptive move, the first salvo of the Cold War? As Charles Kindleberger argues: "What the Machiavellis among us never understood was why the Soviet Union did not join the Marshall Plan and disrupt it. . . . It would not cost anything, as quotas in the IMF and IBRD would have done. It would have been simple to agree in principle and object in practice. The fear in Washington was that the Soviet bear might hug the Marshall Plan to death. Soviet abstention left the West free to operate its own recovery programme with the Soviet Union excluded at its own insistence."[1] Perhaps the father of the Marshall Plan was Joe Stalin, whose refusal to join could be called "the most unintelligent act in history."

The debate about the origins of the plan can likely never be settled, and dozens of studies have presented a case for both views: the United States as benign hegemon or cold warrior. The debate is important, however, because it influences one's judgment about the durability of the postwar rules-based system, including the Bretton Woods institutions and the GATT. Can the system be effectively adapted in the absence of an unchallengeable leader or hegemon? Or will hegemonic decline and the end of the Cold War inevitably lead to a destruction of the regime? The most optimistic appraisal is that the postwar order built by the United States was not imposed on the convergence club but rather reflected a unique "consensual hegemony" based on shared views ("embedded liberalism"), essentially a commitment to international rules that were compatible with a government's domestic objectives.[2] Thus these shared views are durable and can be adapted to ongoing change in the world economy and polity. We shall return to these issues in subsequent chapters.

For some purposes, however, it could be argued that the debate is irrelevant. All government policy stems from a variety of pressures and considerations. Only economists build models that function on the notion that individuals and even governments pursue single-focus or "rational" objectives. In the models, mental or formal, the complexities of the policymaking process and the role of error and accident are impounded in *ceteris paribus*. If one evaluates the Marshall Plan in terms of one aspect of the outcome—its contribution to the creation of the convergence club—it can be argued that the Marshall Plan success was a bit of an unwelcome surprise to some Americans: too true to be good, to borrow from George Bernard Shaw.

Schumpeter asserted that *policy* is a byproduct of *politics* and to understand the impact and aftermath of the Marshall Plan it's important to examine the *political origins* of the initiative. We shall do so first in the context of one element of catch-up, the role of technology and investment in the growth of postwar Europe.

Investment Growth: The Policy By-product of Politics

The speed with which the Marshall Plan was implemented was truly astonishing. Dean Acheson's speech on May 8, 1947, was followed in the same month by a memorandum prepared in the Policy Planning Staff of the U.S. State Department by George Kennan detailing the need for U.S. subsidies for European dollar imports. On June 5, 1947, General Marshall, speaking at Harvard University, suggested that the United States would respond positively if the European countries were "to take the initiative by formulating jointly a recovery programme."[3] A meeting convened by the foreign ministers of France and Great Britain on July 12–15, 1947 (which the Russians and their satellite countries refused to attend), established a Committee of European Economic Cooperation (CEEC). The CEEC produced a comprehensive two-volume report spelling out the details of the policy and institutional aspects of European recovery. On the institutional side, the report recommended establishing a permanent organization, the Organization for European Economic Cooperation, or OEEC. With some minor amendments, these proposals were accepted by the American administration and Congress. The Economic Cooperation Administration (ECA) was established to run the plan in the United States. By April 2, 1948, the Marshall Plan had been launched—less than a year after the historic speech. A quaint footnote to history is that Marshall's initiative "was ignored by the correspondents of the *Times* and the *Economist*, the British establishment in economic matters."[4]

When compared with the long and difficult negotiations required to establish Bretton Woods and the ill-fated International Trade Organization (ITO), the speed with which the OEEC was established seems even more remarkable. One reason for this was the element of unilateralism: the dominant role of the United States was more easily expressed one-on-one, so to speak, in the negotiations with a weak Europe (and an even weaker occupied Japan; see below). Another, more important reason was that by 1947 European recovery had stalled, and the initial weakness of the International Monetary Fund as well as the failure of the special British loan of 1946 made it unlikely that growth would be easily revived. This dismal outlook greatly raised the fear among Americans of a communist upsurge. Communist parties were very strong in both France and Italy, and the Labor party was in power in Britain. Thus speed was essential. President Truman launched the policy of containment (the Truman Doctrine), and Congress provided aid to Greece to prevent a communist victory in the civil war. As a prominent columnist succinctly expressed the answer to "why the rush?": "State Department strategists have now come around—to the point a good many 'visionaries' have been urging all along—that one way of combating Communism is to give western Europe a full dinner pail." This unexpected alliance between "visionaries" and "cold warriors" proved most effective.[5]

Still, it wasn't only fear of communism that garnered the support of Congress for the Marshall Plan. American business, far more efficient than any potential competitors in Europe, saw the opportunities in a stable and more open European market as very enticing. While the formation of the European Economic Community was still in the future, the terms of Marshall Plan aid clearly involved trade and payments liberalization, albeit initially only within Europe, and market primacy in domestic policy. So, like the Treaty of Rome, American business approved the policy as "the sweetest deal."[6] Strict conditionality for the use of Marshall aid was negotiated bilaterally, and the terms for the most part reflected the views of the American business community. The conditionality was much tougher than envisaged under Bretton Woods arrangements.

Early action was undertaken toward the dismantling of restrictions among the European members in trade and payments. This resulted in 1950 in the institution of the European Payments Union (EPU) and the Code of Liberalization of trade. Departing from its prewar policy stance, the United States demanded no reciprocity in this liberalization effort. But American business supported this position as a preliminary measure to full liberalization, which the first GATT negotiations had already begun in Geneva in 1947. Thus the promise of American access to a more prosperous Europe enabled the American government to give up its traditional demand for reciprocity in trade negotiations under the EPU.

Dean Acheson described the chief American negotiator, the former president of Studebaker, Paul Hoffman, as an "economic Savonarola" and compared his role in the Marshall Plan administration to that of an evangelist.[7] (In Japan, the Dodge Plan was even more evangelical, along the lines of Christian fundamentalism!) While American labor was not quite so fervent in its support, the lingering effects of the New Deal were sufficient to forestall serious opposition. (Indeed, the Roosevelt administration had joined the International Labor Organization [ILO] in 1934 to give an international dimension to the New Deal.) And, as is clear from the Technology Assistance program described below, efforts were made from the outset to engage unions in OEEC activity. In addition, a Business and Industry Advisory Committee (BIAC) and a Trade Union Advisory Committee (TUAC) were established. So the politics of consensus in the U.S. context were skillfully handled by the American planners.

In Europe, the situation was more complex. Views about the role of the market and the role of government were by no means homogeneous, as will be noted below. Nonetheless, vivid memories of interwar strife and the destructiveness it engendered—culminating in the war itself—provided a force for consensual cooperation. As Raymond Aron has observed, the postwar institutions were formed by "men walking backwards into the future." Furthermore, European business was eager to rebuild its competitiveness, and the Marshall Plan emphasis on productivity and growth fell on receptive ears. The EPU and intra-European dismantling of bilateral trade barriers provided considerable benefit to European producers protected (albeit temporarily) from American competition. For labor, Marshall Plan aid eased the pain of stabilization measures. And the commitment to full employment, the business promise of high investment and production, social security measures, and a range of protective labor legislation sealed the "social contract," isolating the extreme left.[8] The consensual approach implicit in the social contract (and the memory of the Great Depression) kept wage increases moderate, enhanced profits, and stimulated unprecedented rates of investment. By the late 1960s, memories were fading and the wage moderation of the implicit social contract was eroding. The interventionist labor legislation created structural barriers to adjustment.[9] But more of that later.

As noted, the commitment to full employment was part of the Marshall Plan package. In the Convention for European Economic Cooperation, which established the OEEC,

Article 1, "General Obligations," established the main objectives of the member countries. These were identified as increased production, expanded commerce, full employment, and the maintenance of "internal financial stability." This amalgam of Keynesian and monetarist goals reflected a compromise between employment and price stability objectives and, within the United States, between the Treasury (which favored price stability as the primordial objective) and Marshall Plan administrators in the ECA, who were more concerned with preventing unemployment. (The international monetary arrangements of Bretton Woods also reflect this Keynesian approach, which sought to reconcile domestic policy with rules for international financial stability.)

Thus the dominance of the full employment objective in the "official" stance of the OEEC reflected the Keynesian consensus of the economics profession in the postwar years. While the much-derided notion of "fine-tuning" was more myth than reality,[10] nonetheless the Keynesian view that demand management was a legitimate role of government to offset cyclical fluctuations enjoyed wide support among academics and government officials in many countries and by reducing downside risk influenced private sector expectations, thus encouraging investment.[11] But the consensus negotiated among the member countries and enshrined in the founding convention masked significant differences in views about the role and objectives of government policy not only in the American government but also within the OEEC, ranging from the traditional French penchant for *dirigisme* and planning to the German overriding dedication to price stability. Further, in the United States, despite the passage of the Full Employment Act of 1946, there was no implementation of a comprehensive welfare state as in Europe by the Republican Congress elected that year. Indeed it was not until the 1960s and President Johnson's war on poverty that an effort was made to implement the Full Employment Act and broader elements of a welfare state.

By the end of the 1960s, the Keynesian consensus was under assault in the economics profession. And the fragile consensus among OEEC governments on the role of the state versus the market was also beginning to break down under the pressure of slower growth and structural change. One consequence of the golden age social contract was that government spending in OECD countries rose from 27 percent to 37 percent of gross domestic product from 1950 to 1973, reflecting increased expenditure on social security, health, and education.[12] This rise was most marked in Europe and least in Japan and the United States.

Finally, a number of lessons may be drawn from this brief review of the politics of the Marshall Plan. As pointed out in the previous chapter, an important element in the remarkable growth of postwar Europe was the enormous increase in domestic investment, accounting for as much as one-third of the catch-up with the United States. These investment growth rates, more than twice the prewar level, were to a considerable extent fostered by the Marshall Plan social contract (and also by trade liberalization, as we shall see in the following chapter). The politics of consensus necessary to concoct this successful recipe involved overcoming fundamental differences among the OEEC countries as well as differences within the United States among interest groups and political parties. In the politics of consensus, differences are more easily set aside in a buoyant and hope-filled environment, especially when memories of a bitter past are fresh in the minds of the policymakers. In the 1970s, slower growth, declining productivity, and major structural shocks began to strain both domestic and international consensus on the central issue of the appropriate role of government. Furthermore, in the international domain, as the OECD economies became more open to trade—and financial—flows, the issue of reciprocity, suspended by the United States for foreign policy reasons, was to resurface as an important source of conflict.

Thus, the Marshall Plan's indirect contribution to European investment growth was significant. But of comparable or perhaps greater importance was the direct impact of the Technical Assistance Program of the Marshall Plan, which engaged both American and European business and labor in unprecedented effort and helped to strengthen the social consensus. This aspect of the U.S. role has long been neglected, but recent documentation reveals how significant it was in the building of the convergence club.

Technical Assistance in the Marshall Plan

The diverse origins of the Technical Assistance Program illustrate the role of accident or randomness in the policy process.[13] Jean Monnet, first head of the postwar French Commissariat du Plan (and father of the European Community) had been most impressed by the efficiency of American industry during his wartime stay in the United States. Beginning in 1946 he established a number of committees of economists, statisticians, and engineers to analyze the differences in French and American productivity. Similar statistical studies had been undertaken between 1943 and 1946 by Lazlo Rostas of the British Board of Trade and published by the Royal Economic Society and the Cambridge-based National Institute of Economic and Social Research. The U.S. Bureau of Labor Statistics (BLS) followed up the work of Rostas. In 1948, on the advice of the U.S. secretary of labor, Marshall Plan director Paul Hoffman asked BLS to undertake a series of sectoral productivity industries.

At the request of U.K. officials, BLS undertook to evaluate the policy implications of the U.K. surveys. The conclusions of this evaluation pointed the direction for action, *viz.:*

> In mass production industries the differences in efficiency between plants in the U.K. and the U.S. were so great and involved almost every element of management and production organization and practice that . . . only large-scale visits by U.K. teams of management, supervisors, engineers, labor, and product development personnel visiting a number of comparable U.S. plants could convey an understanding of productivity, increase potential, to the point that industry wide improvements could be undertaken.[14]

Interestingly, the survey showed that U.K. branches of U.S. firms were no more efficient than British corporations. These branch plants in effect reflected American mass production techniques of the 1920s. Thus the war, which *prevented* improvement in European production processes and products, in fact *enhanced* American efficiency through the restoration of full employment, which repaired the damage inflicted by the Great Depression. And defense production, R&D subsidies, and government procurement contributed to the creation of the world's most productive economy in every industrial sector. There was, therefore, considerable scope for European catch-up.

The first Productivity Teams were established by the United Kingdom and France in 1948. Their reports formed the basis for a comprehensive cooperative government, industry, and union Technical Assistance Program launched by the United States under the Marshall Plan. The technical assistance (TA) planning involved the heads of major U.S. corporations plus labor leaders from the AFL and CIO and in each of the European countries, government, business, and labor at the highest level were engaged in similar fashion.

National Productivity Agencies, overseen by tripartite commissions, administered the program in each of the OEEC countries. Overall coordination was provided by the OEEC in Paris and the ECA in Washington.

The chief instrument of technical assistance was the study tour to the United States. Teams were recruited from different plants within an industry. The basis for recruitment was defined by the objective of the program, which was to bring to Europe all the main features of American mass production. These included "new concepts of organization of the work place; new concepts of marketing and business organization; new products, designs, and engineering functions; and new equipment."[15] Hence the teams included industrialists, managers, engineers, foremen, workers, and union leaders. Sometimes parliamentarians joined the team so that government policy issues could be assessed first hand.

The study tours, usually preceded by an intensive orientation course at home, lasted four to six weeks. U.S. firms, trade and labor organizations, government technical experts, and publishers of technical and industrial journals participated in the carefully designed activities. The comprehensive technical reports prepared by each team were widely disseminated in participating countries through plant visits, conferences, and seminars. Follow-up technical services, including technical digests; abstracts and bibliographies; training programs; consultative services; and so forth, reinforced the dissemination process. A particularly effective technique of dissemination was a new technical service called U.S. Factory Performance. Its reports were prepared by BLS with the aid of engineers, accountants, and auditors. Detailed technical data on all factors affecting plant operations were provided to European managers. Perhaps this is the earliest example of what later became *benchmarking*.

Between 1949 and 1957, when the program officially ended, nearly nineteen thousand Europeans went to the United States on productivity study tours (table 2.1). Many of the American experts were engaged in launching European training courses for thousands of workers, technicians and managers. The U.S. cost of the Technical Assistance Program has been estimated at a minuscule 1.5 percent of Marshall Plan capital assistance. Participating governments were required to contribute one-third of the total cost of the study tour. Business contributions took the form of salaries of team members.

But the most extraordinary contribution of the United States to the Marshall Plan Technical Assistance Program was not dollars but the flow of knowledge, mobilized and endorsed by government but provided for the most part by private industry. Why the incredible effort? American business was obviously convinced that, given their overwhelming lead in productivity, it could only benefit from a reconstructed Europe. But there were also more subtle reasons. Raymond Aron, in commenting on the "voluntary contribution" of American know-how, provides a most perceptive and persuasive answer, *viz.:*

> The American propensity to consider their own system exemplary . . . proved most fortunate for the European and Japanese economies; the productivity missions

Table 2.1 Technical Assistance Teams to the United States and U.S. Experts to Europe (participants in TA teams of 8–20 persons, 6–8 weeks)

FISCAL YEAR	EUROPEANS TO UNITED STATES	AMERICANS TO EUROPE
1949	164	3
1950	1,452	36
1951	2,785	36
1952	4,498	37
1953	3,056	172
1954	2,141	220
1955	2,083[a]	165
1956	1,406	273
1957 (through March)	1,157[a]	141
Total	18,742	1,469

Source: James M. Silberman and Charles Weiss, Jr., "Restructuring for Productivity" (Industry Series working paper no. 64, Industry and Energy Department, World Bank, Washington, D.C., November 1992), 15.
[a]Excludes Greece and Turkey.

which toured the United States, and the closely knit relationships which sprang up on both sides of the Atlantic, had beneficial repercussions on the Old Continent. The Americans, by virtue of their philosophy, considered it a matter of course to teach others the secret of their own success. As the predominant economy, the United States had the advantage from its partners' point of view, of believing in freedom and communication rather than secrecy and bureaucracy.[16]

Finally, can we measure the impact of this extraordinary effort? While no formal evaluation was undertaken, the data in table 2.2 are revealing. As may be seen, although investment grew more rapidly after 1960 than during the previous

Table 2.2 Average Annual Growth Rates of Real Products, Real Capital Input, and Total Factor Productivity (percentage)

	1956–60	1960–73
Germany		
Real product	8.2	5.0
Real capital input	6.9	7.0
TFP	4.7	2.8
Italy		
Real product	6.0	4.7
Real capital input	3.3	5.4
TFP	3.3	2.5
France		
Real product	4.8	5.9
Real capital input	4.7	6.3
TFP	2.9	3.0
Netherlands		
Real product	4.8	5.6
Real capital input	4.0	6.6
TFP	2.3	2.5

Source: James M. Silberman and Charles Weiss, Jr., "Restructuring for Productivity" (Industry Series working paper no. 64, Industry and Energy Department, World Bank, Washington, D.C., November 1992), 5.

decade, the rate of change of total factor productivity was higher or approximately the same in the earlier period. Moreover, as will be discussed below, American investment in Europe grew rapidly after 1960 and provided a new and especially dynamic source of technology diffusion, which undoubtedly raised the growth rate of TFP and makes the performance of the 1950s even more remarkable.

Of course, no statistical analysis can isolate the effects of one element—direct technology assistance, in this case— from all the other changes launched by the Marshall Plan.

But as noted in our earlier discussion, the social contract that kept wage growth moderate and investment high was at the heart of European postwar reconstruction, and the TA projects could be called the "fine print" in that contract, building cooperation at the level of the plant. Cooperation and consensus promised higher standards of living to both workers and employers since the aim of TA was to diffuse up-to-date American mass production techniques, honed by wartime production, to European industry, which had been either destroyed or isolated during the war and was far behind American industry long before these events took place. Thus the objective, the process, and the results of the TA were unique and impressive. So much so, that after the Marshall Plan program ended in 1957 productivity programs became well established in Europe, technology issues a major element in OEEC and OECD activities, and technology policies a priority for most European governments. Furthermore, after studying the results in Europe, Japan asked for and received a similar program in 1955 (see below).

The rapidity of diffusion of American mass production techniques by TA involved not just technical or engineering knowledge but production "know-how," marketing methods, enterprise organization, and so forth, or what is termed today "tacit" or noncodified knowledge. The importance of this tacit knowledge to improved productivity is demonstrated in French case studies showing rapid and significant productivity gains with existing plant and equipment.[17] This very important know-how is also transferred (though not so rapidly) by foreign direct investment (but not by other forms of technology access such as licensing). This was certainly the case with the postwar American investment in Europe. And the impact of the surge of foreign direct investment in the 1960s—christened *le défi Americain* by Jacques Servan-

Schreiber—also had significant policy consequences that went well beyond technology issues.

American Investment in Europe

> *Fifteen years from now it is quite possible that the world's third great industrial power, just after the United States and Russia, will not be Europe, but American industry in Europe. Already, in the ninth year of the Common Market, this European market is basically American in organization.*
>
> JEAN-JACQUES SERVAN-SCHREIBER
> *THE AMERICAN CHALLENGE*, 1968

As is so often the case, this forecast was made just as *le défi Americain* was to become much less of a challenge. Nonetheless, the enormous surge of American investment in Europe beginning in the late 1950s was important not only in transferring American technology and management practices but, as was true of the TA program, in furthering the technology gap debate in the OECD, and stimulating European industrial policy in promoting high-tech industries first at the national level in the 1960s and 1970s and then at the community level in the 1980s. American investment also served as a "supply side shock," adding urgency to the need for deeper integration in the EU. Arguably, as was the case with other aspects of U.S. postwar policy, the indirect consequences of American investment on European integration and industrial policy were more important in shaping the international economy than the direct impact of technology transfer.

One of the most important indirect consequences was to shake up complacent, cartelized and inward-looking Euro-

Table 2.3 New U.S. Direct Investment in Europe, New Outflows Plus Retained Earnings (millions of dollars per year)

	1950–52	1953–55	1956–58	1959–61
Europe	129	271	583	1,032
EEC	100	107	229	375

Source: U.S. Department of Commerce, *Survey of Current Business,* various issues.

pean business and to underline the importance of competition policy in the Treaty of Rome. Union National des Industries de la Communauté Européenne (UNICE), the European Community business federation, issued in 1967 a formal statement welcoming American investment in the Common Market but also noted that American firms are too prone to compete by reducing prices. Thus UNICE regretfully notes:

> It has become clear that certain American firms have been badly informed about the price mechanism used in the European market—mechanisms which the various continental rivals respect. A joint study of productive costs has allowed us to set up rules which, while safeguarding competition, prove beneficial to all. We must not allow American firms, from lack of knowledge of our methods, to provoke a price war that would cause serious difficulties in the market.[18]

As Servan-Schreiber wryly observes, UNICE did not even bother to disguise its motive, which was to preserve price-fixing arrangements designed to maintain profit margins without too much effort![19]

As to technology transfer, American firms did not begin their move into Europe to any great degree until after the Marshall Plan had officially ended, even though the U.S. government tried to encourage investment by a special in-

Table 2.3 *continued*

1962–64	1965	1966	1967	1968	1969	1970
1,460	1,867	2,244	1,749	1,457	2,102	2,902
736	854	1,243	893	546	1,163	1,499

surance scheme designed to offset inconvertibility risks.[20] In point of fact, investment began to rise in the second half of the 1950s mainly because of European growth prospects. Thus the Marshall Plan's growth drive and the prospect of the Common Market attracted an unprecedented flow of American investment in manufacturing, which increased well over tenfold between 1955 and 1970 (see table 2.3). Rising investment in technology- and capital-intensive industries such as transportation equipment and electrical machinery as well as in chemicals, which included advanced technology industries such as pharmaceuticals, was reflected in rising acquisition of U.S. technology. U.S. receipts for licenses, patents, royalties—a partial measure of technology transfer—nearly quadrupled between 1957 and 1965, vastly outstripping the rate of growth of gross national product, investment, or industrial production over the same period (table 1.4). Most of the increased transfer was from the U.S. parent to the European subsidiary (table 1.5). And to maximize the benefits from the transfer of U.S. technology, European countries and companies invested increasing amounts in R&D and higher education.

One consequence of American technology exports and European catch-up efforts is illustrated by a study of five hundred major innovations during the 1953–73 period. While nearly 80 percent of the innovations introduced in 1950 were American, by 1973 this proportion had dropped to about 60 percent. And the erosion was concentrated

Table 2.4 Increase in Exports by Technology Intensity, United States and Europe, 1955–1965

TECHNOLOGY CATEGORY OF INDUSTRY SECTORS	UNITED STATES		EUROPEAN UNION	
	1955–60 (1955=100)	1960–65 (1960=100)	1955–60 (1955=100)	1960–65 (1960=100)
High technology	169.7	134.8	190.2	185.5
Medium technology	105.6	150.0	195.2	172.2
Low technology	126.2	118.5	153.9	134.9
All products	130.6	135.6	173.1	164.4

Source: John H. Dunning, "United States Foreign Investment and the Technological Gap," in *North American and Western European Economic Policies,* ed. Charles P. Kindleberger and Andrew Shonfield (London: Macmillan, 1971), 381.

mainly in sectors where the American lead was strongest, such as scientific instruments, electrical and communications equipment, chemicals, and machinery.[21] The American lead in innovations was still enormous, but by the onset of the 1970s, there was growing concern in U.S. policy and business circles about the successful *défi Européen* in some technology-intensive sectors.

Technology transfer also affected European trade. The gap between the growth rates of European and American exports was most marked in medium-technology industries in the 1955–60 period, but the relative improvement was greater in high-technology sectors in 1960–65 (table 2.4). This lag reflects the fact that the more sophisticated the product, the more complex the catch-up process, hence the importance of R&D investment and other complementary policies in Europe.

Thus while many factors other than American foreign investment affected European export performances, a virtuous circle was at work. As analysis of the data behind the summary measures in table 2.4 reveals, export performance in research-intensive products was better in countries with higher proportions of American investment, and in turn, American investment tended to flow to countries and sectors with better export performance. While American subsidiaries accounted for part of the changing export pattern of European industry, the major portion of the improvement in technological content stemmed from domestic firms.[22]

Furthermore, U.S. exports to Europe were also an important source of technology transfer. Estimating the technology content of all manufactured products by R&D expenditures per sales dollar (rather than estimating technology intensity by industry, a cruder measure that spans a wide range of products) shows that in 1968 the average technology intensity of U.S. manufactured exports was well over twice that for Europe, underlining U.S. dominance in this period.[23] Nor, in fact, did American dominance as measured by export shares erode over time (table 2.5). The relative "erosion" in the U.S. position showed up in the trade balance, as technology-intensive imports grew more rapidly than exports after the mid-1960s.

Finally, the increased presence of American firms in Europe strengthened the resolve of both politicians and opinion-makers to push European integration and improve the competitiveness of European business by various types of industrial policy. This was clearly the aim of Servan-Schreiber's provocative and influential tract. But more moderate voices echoed the same message. The well-known and well-regarded liberal, Raymond Aron, writing in 1973, cited the fate of Canada, "an economic colony of the United States," as a warning against inaction by European governments, *viz.*:

Table 2.5 U.S. Position in Trade by Technology Intensity

	TOTAL	LOW	MEDIUM	HIGH
U.S. share of exports				
1966	22.0	20.0	22.0	25.0
1978	23.1	24.8	21.3	25.2
1982	24.9	24.2	23.0	28.6
U.S. trade ratios				
(Exports over imports)				
1966	1.17	0.80	2.17	2.28
1978	0.78	0.84	1.10	1.52
1982	0.83	0.86	1.09	1.53

Source: United Nations, *International Trade Statistics Yearbook,* various issues; technology categories based upon categorization used in OECD, *Science and Technology Indicators,* April 1992.

The real danger lies in a further expansion of the wave of United States direct investments in Europe, the reinvestment of profits, and additional outflows of capital to swell the "industrial America" established on the Old Continent, to such a degree that the Atlantic may become as easily spanned and as little visible as the border between the United States and Canada.[24]

This account of the American role as master-builder of the European wing of the convergence club suggests that while the main contribution to catch-up stemmed from the Marshall Plan and the role of American government and business, both the process and the outcome were far more complex than either the "idealists" or the "cold warriors" could have imagined. The implementation of the grand overriding vision that underlay the Marshall Plan required American and European agreement on the broad overall goals, so the term "consensual hegemony" is appropriate at the highest level of generalization. But, as always, the devil is in the details. The erosion of the multilateral trading system in the 1970s and the 1980s revealed, as will be discussed in the following chapters, how fragile the consensus proved to be when put to the test.

The American role in the postwar reconstruction of Japan presents a different story but with a similar message.

The United States and the Japanese Postwar Miracle

If Joe Stalin should—ironically, of course—be considered the father of the Marshall Plan, then a similar title might be conferred on the North Korean dictator Kim Il Sung and the Japanese postwar growth miracle. The Korean War fundamentally altered American policy in occupied Japan and shaped the nature of the catch-up process by which it gained admission to the convergence club.

In November 1945, barely three months after the signing of the surrender document on the U.S. battleship Missouri, General MacArthur, the supreme commander of the Allied powers (SCAP) issued a set of directives to the Japanese prime minister. They captured the overall aim of the U.S. government, which was to transform Japan into a peaceful, democratic, liberal market society. The reforms included female suffrage, trade union rights, a new liberal education system, land reform, and deconcentration of industry. American policy was not directed to rebuilding the Japanese economy through the provision of foreign aid, as was the case for Europe through the Marshall Plan. Indeed, the original Truman policy statement emphasized that "the plight of Japan is the direct outcome of its own behaviour, and the allies will not undertake the burden of repairing the damage." And the presidential instructions to SCAP, which prompted MacArthur's reform prescription, states in part that "you will make it clear to the Japanese people that you assume no obligation to maintain any particular standard of living in Japan."[25]

The economic program for Japan was set out more extensively by the U.S. ambassador for reparations, Edwin Pauley, who visited Japan in November–December 1945. Pauley recommended that no action should be taken that would assist Japan "in maintaining a standard of living higher than that of neighbouring Asiatic countries injured by Japanese aggression."[26] To this end he spelled out a scheme for the general restructuring of East Asia designed to prevent any recurrence of Japanese economic domination of the region. Japan should not only pay reparations but also send part of its industrial equipment to other countries, to assist in their development to the same economic level as Japan.[27] Thus the initial American proposal for postwar Japan was to build a peaceful, democratic, liberal, *third world country*. It was clearly never intended to produce a member of the convergence club!

But this overall policy objective, even when enunciated at the end of 1945, masked a number of conflicting views about Japan in the U.S. government and in business circles. Indeed, by the time Pauley's report was submitted by the U.S. government to the inter-Allied Far Eastern Commission (FEC), Washington had revised its policy, and most of the reparations proposals and other aspects of Pauley's orientation were in the course of revision. As early as December 1945, a senior member of MacArthur's General Staff wanted a stronger Japan as an ally of the United States in "the coming war with Russia."[28] But the first sighting of the Cold War was not the only reason for a gradual reversal of American policy. Indeed, once the Cold War became the single focus of American foreign policy, the U-turn in policy toward Japan was not gradual but dramatic, as we shall see below.

In fact, discontent over the role of SCAP began almost immediately after surrender. American business was becoming aware that a rehabilitated Japan would be a good, growing customer. Following Pauley, a new reparations mission was sent to Japan in January 1947. The head was Clifford Strike, owner of a big New York engineering firm, who earlier that year had published an article entitled "Revenge is Expensive." This was followed by a blue-ribbon mission of American business executives in March 1948 led by William Draper, Jr., undersecretary of the army. The reparations issue was "settled" by virtually *no reparations* (table 2.6). After the San Francisco peace treaty in 1951, Japan agreed to make "reparations" payments to certain East Asian countries but it was also agreed these could be counted as official development aid. In sum, "war reparations for Japan resulted in the establishment of the foundation for the expansion of commercial activities (in East Asia) some years later."[29]

Reversal was not confined to reparations. As noted earlier, a major objective of reform cited in MacArthur's directives was deconcentration of Japanese industry, or dissolution of the giant combines called *zaibatsu*. American business and some American officials in Washington were less than enthusiastic about this reformist zeal. James Lee Kauffman, an attorney for most of the major U.S. companies in Japan before the war, wrote a report after a visit to Japan in the summer of 1947, which blasted deconcentration as "socialistic." The Kauffman Report prompted George Kennan, head of Marshall's Planning Staff, to note: "The ideological concepts on which these anti-zaibatsu measures

Table 2.6 Successive Reparation Proposals (millions of yen in 1939 prices)

| | DATE OF REPORT | REMOVALS OF | | TOTAL |
		INDUSTRIAL EQUIPMENT	MILITARY EQUIPMENT	
Pauley proposal	November 1946	990	1,476	2,466
Strike proposal	March 1948	172	1,476	1,648
Draper-Johnston proposal	May 1948	102	560	662
Actual removal	(before removals were stopped in the spring of 1949)			160

Source: Shigeto Tsuru, *Japan's Capitalism: Creative Defeat and Beyond* (Cambridge: Cambridge University Press, 1993), 39.

rested bore so close a resemblance to Soviet views about the evils of 'capitalistic monopolies' that the measures could only have been eminently agreeable to anyone interested in the future communization of Japan."[30] By April 1948 the U.S. government had abandoned most of the original zaibatsu reform intent. The list of companies to be dissolved was reduced from 325 to 100. The banks were exempted. The old zaibatsu family heads were replaced by younger government bureaucrats, who were assisted by the banks in restructuring the combines to make them more efficient. After the occupation ended in 1952, the antitrust legislation that had been introduced under SCAP orders was modified and some combines, including the trading companies of Mitsubishi and Mitsui, were restored. As has been noted by a historian of modern Japan, "the effect of the American policy was to increase rather than to diminish the concentration of control."[31]

SCAP, as we have seen, was also concerned with labor reform. In December 1945, the Trade Union Act, modeled on the American Wagner Act, was passed. This gave Japanese workers the right to organize, to bargain collectively, and with minor exceptions in the public sector, to strike. Union membership surged. By 1949 it was more than twelve times the prewar level. Many of the new unions were extremely militant. In February 1947 a general strike was announced. It was banned by the order of General MacArthur. When the Cold War began in 1948, SCAP's reformist vision dimmed once more. The Trade Union Act was revised in 1949 to encourage enterprise unions. A dual labor market was to emerge: high wages and lifetime employment in large establishments, lower wages and fewer benefits in smaller ones.[32] This labor market structure—unimaginable under the industrial bargaining pattern fostered by the Wagner Act— was to prove remarkably adaptable and growth-friendly. The workers in the large firms of the conglomerates—now termed the *keiretsu*—became "devoted to their master and employer at all costs, as if they were loyal warriors in feudal times."[33] In fact, the new younger managers in many of the keiretsu found much of their wartime experience relevant— seniority and lifetime experience, loyalty and consensus, and so on.

The aftermath of the American Occupation also had a lasting effect on Japanese politics. In this instance, the issue was land reform. While one consequence of the redistribution of land from prewar landlords to small farmers was to reduce the rural populations, the politicians in what was to become the Liberal Democratic party (LDP) persuaded SCAP that the electoral constituencies should be maintained "on the basis of the 1950 population figures."[34] This decision ran counter to one of the basic principles of electoral democracy, and certainly to the practice of the United States. One consequence was that the LDP remained in power for nearly forty years, heavily reliant on rural support. This long period of one-party rule likely facilitated Japan's development strategy but also contained the seeds of future policy disputes—not least with the United States.

These examples of policy dissonance with respect to the American role in the early years of Japanese reconstruction stand in marked contrast to the carefully orchestrated politics of consensus that launched and managed the Marshall Plan in Europe. It's not clear why this is so. Some have attributed the zig-zags in Japanese policy to the power and personality of MacArthur, whose "vanity made him vulnerable to flattery by Japanese, economic and journalistic figures" and whose personal regime in Tokyo allowed him to "exclude or downgrade civilian personnel prepared by the State Department."[35] There was, moreover, almost no wartime preparation for Japan's surrender, unlike the extensive planning for the reconstruction of Germany. MacArthur more or less left the Japanese bureaucracy to govern on a day-to-day basis. SCAP had no planning capacity and few interpreters. The U.S. government intervened by special missions, as we have seen, and tried to keep a check, from time to time, on MacArthur's actions. All this suggests a kind of indifference—or underestimation of the potential importance of Japan, or perhaps of Asia as a whole. It seems fair to say that "the Japanese ruling class probably understood the nature of the U.S. occupation far better than the latter understood the former."[36]

Another fascinating example of America's zig-zag attempts at reform of the Japanese system, which was also to have very long-run consequences, was the failure to follow through on administrative legal reform. SCAP insisted on an Administrative Procedures Act in 1946 but then, in accordance with MacArthur's policy of giving the Japanese bureaucracy full power to run things, no follow-up took place. The result was to enhance the power of Japanese bureaucrats to operate in a fundamentally opaque system with little sunlight and little control—that is, the system that elicited growing anger and frustration about "structural impediments" in the 1980s (see next chapter). It took until October 1, 1994, for the Japanese to pass an Administrative Procedures Act and *begin* the real reform process "launched" by the Americans in 1946![37]

But American policy dissonance or perhaps indifference to Japan and to Asia began to change in 1948 as word of Mao Tse-tung's long march reached Washington. The change was not in the direction of reform, however. The first signal of change came from the military. Kenneth Royall, secretary of the navy, in a speech in January, warned that were the Kuomintang to fall, America's attitude to Japan would have to be reexamined. Once U.S. policy shifted to restoring Japan's prewar position as "the workshop of Asia," a clear economic plan centered on price stabilization, exchange convertibility, and fiscal probity became imperative. It was called the Dodge Plan.

Joseph Dodge was a Detroit banker who had played a key role in the postwar German currency reform. What he faced in Japan was a collapsed economy and rampant inflation. The Dodge Plan included an extremely tough budget, control of the money supply and elimination of government subsidies, a form of "tied aid" by establishment of a Counterpart Fund Special Account to finance investment in plant and equipment, and very important from Dodge's viewpoint, a fixed exchange rate. The value was fixed to *encourage Japanese exports* and was considerably *lower* than the target suggested by the Japanese government. This is simply one more example of how—quite inadvertently, one presumes—the postwar development model of Japan (which, given the shortage of raw materials in that country, required an export orientation in manufacturing) was facilitated by American policy.

The Dodge Line, as the Japanese termed it, was highly deflationary. It was most successful in its primary objective of stabilization but also created mass bankruptcies of many small- and medium-sized companies. This had the effect of rationalizing Japanese industry by favoring the former zaibatsu (keiretsu), as did the undervalued exchange rate, which provided a kick-start for Japanese export growth. Japanese industry emerged from the Dodge Plan leaner, meaner, and more concentrated. The high level of unemployment quieted union militancy, strengthened management power in large-scale firms, and set in motion the changes in labor law mentioned above that created enterprise unionism. Dodge came back to Japan later to check up on the progress of his program and commented, with satisfaction, that "it's a textbook example of how a budget can stop an inflation cold."[38] It proved to be more than that. One major consequence of the Dodge Plan was that it laid the groundwork for the success of a unique development strategy by forging close cooperation between "Japanese big business elements and their bureaucratic and political allies in Japan."[39] The Korean War then elaborated the full dimensions of that strategy.

The "successful" Dodge Plan had left the Japanese economy in the doldrums of deflation. But the Korean War injected a massive dose of demand from American military procurement. As one businessman expressed it, "the kamikaze (divine wind) has at last begun to blow in our favour."[40]

The U.S. Army turned Japan into a multi-purpose base

for its military operations in Korea. The economic impact was dramatic and worth describing:

> Rush orders for large quantities of all kinds of support supplies [came from] the U.S. military to the Japanese producers, from galvanized iron sheets and cotton duck to prefabricated buildings and chemicals. These were called "special procurements" paid for in dollars; and the list of goods and services demanded soon were expanded to cover a wide field of economic activities. . . . In fact, Japan's automobile manufacturing . . . acquired the momentum of its early growth from orders for repairing U.S. Army vehicles. Already in October 1950 both Yawata Steel and Nippon Kokan made public a three-year program of modernization; and in November Kawasaki Steel announced the projected construction of an integrated steel plant, the first of its kind in Japan.[41]

In all, the Korean War effort proved to be a *major Marshall Plan.* U.S. "aid" amounted to more than $31 billion while Marshall Aid was $16 billion. But Marshall Aid carried carefully delineated *conditions for economic policy.* The only "condition" for Korean War "aid" was to make Japan a bulwark against communism in Asia, "an essential base for the deployment of American power."[42]

The Korean War marked a watershed for Japan's future developments. A coherent policy focus on productivity and growth was enunciated by the Yoshida government including industrial policy, investment policy, trade policy, and technology transfer: "productivity ideology" reigned supreme (see below). The government did not start from scratch since during the war several groups had begun to work secretly on postwar reconstruction plans. As early as the summer of 1946, an informal advisory group to Yoshida had been established and a fully coordinated strategy was ready by late 1949.[43] The reconstruction of private industry did not start from scratch either. Despite the wartime devastation, there existed large resources of well-educated manpower and spillover from some wartime technology.[44] Thus Abramovitz's "social capabilities," necessary for catch-up, were in a sense invisible but nonetheless available. Hence, after the Korean War, "lift off" economic reconstruction took place at a rapid pace. In 1956 the Ministry of International Trade and Industry (MITI) Economic White Paper declared Japan was "no longer in the postwar era." In their view, reconstruction was over and the path to convergence had begun. Catch-up depended not only on domestic policy, however, but also—as in Europe—on access to technology.

Technology Transfer

As in the case of Europe, technological catch-up fostered by the Marshall Plan included both *direct* and *indirect* mechanisms. The *direct*, the TA project, fostered rapid diffusion of American "know-how" in mass production. The *indirect* mechanisms were essentially knowledge spillovers from trade and American direct investment. Japanese postwar development was unique in many respects but perhaps most of all in the area of technology transfer. While the import of American capital equipment was important in the early stages of reconstruction, financed mainly by Korean War aid funds, foreign direct investment was tightly controlled and the key element in Japanese development strategy was the licensing of foreign (mainly American) technology. Below

Table 2.7 Contributions to Output Growth in United States, Japan, and Germany, 1965–1973

	ANNUAL GROWTH (PERCENT)	LABOR	CAPITAL	R&D	TECHNICAL CHANGE	RESIDUAL
United States	3.74	0.99	0.88	0.12	1.58	0.17
Japan	8.71	0.23	3.01	0.19	4.51	0.77
Germany	4.21	−0.13	1.61	0.14	2.58	0.01

Source: M. Ishaq Nadiri and Ingmar R. Prucha, "Sources of Growth of Output and Convergence of Productivity in Major OECD Countries" (New York University, Department of Economics, December 1992, mimeographed), 15.

we shall briefly review Japanese investment and technology transfer policies and then turn to the American-sponsored TA program, which was based on the Marshall Plan model.

First, however, it is important to note that Japan not only restricted *inward* investment during the catch-up phase but also controlled *outward* flows, in order to increase the rate of domestic capital accumulation. Over the period 1965–73, domestic investment played a much greater role in the Japanese than in the German "growth miracle" (table 2.7), setting a pattern followed later elsewhere in East Asia, as we shall discuss in chapter 5. Various measures were adopted to increase domestic savings and, mainly through foreign exchange controls until the mid-1960s, case-by-case screening was applied by the Finance Ministry, in cooperation with MITI, for each new investment outside of Japan. No published guidelines were available, but investments related to natural resource development or export promotion were favored.

After the mid-1960s, when Japan joined the OECD and the International Monetary Fund, these restrictions were gradually lifted although screening continued until the 1980s.[45] This impact of the gradual liberalization (table 2.8), was rather modest until the enormous outward surge in the

Table 2.8 Direct Investment Flows Japan 1950–1987

FISCAL YEAR	INWARD	OUTWARD
1950–55	29	447
1956–60	62	447
1961–65	181	494
1966–70	324	2,628
1951–69	596	2,672
1970–75	808	22,269
1976–79	1,172	6,861
1980–85	557	6,525
1986–90	2,037	36,493

Sources: A. E. Safarian, *Multinational Enterprise and Public Policy: A Study of Industrial Countries* (Aldershot, U.K.: E. Elgar, 1993), 238, and United Nations Conference on Trade and Development, *World Investment Report* (Geneva: United Nations), various issues.

second half of the 1980s. But the contrast between Japan and Europe with respect to both inward and outward investment, in this as so many other respects, was to have long-lasting consequences. Thus, in the immediate postwar period, there was a large-scale expansion of European investment abroad, especially in the United States, where the European investment stock increased nearly sixfold between 1950 and 1972. This symmetry of presence gave European industry—and, indirectly, governments—a "voice" in the United States that Japan lacked. But more to the point in the current context, as table 2.8 shows, there was virtually no inward foreign investment in Japan during the catch-up period following the war. Japan needed American technology, but chose *licensing* as the preferred mechanism.

Japan's restrictive policies toward foreign investment have a long history, going back to the Mejii restoration of 1868.[46] The few foreign-controlled firms established in the interwar period had disappeared by 1941 so there were significant opportunities open to the U.S. occupation authorities. Yet liberalization of investment (or, for that matter, trade) was evidently not a top priority for SCAP or even Dodge, the banker. Under the Foreign Exchange and Foreign Trade Control Law of 1950, entry was controlled except, in rare cases, by licensing or perhaps joint ventures with foreign minority interest. The criteria for entry were described by one foreign businessman: "The product or process should be new to the country, may not be 'unfairly' competitive with existing locally-controlled counterparts, and should fit into the overall plans for the expansion of Japanese industry."[47] The process was sufficiently cumbersome that most potential investors gave up.

Overall investment policy was directed to technology licensing—that is, an unbundling of the foreign firm's assets. More than twelve thousand technical-assistance contracts were negotiated between 1950 and 1972 at a cost of $3.3 billion. Alone among the OECD countries, Japan classified technology-transfer arrangements as a form of foreign direct investment included under the Foreign Investment Law so that contracts were carefully monitored. The $3.3 billion cost seems a pretty good deal for the Japanese if one considers the contribution to catch-up as shown in the table 2.7 estimates! But from the viewpoint of the United States, the deal was termed a "disaster" in a report prepared for the U.S. Treasury in 1978. It's worth quoting:

> The U.S. private corporations will ultimately determine the level of U.S. penetration of the Japanese market. As has been discussed, Japan has been doubly protected in the past from foreign products and investment—

first by its own system of protectionism and controls
but also by the indifference of a great many U.S. companies toward Japan. These factors compounded, and
the enormous flow of U.S. technology to Japan in the
1950s and 1960s reflected both protectionist trends. On
the one hand, entry to Japan was difficult and the Japanese were eager to buy technology. On the other hand,
the foreign company often had no real determination
to enter Japan. The market seemed small and remote.
Technology seemed inexpensive. The income from
written-off R&D investment was attractive.

The result has been a disaster. The cumulative cost
to date for technology purchases by Japan from
abroad—more than 25,000 contracts covering essentially all the technology the West had to offer and most
from the United States—has been about $5 billion.
That is a little more than 10 percent of the annual
R&D expenditure of the United States. More to the
point, that technology has nurtured competitors who
now enter or threaten U.S. markets. And as a final
irony, technology which might have been a lever to enter the Japanese market has been surrendered, and
with it the advantage that might have made entry successful.[48]

The puzzle to which there is no simple answer is why
the U.S. government and U.S. business, which together had
pushed for liberalization as a basic principle of the Marshall
Plan, failed to do so in Japan. And then were shocked to find
a "disaster."

The Treasury report attributes a good deal of the problem to the shortsighted view of American business, which
was satisfied with its huge domestic market and for which

"Japan seemed pretty unimportant."[49] This combination of indifference and underestimation of Japan's potential by American business no doubt also affected U.S. government policy, which as already noted, was generally haphazard and ill-coordinated in Japan after the war. The verdict of Kent Calder on SCAP's role in Japanese financial policy is similar:

> Initially SCAP supported five major reforms relating to credit allocation:
> 1. General democratization of the economic structure, including the broadening of ownership of securities and access to capital markets.
> 2. Creation of a market-oriented financial system.
> 3. Creation of a financial system based, like that of the United States, on direct finance via stable and liquid securities markets.
> 4. Reduction in the powers of the bureaucracy over the financial system. This was to be accomplished through deregulation or decentralization of regulation, and via the establishment of independent regulatory commissions analogous to the U.S. Federal Trade Commission, Securities and Exchange Commission, and Federal Reserve Board.
> 5. Reduction of the role played in the Japanese financial system by government banks and other public institutions, particularly those formerly associated with the military.[50]

After the onset of the Cold War, enthusiasm for financial reform evaporated. Dodge, insistent on fiscal austerity, created a unique Fiscal Investment and Loan Program (FILP), which "provided off-budget support for industry and other sectors through an elaborate network of government banks.

To obviate inflationary pressures, these were funded through a highly developed postal-savings program rather than through the national budget."[51] The combination of FILP, the postal savings system, and other *ad hoc* and uncoordinated measures served to encourage a source of *low cost domestic savings to fuel investment, a highly regulated financial sector, and a corporate governance structure dominated by domestic banks.* And the financial market regulation made entry by foreign financial services firms extremely difficult. Bank-centered corporate governance structure later became a focus of fierce dispute over "structural impediments" to market entry by investment in nonfinancial sectors. And when Japanese investment flooded into the U.S. market in the 1980s, the asymmetry of investment presence in the two countries added to the friction generated by the large and growing trade imbalance (see chapter 5).

Finally, another very important consequence of the choice of licensing rather than foreign investment to access American technology was the absence of the "supply shock" effect or *le défi Americain.* The tacit knowledge of Fordism was not diffused in Japan (except via the TA project) and this may be another reason why a different form of enterprise evolved. More broadly, the absence of foreign investment helped to insulate Japanese business and to preserve long-established values and attitudes, unlike the situation in Europe described earlier. Michu Morishima asserts, that the outcome of the American role in the postwar reconstruction of Japan was that "Japanese capitalism re-emerged like a phoenix in a form almost identical to that of the pre-war period."[52] Except, of course, that the focus was not military but entirely economic. Perhaps this assertion by Morishima is a trifle strong: and, in any case, the outcome was clearly not intended by the Americans.

The Productivity Movement in Japan

In December 1953, the U.S. government suggested that the Technical Assistance Program launched in Europe under the Marshall Plan might be extended to Japan.[53] Japanese industry was flush with profits from the Korean War boom. However both business and government in Japan were well aware that industrial efficiency lagged behind that of the United States, and that Europe, under American leadership, was engaged in a concerted catch-up effort. A group of Japanese economists had formed the "Economic *Doyukai*" (fellowship) after the war with the aim of management reform, and one of its most influential members, Kohei Goshi, had observed the European developments on a trip abroad. His emphasis on the need to institute a similar effort in Japan fell on receptive ears. MITI had received translations of the BLS, British, and other productivity studies from the International Labor Organization (ILO) in 1950 and 1951 and had established an "Industry Rationalization Council," which produced its first report in 1951, stressing, *inter alia*, "management methods" and the "acquisitions of superior technology." The "productivity ideology," which MITI and business together were forging was sympathetically received by the United States and hence the suggestion to replicate the Marshall Plan approach to help foster this drive for greater efficiency in Japan. In March 1955, the Japan Productivity Centre was established as a private tripartite organization among management, labor, and academics. A brief history of this development, little known outside Japan, is worth relating.

The MITI White Paper of 1956 was entitled "Growth and Modernization of the Japanese Economy." Its emphasis on a "productivity ideology" based on modern technology and management efficiency was strongly influenced by the same events that had led to the establishment of the Japan Productivity Centre the previous year. Access to technology was seen as a necessary but not sufficient condition for rapid development. Equally important were "modern" management techniques and effective "utilization of the labour force" including job training and "efficiency-based compensation schemes."

MITI's productivity ideology originated from the Ministry of Labour's translation of the International Labor Organization documents on labor productivity and the European Productivity Centres in 1950 and 1951, and from discussions between the U.S. and Japanese governments (in anticipation of the 1951 Peace Treaty) on plans for economic cooperation after the end of the Korean War. From these discussions, the Japanese understood that when the war boom ended, economic relations with the United States would no longer be based on military procurement and that in order to compete on commercial grounds in both the American and Southeast Asian markets, Japanese industry would have to be fundamentally restructured, or rationalized, as the Japanese put it. As early as 1951, the Industry Rationalization Council, which had been established by MITI, recommended the creation of a Japan Productivity Centre. Although this was premature, the idea was planted in the Japanese ministry.

While these views were being explored in government and business, the Economic Doyukai, a group of "progressive economists" formed after the war, was preaching the need for management reform. Their bible was James Burnham's *Management Revolution,* which had been translated by one of their members. The message they took from Burnham was that competent managers, supported by technology experts, are "important national treasures and must be protected from the selfish whims of capitalists." When Kohei Goshi, an executive of the Doyukai, visited Western Germany in early 1953, another part of the gospel was added: harmonious labor relations. His report emphasized the importance of the "family relationship" between management and unions in German industry, which he saw as a key to the impressive productivity performance of German firms. (Indeed, more generally, the evolving German model of social partnership—that is, cooperation between government, business, and labor—greatly impressed the Japanese.) Finally, Goshi's European visit also took him to England, where he studied the papers prepared for the 1953 Anglo-American Productivity Conference, which described in great detail the study trips to the United States. He describes himself as "awestruck."

From the end of 1953 to the spring of 1955, all these separate developments came together. Upon his return from Europe, Goshi met with an official in the commerce division of the American embassy. This official emphasized the need for technological exchange between Japan and America and lauded the success of the European efforts. He offered to provide funds to bring American technicians to Japan. Goshi then brought together with the Doyukai the main industry organizations in Japan (the Keidanren, Nikkeiren, and Nissho), and by March 1954 they had established a private-sector Japanese-American Productivity Enhancement Committee. The committee's original proposal was to hold seminars on management issues with senior executives, technicians, and workers to spell out the main problem areas impeding productivity improvement and to send delegations to the United States to study effective methods to overcome these problems. The costs of the operation were to be jointly covered by American grants and the industry organizations, with the Japanese contribution limited to 20 percent of the total.

MITI welcomed these developments but was eager to establish a government presence in the activities. The American government, on the basis of its European experience, agreed that this was essential. An official was sent from Washington in September 1954 to convey these views to the Japanese government. After discussions and negotiations over funding and operational details, in March 1955 the Japan Productivity Centre (JPC) was established as a private nonprofit organization representing management, labor, and academics. A parallel government group, composed of deputy ministers of the relevant ministries and private sector representatives of the JPC, was also established to ensure a linkage between the productivity enhancement program in industry and the government's modernization policy outlined in the 1956 White Paper.

The productivity movement in Japan replicated the TA program in Europe. Groups from all sectors of industry were sent on study tours and American specialists came to lecture and advise in Japan. Even after the termination of U.S. aid in 1961, the study tours continued on a self-funded basis. By 1960 a network of regional productivity centers had been set up. In 1961 Japan invited eight Asian countries to a meeting in Manila to found the Asian Productivity Organization (APO) and pursued an active policy of productivity enhancement in that region, including a JPC China Office established in 1978. The APO today includes eighteen countries.[54] (And, as we shall see in chapter 5, it is now actively engaged in upgrading the technological capabilities in East Asia to improve the "supply base" for new Japanese investment in the region.)

As was the case in Europe, it is impossible to assess in any rigorous fashion the effects of the American contribution to Japanese development through the productivity movement. As stressed earlier, the transfer of "tacit knowledge," including management methods and enterprise organization forms, are today recognized as essential elements in technology diffusion. In the Japanese case, the diffusion of tacit knowledge took place mainly through the productivity enhancement efforts of the JPC rather than through several channels including foreign direct investment. The resulting enterprise form and labor-management relations turned out to be very different from the American mass production model of Fordism. The question is why? We have suggested that the absence of foreign investment provides one clue. But perhaps that is not an adequate explanation.

More importantly, and more broadly, as this brief account of the history of the JPC illustrates, Japan was obviously not a *tabula rasa* upon which a new market model could be engraved: the embedded "social capabilities" or institutional and behavioral systems were not wiped out by the physical devastation of the war. (Indeed, this also applied to Western Europe.) Thus the *new* knowledge, crudely termed technology assistance, was filtered through a fine web of *inherited* knowledge—culture, institutions, values and behavior—and thus was transformed during the process of acquisition. The result was inherently unpredictable for the American administration or American business.

Conclusion

This chapter has analyzed the contribution of the United States to two key forces of postwar catch-up in Europe and Japan: domestic investment and technology transfer. But as was clear in the Marshall Plan, the Korean War boom in Japan, and the direct technology transfer projects, the processes of catch-up were strongly influenced by the institutional context of each country (Abramovitz's "social capabilities"), as well as by accident and error—essentially random factors. The outcomes—either in terms of convergence or market systems—were thus essentially unpredictable.

Does this unpredictability matter? The answer has to be a cautious yes because by the 1970s the existence of the convergence club was a rather unwelcome surprise to many Americans, and even more so was the fact that there were several "flavors" of capitalism. Both results fed a sense of unfairness. The view that the rebuilding of Europe and of Japan, after the onset of the Korean War, depended on American leadership is incontestable. But the Americans also believed that what was being created—as a bulwark against communism—was a replica of the United States. The inherent unpredictability, or what economists term path-dependent development, ruled that out from the beginning. And as we shall see in the following chapter, there was also a considerable gap between intent and outcome in the third force speeding postwar catch-up—the liberalization of international trade.

Three

The GATT House: Termites in the Basement

The liberalization of trade in the decades following the war played an important part in catch-up. The large and largely closed domestic market of the United States had provided the necessary conditions for its lead in mass production industries since the beginning of the twentieth century. For European and Japanese business to capture the economies of scale essential to competitiveness in many of these industries, home markets were too small. So the trade barriers erected during the thirties had to be dismantled and a new liberalization momentum set in play. Export growth outpaced output growth by a wide margin during the 1950s and 1960s for both Europe and Japan. This in turn stimulated investment and raised productivity. Furthermore, trade was also a channel for technology transfer: the spillovers from American R&D investment, embodied in leading-edge capital goods, added to the growth effects of the postwar investment boom in the defeated countries. And penetration of the dynamic and sophisticated American market also added to the knowledge base of the exporting firm valuable information about consumer preferences and the strategy of competition.

The United States took the leading role in building a new trading system. Memories of the protectionist battles of the 1930s, initiated by the notorious 1930 Smoot-Hawley tariff, were still vivid. Cordell Hull, Roosevelt's secretary of state, had reversed the longstanding U.S. protectionist policy in 1934 by the passage of the Reciprocal Trade Agreements Act (RTAA), which authorized the president to negotiate tariff reductions with foreign states on a nondiscriminatory basis. (The Constitution of the United States gives Congress exclusive power "to regulate commerce with foreign nations," but Congress may delegate trade policy powers to the executive branch.) Hull was convinced that freer international trade was essential to U.S. prosperity, to world recovery, and to the maintenance of world peace. From 1934 on, Hull's vision became "the core mythology" of American foreign policy.[1]

The importance that the United States attached to trade was apparent at the outset of the Bretton Woods negotiations. Indeed, freer trade was considered to be an essential component of the Bretton Woods plan. Just as a stable international monetary system was considered essential to long-term growth, the link between the monetary and trading systems was well understood by the Bretton Woods creators, Lord Keynes and Harry Dexter White. The beggar-thy-neighbor devaluations were as pernicious as the tariff wars of the 1930s. Both Keynes and White agreed that a stable, rule-based payments system required a stable, rule-based trading system—and vice versa. But, whereas achieving consensus on the monetary rules proved difficult but doable, the profound disagreement between the U.K. and U.S. Treasuries over trade rules proved insuperable. It's of interest to note that it was easier for these macroeconomists to deal with monetary issues. They shared a convenient kind of macromyopia that allowed them to delegate the detailed, messy, "political" micro issues to people in other government departments, not in treasuries. Thus only the broadest generalities on trade were included in the International Monetary Fund (IMF) Articles of Agreement.[2]

So the trade debate followed a separate track. But it still involved a negotiation between the United States and the United Kingdom. Although the United States took the leading role, the State Department evidently felt the need for British support. And the British view was probably best summed up by a popular rhyme of the day: "In Washington Lord Halifax whispered to Lord Keynes, 'They've got all the money bags but we've got all the brains.'" Keynes kept an eye on the trade negotiations, which were handled by two British professors on loan to the Economic Section of the War Cabinet, Lionel Robbins and James Meade. Early in the talks, which began in the summer of 1941, Keynes referred to the initial American provisions as "the lunatic proposals of Mr. Hull."[3]

The disagreement between the British and Americans, which was to shape the final outcome of the trade negotiations, concerned two fundamental issues: nondiscrimination, or the most-favored-nation (MFN) rule, which would accord all countries' equality of treatment of imports and exports; and the extent and nature of "escape clauses" to permit temporary import barriers for protection of the domestic economy. The British wanted to maintain their system of preferential treatment of Commonwealth Countries for political reasons. This request for discrimination or preferential arrangements for imports and exports for certain countries flew in the face of Hull's vision.

Even more difficult, however, was the demand for the right to regulate imports, for this represented a test of the "Keynesian consensus," the need to resolve the conflict between domestic policy, dedicated to the maintenance of full employment, and the more laissez-faire international rules of free trade. For the British, as stated in the 1944 White Paper on Employment Policy, the government's role in preventing unemployment was primary, and there was no mention of trade policy. Even the *Economist*, the traditional champion of laissez-faire and free trade, declared "that it did not challenge the old principle that international exchange and division of labour leads to the highest possible national income, but modifications were necessary, because the modern community had acquired economic needs other than maximum wealth."[4] The desired "modification" was the right to take temporary trade restrictive measures when faced with balance-of-payments difficulties. The alternative—domestic deflationary policies—was unacceptable to the British government (and to most governments in Europe, as well.)

There were some Americans, especially Keynesian academics, who also gave priority to full employment. But this was not the prevailing view. As Jacob Viner notes:

> The zeal of the United States for the elimination of special and flexible controls over foreign trade is in large part explained by the absence of any prospect that the United States will in the near future devise or accept a significant program for stabilization of employment or for the planning of investment, the confidence prevailing in this country that our competitive position in foreign trade and the exchange position of the American dollar will continue to be strong, and the availability of the cache of gold at Fort Knox to tide us over even a prolonged and substantial adverse balance of payments if perchance it should occur.[5]

The depth of disagreement on this crucial issue of the role of government deserves underlining. There was no government-constructed postwar "social contract" in the United States. While an Employment Act was passed in 1946 (and the Council of Economic Advisers created as an instrument of the Keynesian policy approach), after the 1946 elections the Republicans dominated Congress and the role of the council in this respect was somewhat limited. Most of the American social contract was negotiated by the mass production unions in the golden age of growth. Furthermore, the European "social compact" involved more than Keynesian demand management: it included a commitment to income redistribution involving an expanded role of the state in both taxation and expenditure, alien to the historical and deeply embedded U.S. conception of the government's role. The New Deal represented a departure dictated by changed circumstances but not a fundamental transformation of the vision of the Founding Fathers. Thus the romantic ideal of the Hull vision was undergirded not by a widely held consensus about the nature of the relationship between the international trading system and domestic policy shared by the United States and the other OECD countries. Rather, as Jacob Viner noted, American support for the GATT stemmed from investment abroad because of America's lead in the world economy.

The separate trade negotiations between the United States and the United Kingdom began in 1943. It was not until the end of 1945—well after Bretton Woods—that a document was released in Washington entitled "Proposals for Consideration by an Intergovernmental Conference on Trade and Employment." The Anglo-American compromise involved dropping Commonwealth Preference but including provisions for balance-of-payments restrictions. The proposals included a charter for an International Trade Organization (ITO).

To create a more global system, the U.S. proposals were sent to the newly formed United Nations where, in February 1946, its Economic and Social Council (ECOSOC) called for a conference to establish the ITO. A preparatory committee of eighteen countries (the Soviet Union declined membership) was formed and four preparatory meetings were held to complete the draft ITO Charter, the first in London in October 1946 and the last in Havana in 1948. The principal meeting was held in Geneva from April to November 1947. The Geneva meeting had three aims: continuing the preparation of the charter; negotiation of a multilateral agreement of tariff reduction; drafting "general clauses" of obligations related to tariff negotiations. The second and third parts became the General Agreement on Tariffs and Trade, or GATT.

The details of the draft GATT will be discussed below. GATT was intended as part of the ITO charter. The U.S. administration, after criticism and questioning from congressional communities during 1947, defended their negotiating authority under the 1945 extension of the 1934 RTAA. To placate Congress the negotiators used the term "contracting parties" to make clear no international organization had been established. The ITO charter, the main objective of the preparatory process, was to be completed at Havana the following year.

At Havana the charter of the ITO reflected the many compromises negotiated during the preparatory process. In contrast to the Bretton Woods institutions, weighted voting (according to economic clout) was dropped for a one-country vote rule. Chapters on employment, development, antitrust, investment, agriculture, and a number of exceptions to liberal trade rules were included. The battles among both developed and developing countries were over exceptions and exceptions to exceptions. Even Commonwealth Preference was included under a "grandfathering" of existing preferential arrangements.

The negotiated compromise that produced the ITO reflected the pragmatic, nondoctrinal bent of the State Department. It was presented as a singular victory, as "a middle way" between an approach too rigid to withstand strain and the "near anarchy" that would be likely in the absence of any agreement.[6]

But all the compromise and difficult negotiations leading to agreement in Havana were overtaken by events. At the time of the Havana meeting, the Marshall Plan was launched. The trade and payments liberalization of the OEEC, based on discrimination against the United States, settled the issue of nondiscrimination without debate. The ITO was not ratified after Havana by any country because all were waiting for the leader to ratify first.

The president required another extension of negotiating authority in 1949 so decided not to send the ITO to Congress that year. But in his message to Congress on January 4, 1950, President Truman declared that "we should promptly join the International Trade Organization."[7] However, opposition was building from many quarters—and support from few. As well, the Korean War had started. Interest in global cooperation had waned. Truman judged there was virtually no chance of approval of the Havana Charter. On December 6, 1950, a press release was quietly issued:

> The interested agencies have recommended, and the President has agreed, that, while the proposed Charter for an International Trade Organization should not be (re)submitted to the Congress, Congress be asked to consider legislation which will make American participation in the General Agreement more effective.[8]

President Truman's judgment that the ITO would be rejected can, of course, never be tested. Yet the basis for the judgment seems pretty plausible: no strong support, lots of strong opposition. Why did Bretton Woods get by Congress? And the Marshall Plan? No strong opposition, seems to be the answer. Bretton Woods was about money and the dollar. Americans were not worried about the dollar—as Viner noted, they knew there was lots of gold in Fort Knox. The Marshall Plan was about the Cold War. There was little opposition to the Cold War. But as William Diebold has observed, the ITO was killed by a "perfectionist/protectionist" coalition. There were too many loopholes, far too much government intervention for free traders, and too much free trade for protectionists. Consensual hegemony lacked consensus in the hegemon's own domain. This is worth spelling out.

Much of the most effective business opposition was not based on fear of import penetration (although there was, as always, some of that). Diebold explains:

> Business opposition to commercial policies that are alleged to go too far in removing trade barriers is an old story. The new element in this case was the opposition the Charter met from businessmen who felt it did not go far enough in removing trade barriers. The people who took this view were not primarily concerned about the effect of the Charter on American trade barriers. Their objection was that the Charter would do little to remove the trade barriers set up by foreign countries and might even strengthen some of them. The essence of this view was that the exceptions to the Charter's general rules, and the escape clauses applicable to special circumstances, were so numerous that most foreign countries could comply with the Charter without actually freeing trade from existing restrictions. More-

over, the businessmen who took this view usually believed that the Charter went too far in subordinating the international commitments of signatory countries to the requirements—real or imagined—of national economic plans and policies. They believed, too, that the Charter was too heavily laden with the ideological and practical paraphernalia of government regulation and control, so that it would not help, and very likely would hinder, the development of private enterprise. In short, the businessmen who took these views held that the Charter was not "liberal" enough and not "internationalist" enough.[9]

The business opposition was particularly strong in the matter of full employment, exchange controls, and quotas. These parts of the charter, to them, smacked of planning and could lead to inflation. The failure to provide full protection for foreign investment was another stumbling block. But what lay at the heart of the opposition of powerful business lobbies was a rejection of the idea that there can be many variants of market systems, with different institutional arrangements including different mixes of government and business roles. And where such differences existed, they were, in the view of American business, probably unfairly protectionist. The support for trade liberalization by many U.S. business groups was based on support for access to foreign markets, which were seen as less open than those of the United States, in part because of government intrusiveness. This was not unfamiliar rent-seeking by industrial lobbies who stood to gain from their lead in mass production, which would be enhanced by increased market share. It is by no means unusual behavior in any country. But it should not be confused with a policy based on the overall benefits flow-ing from a liberal, global trading system. A statement by the U.S. Council of the International Chamber of Commerce pretty well summed it all up:

> It is a dangerous document because it accepts practically all of the policies of economic nationalism; because it jeopardizes the free enterprise system by giving priority to centralized national governmental planning of foreign trade; because it leaves a wide scope to discrimination, accepts the principle of economic insulation and in effect commits all members of the ITO to state planning for full employment. From the point of view of the United States, it has the further very grave defect of placing this country in a position where it must accept discrimination against itself while extending the Most-Favored-Nation treatment to all members of the Organization. It places the United States in a permanent minority position owing to its one-vote-one-country voting procedure. Because of that, membership in the ITO based on this Chapter would make it impossible for the United States to engage in an independent course of policy in favor of multilateral trade.[10]

Added to this "perfectionist" opposition was the more traditional line-up of protected industries and an alliance of some of these industries with trade unions: the National Labor-Management Council on Foreign Trade. A new argument was presented by these groups: the alleged unconstitutionality of delegating power to an international body. (Sound familiar?) And against this formidable array of opposition lobbies, the only voices supporting the ITO were "the bureaucrats and college professors."[11] They, if few others, shared the Hull vision. It is also important to underline that this "vision" was fundamentally different from the nineteenth-century neo-classical "vision" of unilateral free trade, which so impassioned the British and led to the repeal of the Corn Laws in 1846. The Hull vision rested on reciprocity, broadly defined, as the motor for liberalization, not selfless and self-beneficial unilateral free trade.

Be that as it may, American leadership in the trade arena did not fail with the death of the ITO. It was American initiative that launched the negotiations in Geneva. An important motive for this initiative was the view that the Havana Conference would be facilitated if concrete tariff reductions could be presented as evidence of the benefits of trade liberalization. The administration was also concerned to start negotiations as soon as possible before the powers of president to reduce tariffs expired in June 1948. The GATT, signed by twenty-three "contracting parties," was not opposed by the U.S. Congress—but neither was it endorsed, as was made plain when the Reciprocal Trade Agreements Act was extended again in 1951. Since GATT was much narrower in coverage and because the commitments contained in the Agreement were less binding,[12] it did not elicit the widespread opposition of the ITO. Its weakness was its strength—at least at the outset.

Termites in the Basement

The ITO died in the United States not simply because there was a great deal of opposition to the compromise proposal for a world trade institution to complete the Bretton Woods architecture. Equally important, there was little support to accept the negotiated compromises. The GATT, narrower and weaker, at the outset elicited little in the way of real opposition or support. Some of the negotiated compromises were still there, but because it covered the narrower area of commercial policy, they were far less obtrusive. And the threat to "sovereignty" was avoided because formal ratification in the U.S. Congress was not needed. This was another good example of the American genius for creative ad hocery, which resulted in a powerful trade liberalizing drive through successive rounds of negotiations led by the United States. But under the ad hoc edifice of the GATT were a number of termites gnawing away at the foundations.

The essential compromise embedded in the GATT—as in the Bretton Woods arrangements—concerned the balance between domestic policy objectives and international obligations, in this instance the reciprocal reduction of trade barriers. The extent and nature of "escapes" from negotiated commitments to liberalization are carefully spelled out in the GATT rules—or as exceptions to the overriding "rule" or "norm" of liberalization. These exceptions were considered essential as a means of promoting liberalization, for in the absence of legitimate "escapes," governments would be reluctant to undertake any significant reduction of trade barriers. The same idea is expressed in another way: "escapes" provide modest protectionist "safety valves" as a way of avoiding worse protectionist policies. While the overall aim of the GATT was to reduce barriers (and, see below, eliminate discrimination in international trade) by promoting the negotiation of tariff bindings (a commitment not to raise agreed tariff levels) and banning the use of other barriers, such as quotas, a wide range of exceptions to these rules was also part of the agreement. These included the "trade remedy" rules such as antidumping and countervailing duties against unfair trade based on longstanding American legislation about the importance of "fairness" in trade (Article VI), the so-called Escape Clause against import surges (Article XIX), the balance-of-payments exceptions (Articles XII–XV and XVIIIB), the national security exception (Article XXI), the waiver provisions (Article XXV), and the renegotiation provision (Article XXVIII). There were also various provisions to protect agriculture from the liberalization commitment. While some of these "escapes" were little used, others, especially those against "unfair" trade, eventually resulted in significant abuse of the GATT's *raison d'être* of liberalization.

Another primary objective of American leadership was nondiscrimination, or MFN. In the interest of achieving consensus, exceptions to MFN were permitted for custom unions, free trade areas as well as continuation of existing preference systems. The Americans were willing to accept this exception to what was considered a fundamental pillar of the Hull vision because of their concern with the stability of postwar Europe. It was not possible to foresee at the time how far the MFN principle would be eroded by this exception, not only by the formation of the European Economic Community and the European Free Trade Association (EFTA) but by a number of preferential arrangements made by the Europeans with their former colonies. Indeed, discrimination became an "established" element in the Community's policies.[13] Further, since agriculture was not, from the beginning, an integral part of the liberal trade regime, and the United States had undermined even the ambiguous rules that existed by a waiver for its own domestic policy in 1955, there was nothing to prevent the launch of the community's grossly distorting Common Agricultural Policy (CAP).

As has been noted, the notion of reciprocity—that is, a

balanced exchange of export opportunities and import openings—was a key and basic premise of the American approach to trade liberalization. Reciprocity was the governing principle in the bilateral negotiations under the RTAA and under the GATT it involved essentially bilateral negotiations multilateralized via the MFN clause. For political reasons, reciprocity was essential to the American approach because it minimized "free riding"—that is, getting the benefits from the system without any concessions. The multilateralization of negotiations sought to constrain free riding by techniques such as principal supplier negotiations whereby bilaterals concentrated on categories of imports that originated mainly in the partner countries.

But as was the case in nondiscrimination, the United States relaxed the rules of reciprocity to help the postwar reconstruction process. Thus, in the rounds in Geneva and Annecy in 1947 and 1949, "the United States, armed with an authorization to reduce tariffs by 50 percent, exchanged real tariff concessions for fake ones from the Europeans. The latter, in fact, had ceased to use tariffs to regulate trade and instead imposed quantitative restrictions to limit imports."[14] Indeed, there were no truly reciprocal trade negotiations under the GATT until the Kennedy Round of the 1960s. All this was part of American foreign policy, as we stressed in the discussion of the Marshall Plan, and only foreign policy concerns were powerful enough to override the deeply entrenched concern with unfair "free riding." *But the lack of reciprocity in the early rounds of the GATT was to add to the feeling in American business circles that the trading system was "unfair."* Once European and Japanese convergence was apparent, the Cold War *raison d'état* seemed a far less compelling basis for trade policy, and there was growing resentment over the role of the foreign policy "establishment." Of course, with the Cold War over, this powerful "high policy" constraint has vanished.

Another basic flaw in the GATT compromise was the dispute settlement mechanism. The GATT was, as stressed, based on the notion of *flexibility*—that is, basic rules but lots of escapes. And the GATT's legal status in member countries, especially in the United States, was ambivalent, to say the least. Furthermore, the rules themselves were often "constructively ambiguous," but in the early years the drafters were often still representing the contracting parties so that there was a shared understanding about their implicit meaning. Disputes could be settled by conciliation and persuasion, which really amounted to further negotiation, rather than by more transparent, legal procedures. But as the number of contracting parties grew—including the accession of Japan at American insistence over European objections—and the rules became more complex, the dispute settlement mechanism proved increasingly impotent. Noncompliance became widespread, and the mechanism was virtually abandoned by the 1960s. It was frustration with the inadequacy of the system that lay behind the U.S. Section 301 law in 1974, which sanctioned American unilateralism (see chapter 4) and also generated a major effort in the Tokyo Round to revive and strengthen the GATT procedures. There is, of course, an inherent contradiction between congressional criticism of the GATT's legal weaknesses and the unwillingness to yield "sovereignty" to international institutions, and that contradiction has not yet been resolved, as was evident in the debate over the implementation of the Uruguay Round.

The GATT represents a historic achievement of American leadership, but it is difficult to accept the view of many international scholars that the founders had a shared vision of a liberal trading system or even that most Americans had such a vision. Those who negotiated the GATT for the United States did, indeed, seek a "free" and "fair" trading system, but support from business and labor lobbies was lacking. The push to open foreign markets was on the whole based on rent-seeking behavior by competitive mass-production industries, but this of course made reciprocity essential to reduce free riding. All things considered, the view that Hull's vision underlay the creation of the GATT does not stand up to careful examination.[15] The crux of the matter concerned the role of government.

The consensus reflected in the GATT rules and the exceptions masked significant differences on this basic issue, which was the *nature and extent of government intervention to achieve domestic objectives*. Framed by the optic of the Cold War, there seemed to be only two, opposed, economic "systems": capitalist or communist, market or planned. Outside this line of sight, however, a number of market economy variants were already emerging after the war. And, as we saw in the previous chapter, America's role in postwar reconstruction unintentionally fostered these different variants. The consensus, which the GATT represented, was forged by this astigmatic affliction. This does not negate the fact, of course, that when all is said and done, no other approach was feasible: Viner's "flexibility" or "anarchy" was the choice. Nor does it negate the fact that the United States and all other countries greatly benefited from the multilateral negotiations that liberalized world trade. But it is also inescapable that the compromise embedded in the GATT was subjected to ever increasing strain over the 1970s, a subject to which we now turn.

Erosion in the 1970s

The 1970s could not have presented a starker contrast to the golden age of catch-up. Instead of buoyant growth there was stagflation, an ugly new term to describe the unique combination of rising inflation and rising unemployment caused by the unprecedented supply shock from the quadrupling of prices by the OPEC cartel, which spawned unprecedented macroeconomic imbalances. A combination of slowing growth and declining productivity (still not fully explained), as well as increasing change in information and communication technologies (ICT), created powerful pressures for structural adaptation. Yet structural adaptation, especially in Europe, was made much more difficult by many of the features of the welfare state, the product of the postwar social contract. Within the OECD countries, the politics of consensus evaporated and among them policy dissent heightened. The puzzle of how to deal with stagflation eroded the Keynesian consensus in both governments and among economists as monetarist ideas became more attractive.

With the scope for both fiscal policy and monetary easing greatly reduced, and faced with the political difficulties of tackling the "structural rigidities," which impeded adjustment, the attractiveness of a range of protectionist measures became more appealing. This political attractiveness of protectionism as a policy option was fortified by the increasing importance of trade, especially in manufacturing products. The challenge from Japan as a powerful competitor and the rise of new actors such as the Asian "dragons," or newly industrializing economies (NIEs), of Hong Kong, Singapore, Taiwan, and Korea not only added to structural pressures for adaptation but lent plausibility to the popular view that a basic cause of the unemployment and slower growth was foreign competition.

This clash between the "irresistible forces" of increasing structural change and the seemingly "immovable object" of the postwar social contract gave rise to the "new protectionism" of the 1970s (see below). But the new protectionism, which violated the spirit if not the letter of the overall GATT norm of liberalization, was also symptomatic of a more fundamental fault line in the postwar international system where the termites were breeding: the tenuous nature of the consensus concerning the respective roles of domestic policy and international rules.

The first sign of the fault line came not in the trade arena but in the break-up of the monetary arrangements of Bretton Woods. The threat of a massive request for convertibility of official dollar holdings into gold, which had been building up for some time, and was exacerbated by U.S. domestic policy failure in choosing not to raise taxes to finance the Vietnam expenditures in the late 1960s created the crisis. On August 15, 1971, President Nixon suspended the convertibility of the dollar into gold and placed a 10 percent surcharge on imports into the United States. Faced with the need to tighten monetary and fiscal policy and a growing trade deficit stemming from an overvalued dollar and excessive government spending, the United States chose instead to devalue the dollar by closing the gold window and imposing the surcharge to force negotiations on a new exchange-rate alignment.[16] In the discussions that followed the August events, Treasury Secretary Connally stressed the importance of opening the European and Japanese markets to American exports and also the need for those countries to accept a bigger share of the costs of overseas defense (fairer burden-sharing, as it came to be called). In the event, efforts at monetary reform failed but the discussions were important in helping U.S. efforts to launch a new round of trade negotiations to redress what was felt to be an imbalance in market liberalization in earlier rounds. Another, equally important concern of the U.S. administration was the rise of the "new protectionism." This commitment of the American administration to trade liberalization by using multilateral negotiations to offset rising protectionist pressures—sometimes called the bicycle theory—was still clearly evident in the 1970s.

The New Protectionism and the Tokyo Round

In June 1978, OECD Ministers announced a new policy approach to cope with stagflation. This marked the "official" demise of the postwar Keynesian consensus and represented an effort to forge a new consensus combining macroeconomic, microeconomic or structural, and international trade policies. The new approach was spelled out in a report entitled *Positive Adjustment Policies: Managing Structural Change.*[17] A major theme of the report was the need to tackle the "socio-economic rigidities" of the OECD economies, which were impeding adjustment to structural change; exacerbating stagflation; and fostering new forms of protectionism.

The OECD outlines the "basic origins" of these structural rigidities:

> First, they reflect attitudes and institutional developments which evolved during the period of uninterrupted high levels of employment, and which were slow to change under the entirely different circumstances of the 1970s. Second, they reflect the rapid

growth of the public sector and of social programmes
and regulations which, however desirable in themselves, have sometimes had unintended adverse side effects on incentives to work, save and invest. Third, they
derive from attempts by governments to alleviate the
social consequences of structural change by preserving
given production and employment structures. Fourth,
and most importantly, slow growth itself makes structural adjustment more difficult.[18]

The self-reinforcing virtuous circle of the 1950s and
1960s, was replaced by a self-reinforcing vicious circle in the
1970s. But the extent and nature of the rigidities were not
uniform among the OECD countries. The role of government was more pervasive in many European countries than
in the United States, and in Japan one role of government
was to facilitate adjustment. However, both Europe and the
United States were subject to protectionist pressure, and the
target was often Japan.

The term *new protectionism*, which was coined in the
1970s, consisted of border nontariff measures (NTMs) such
as voluntary export restraints (VERs) and domestic nontariff measures such as subsidies. By definition, the border
measures were difficult to quantify or, often, even to detect
when they took the form of quasi-legal market-sharing
agreements (orderly marketing arrangements, or OMAs)
among companies. Despite the absence of rigorous quantitative estimates, however, various studies suggested that as
much as one-fifth of OECD manufacturing imports was affected by quantitative restrictions at the end of the 1970s, a
quadrupling over the decade.[19] These quantitative barriers
were concentrated in certain sectors; in addition to agriculture, textiles, footwear, iron, and steel showed the greatest

prevalence early in the period, beginning in the 1960s, but by the end of the decade consumer electronics and automobiles were added. The main target countries of the restrictions were Japan and the Asian NIEs. This summary may be seen in figure 3.1.

The "new protectionism" arose because the GATT itself was not designed to deal with structural change. The GATT safeguard clause (Article XIX) was intended to deal with short-term import surges but not with the fundamental structural adjustment of the 1970s. Moreover because it was to be applied on an MFN or nondiscriminatory basis and required proof of serious injury as well as "compensation" (or lowering of other barriers) by the invoking country, it was rarely used. The "new protectionism" involved selective, nontransparent measures and was more attractive to countries that wished to preserve the appearance if not the practice of adherence to GATT principles. Sometimes governments, especially in Europe—where antitrust policy and ethos was still weak—simply closed their eyes to cartel-like price or market share arrangements made by private firms.

Quantitative restraints or quotas created a political constituency for their maintenance in both the importing and exporting countries through the generation of scarcity "rents." And, most importantly, by fostering trade diversion, both geographic and product-oriented, they built in a *dynamic for extension.*

Thus while the NTMs were first applied mainly in labor-intensive industries such as textiles and footwear and were porous enough to permit significant growth in trade during the 1970s, it was the extension to more capital-intensive, high-wage sectors such as steel, automobiles, and consumer electronics that most affected the trade policy climate in the United States and Europe. Indeed, the spread of trade re-

Figure 3.1 The Spread of NTBs Facing Major Import Categories, 1968–1984

Product

Automobiles
  U.S.

  EU
  Germany
  France
  Italy   VER: Japan 1956 2,200 units
  U.K.

(U.K.) 1975–78 Monitor
imports for Japan; Prudent
Market Agreement:
1978—Set at 1977 level =
11% domestic market

  Canada

  Japan   Discretionary licensing (date of origin?)

Steel
  U.S.   ⎰ VER: Japan, EC 1969–74 (carbon steel) 1969:
      ⎱ Imports to 5.75 million tons, w. permissible increase

  EU

Textitles
  U.S.   Long-Term Agreement 1962 renewed twice   Multi-Fiber Agreement 1974–1978
  EU   Long-Term Agreement 1962 renewed twice   Multi-Fiber Agreement 1974–1978
  Canada   Long-Term Agreement 1962 renewed twice   Multi-Fiber Agreement 1974–1978
  Japan

Footwear
  U.S.
  U.K.
  France
  Italy
  U.K.
  Canada

Consumer electronics products
  U.S.
  EU

  France
  Italy

(It.) Quota: Japan: Radio, TV,
communications equipment

  U.K.

Motorcycles
  U.S.
  EU
  France

  Italy

| | | | | | | | | |
| 1968 | 1969 | 1970 | 1971 | 1972 | 1973 | 1974 | 1975 | 1976 |

	Termination Date
(U.S.) VER: Japan 1981 -3/1984 1.68 M passenger Cars including light trucks = 3/85 1.85M	3/85
(EU) VER: Japan 2/1983	
(Ger) UR by Japan 6/1981: Growth limited to 10% yr	6/84
(FR) Japan: Sales restrained to 2.5–3.0% of domestic market	
(Can.) VER: Japan 1981: 23% domestic market 1982: Varying units permitted	4/84

┌ (U.S.) VER: EC 10/82 (carbon steel)   10/85
└ Specialty steel (section 201) 7/83   7/87

┌ (E.U.) Basic Price System (BPS) VER/13 major suppliers (cabon steel)
└ Basic Price System (BPS) VER/13 major suppliers (Specialty steel)

	Termination Date
Renewed with additional protocol to 1982—Accept new protocol of extension of MFA to	7/86
Renewed with additional protocol to 1982—Accept new protocol of extension of MFA to	7/86
Renewed with additional protocol to 1982—Accept new protocol of extension of MFA to	7/86
(Japan) Restrictions on textile imports from LDCs were in effect in 1980	

	Termination Date
(U.S.) OMA: Taiwan, Korea Nonrubber footwear 1977	6/81
(U.K.) OMA: Taiwan, Korea Nonrubber footwear 1978 . . .	
(FR) VRA: Taiwan, Korea Nonrubber footwear 1981	
(It.) Quotas: Nonrubber footwear 1979 . . .	
(U.K.) OMA/VER: Poland, Korea rubber footwear 1979–80	
(Can.) Quotas: General footware restraint/Third World Nations, Leather Footwear 1978	1985

	Termination Date
(U.S.) OMA: Taiwan, Korea (color TV receivers)	
(EU): QR: Japan/VTRs, color TV tubes	2/86
(France) Quotas: Discretionary licensing/Global (in effect in 1980)	

(U.K.) VER: Taiwan, Korea: Radio, TV, communications equipment

	Termination Date
(U.S.): Tariff rate quota	4/88
(EU): VER: Japan	2/86
(France) Import Surveillance—Japan cylinder capacity—50 cm	
(Italy) Quota: Japan (includes bicycles as well)	

1977	1978	1979	1980	1981	1982	1983	1984

strictions from labor-intensive to more capital-intensive industries reflected the diversification of exports, especially in the rapidly growing Asian NIEs, which had been fostered by the new protectionism—that is, reflected the built-in dynamic noted above and helped spur rapid growth in the NIEs by accelerating export-led structural transformation (see chapter 5). The latter can be illustrated by the U.S. color television OMA initially aimed at Japan, which encouraged Korea and Taiwan to become alternative suppliers and therefore targets of quantitative restrictions. Thus in a period of slower growth and lagging productivity, both Europe and the United States faced a growing challenge not only from Japan but also from new players in the world trading system outside the OECD. Because the EU continued to maintain discriminatory barriers against Japan even after it entered the GATT in 1955, the Japanese export juggernaut hit the United States harder than Europe, and to some degree this was also true for the NIEs as well. Both developments were to raise American concern about the bilateral trade balances with Japan and also about the basic fairness of the GATT system. Other aspects of the EU's trade policy added to this concern (see below).

Another aspect of the new protectionism also fed American disillusionment with the GATT. The combined impact of slower growth (causing overcapacity) and increasing imports in sectors such as steel and autos began to erode the monopoly rents embedded in the above-average wage and benefit levels of these heavily unionized sectors. As noted earlier, in contrast to Europe, the American postwar social contract was, to a considerable degree, "privatized": the rich health care, pensions, and other benefits provided by governments in most OECD countries were negotiated on an industry basis in the booming mass-production sectors after the war.[20] Largely as a consequence of the erosion of these benefits, the AFL-CIO became overtly protectionist by the 1970s, sponsoring legislation to impose comprehensive import quotas, for example. When labor's voice was added to that of U.S. agriculture, enraged by the EU's Common Agricultural Policy, it was clear that domestic political support for liberal trade in the United States was seriously unraveling.

It's of interest to note, however, that the new protectionism spawned allies for more open markets. A number of analyses of the sectoral pattern of border restraints stressed that they were largely confined to standardized, basic industries or those with high capital requirements but had not affected newer technology-intensive, innovative sectors.[21] Indeed, these analysts stressed that growing intra-industry trade in these sectors, dominated by the OECD countries, would increasingly provide a fundamental liberalizing thrust to the trading system.[22] However, this was not exactly how it all played out in the 1980s, as we shall see in the following chapter.

In addition to border measures, the new protectionism included domestic "barriers" to trade, especially subsidies. During the 1970s, the use of subsidies had also increased as a consequence of structural pressures. But both the absolute amount and rate of increase of subsidies was considerably higher in the EU than in the United States or Japan (table 3.1). Indeed, in the United States subsidies declined over the decade. Of course, not all the subsidies were protectionist in intent or impact. No comprehensive data on targeted, sector-specific subsidies are available, but more detailed country studies of specific sectors do show that there was an increase in subsidies to industries experiencing severe adjustment difficulties: steel, shipbuilding, textiles, and at the

Table 3.1 Subsidies Applied by Selected Countries, 1960–1980 (percent of GDP in current prices)

	1960	1965	1970	1975	1980
United States	0.2	0.4	0.5	0.3	0.4
Japan	0.5	0.7	1.1	1.5	1.5
European Union	1.2	1.5	1.8	2.5	2.6

Source: OECD, *National Accounts Statistics, 1960–1980* (Paris: OECD), various issues.

end of the decade, automobiles.[23] The effectiveness of these subsidies in improving efficiency is highly dubious. Nonetheless, American industry became convinced that foreign governments were unfairly providing support to their own firms to enhance their competitive advantage in world markets. These arguments echoed the views expressed in opposition to the ITO. As one U.S. senator put it: "The United States has been a patsy for what our trading partners have been doing for too long."[24]

The difficulties of coping with slower growth and powerful forces of structural change that gave rise to the new protectionism in the 1970s were not the only reason for growing American disenchantment with the GATT system. As was evident in the construction of the postwar architecture of international cooperation, U.S. foreign economic policy had a decidedly Euro-Atlantic focus. Japan was visible out of the corner of the eye, so to speak, and becoming more so as the catch-up process ended in the 1970s. But Japan only came into full view in the 1980s. In the 1970s Europe and especially the European Union were still the prime concern for American trade policymakers. So the European "system" came under close scrutiny. Because the structural rigidities built into the system through the postwar social contract were more pervasive in Europe than in the United States, they were more difficult for governments to tackle in the stagflation environment of the 1970s. Further, the European view of the role of government placed more emphasis on domestic "adjustment" measures (subsidies or even government-sponsored cartels in sectors such as steel) than the Americans considered legitimate and, hence, "fair." Oversimplified as it may be, the Hirschman distinction between Exit and Voice captured the transatlantic differences in response to the structural pressures of the 1970s. Exit relies more on decentralized market mechanisms whereby winners are rewarded and losers are supposed to disappear: it is a fluid, flexible, and disposable paradigm. Voice involves a process of negotiation among private and public players designed to mitigate the cost of change.[25] It is more rigid and accords more weight to equity and political cohesion and less to efficiency.

These transatlantic differences in market models were largely masked in the period of rapid growth following the war. They were more clearly evident as growth slowed. For Americans, they raised the question: were we "patsies" when we created the GATT? To this was added another question: were the Europeans abusing another fundamental principle of the postwar system—nondiscrimination? Having achieved the right to preferential trading arrangements in Article XXIV of the GATT—conceded by the Americans for foreign policy reasons—the EU over time entered into a number of preferential arrangements with former colonies in Africa—also largely for foreign policy reasons—and with the European Free Trade Area (EFTA) so that a shrinking portion of EU trade was based on the MFN principle. Article XXIV was so loosely applied that none of these arrangements were subject to any scrutiny. Another—and probably more egregious flouting of the "liberalization norm" of the GATT—was the Common Agricultural Policy (CAP). Once again, a policy that was fundamentally political in origin, designed to reinforce European integration by strengthening the bonds between France and Germany, had major perverse consequences, which greatly diminished access to European and third-country markets and distorted world agricultural markets through vast subsidy expenditures. Despite these extreme negative international spillovers, however, the political and social policy dimensions of the CAP made it strongly resistant to reform, however incomprehensible this appeared to outsiders more attuned to ideas of market rationality.

As mentioned earlier, the Kennedy Round (1963–67) was the first in which there was significant (for the United States) reciprocal exchange of benefits, and the economic results were substantial, involving about 35 percent reduction on nonagricultural tariffs covering about 80 percent of industrial trade.[26] It was also the first time the EU, consisting of the original six members, engaged in international negotiations. But the United States was still the most dominant trading power. After the Kennedy Round, however, more rapid integration and the inclusion of new members, especially the United Kingdom, created a trading power equal in size and with a similar standard of living to that of the United States. So in the Tokyo Round, negotiations were essentially bipolar, a rather dramatic illustration to the Americans of the consequences of convergence.

Despite the growing power of the EU and the increasing evidence of protectionist pressures, there was little interest in Europe in another set of multilateral negotiations following the Kennedy Round. As already pointed out, it took the events of August 1971 and the breakup of Bretton Woods to energize the inward-looking EU to agree to discuss a trade agenda. But, once again, Americans had to provide the leadership. Despite the rise in protectionist pressures and the growing disenchantment with the GATT, expressed by many interest groups in the United States, the American executive had maintained a commitment to the broad liberalizing norms of the postwar system, which differentiated it from its trading partners. Continuity in policy was also reinforced by the presence, both in and outside government, of a still significant number of individuals who had made major contributions to the building of the postwar system. In the United States, the club that built the convergence club was still around at the outset of the 1970s.

But, at a time of rising protectionist pressures, there was a price to be paid for securing from Congress the presidential authority for multilateral negotiations. What has been termed "neo-nationalism" in trade policy reflected a growing view in Congress that "the United States has given away, in purely commercial terms, much more than it has gotten in past trade negotiations" and that there was no longer "any need to help support the economies of the other industrialized countries through expanding our imports from them."[27]

This view was reinforced by a growing trade deficit that, as described, helped prompt the Nixon shock. Many in Congress were, therefore, increasingly skeptical that the executive could be trusted to negotiate a "fair" deal for the United States or that GATT itself adequately protected America's national interest. Included in the 1974 Trade Act authorizing negotiating authority for the Tokyo Round were tougher measures to protect against unfair (dumped or subsidized) imports and to reduce executive discretion in applying penalties. And a new instrument, Section 301, dealt with other countries' "unfair" trade policies and gave the president broad and virtually unconstrained authority to deal with "unreasonable" and "unjustifiable" trade practices. In part, this authority also reflected growing dissatisfaction with the GATT dispute settlement mechanism, which had pretty well fallen into disuse by the late 1960s. On the other hand, in an effort to deflect protectionist pressures by co-opting lobbyists, the 1974 act established a new private sector advisory committee structure, which greatly assisted endorsement of the round results.

The Tokyo Round agenda itself mirrored this deeply entrenched and growing view in the United States that other countries were basically unfair, especially in the way their governments behaved. In trying to tackle the new protectionism, the negotiations, for the first time in GATT history, included nontariff measures (NTMs)—not only at the border but trade-impeding barriers arising from domestic policies such as government procurement and standards regulation and, most important from an American vantage, both industrial and agriculture subsidies (the CAP). Also, an effort was made by the United States to strengthen the dispute settlement system of the GATT in an effort to counteract the growing American business view that the rules-based system was ineffective since rules of the road have little meaning when there's no traffic cop to enforce them.

As noted, by and large, the Tokyo Round was a bipolar negotiation between the United States and the EU. It's fair to regard it as a genuine attempt by the American executive to stem the tide of growing disaffection with the postwar multilateral trading system and to retrieve the shared consensus that some, both inside and outside the administration, still firmly believed had created the GATT (albeit termites and all).

The round did achieve a significant reduction in tariffs, comparable to that of the Kennedy Round. But on NTMs the outcome was rather different. The EU was unwilling to yield on CAP so virtually nothing was achieved in agriculture. Similarly, the EU skillfully blocked any meaningful reform on dispute settlement, thereby ensuring that its preference to handle disputes bilaterally through (nontransparent) negotiations could continue.[28] On safeguards, EU insistence on the right to apply safeguards selectively (which was resisted by developing countries and Japan) precluded agreement. The failure to reform the safeguards code and to eliminate quantitative restrictions such as VERs left the border barriers of the new protectionism pretty well untouched.

But the real battleground of the Tokyo Round was the European Union–United States dispute over subsidies, exemplifying as it did differences in view about the proper role of governments.

Ostensibly, the main issue in the subsidy dispute concerned the U.S. domestic legislation that permitted the imposition of countervailing duties without a prior determination that the subsidy had injured domestic firms. The EU (and others) argued that this legislation was inconsistent with GATT principles even though technically legal under the original terms of the agreement that "grandfathered" existing legislation. The United States was not prepared to budge on its right to countervail because its main objective to the Tokyo Round was to constrain the increasing use of domestic (as opposed to export) subsidies by other countries, especially the EU, in agriculture, in industry, for regional development, and other purposes. But the United States lacked allies on this stand except on agriculture, where it was supported by exporting countries like Australia and New Zealand. One might say that support for Exit was weaker than support for Voice. The result was yet another compromise of "constructive ambiguity," which was intended to constrain U.S. use of countervail and reduce "impermissible" subsidies. By and large, it did neither, so the issue turned up again in the Uruguay Round.

Similarly, differences between the United States and the EU and others—which centered on the issue of transparency of procedures—were glossed over in the negotiations on standards and government procurement. In both items the United States argued that its own system was more open and competitive, and therefore fairer, than the less transparent arrangements in Europe and most other countries. Once again left unsettled by the Tokyo negotiations, this same theme was to recur with increasing intensity in the 1980s.

So how does one evaluate the Tokyo Round in terms of the GATT system—that is, the rules-based system fundamentally underpinning a broadly liberalizing norm? On the issue of tariffs, liberalization continued. For transparent border barriers reciprocity worked. But in terms of the new protectionism, little progress was made, although it could be argued that without the round the situation would have been far worse. In any case, the failure to deal with basic conflicts over domestic policy stored up problems for the future trade relationship between the United States and the EU.

But at a more fundamental level, the results of the round initiated a transformation of the nature of the rules and the principle norms of the system itself.

Whereas the GATT had been built essentially by a transatlantic alliance with only a few "outsiders" involved, by the end of the Tokyo Round the number of contracting parties had grown from the original twenty-three to eighty-nine. Except for Japan, the newcomers were mainly developing countries who sought and to some degree secured, differential treatment, which further eroded the reciprocity and non discrimination principles. Securing differential treatment represented a Pyrrhic victory. Further erosion of nondiscrimination in the Tokyo Round was manifest in the many new codes, covering a range of NTMs, which applied only to code signatories, for the most part developed countries. This introduced a new GATT principle termed "conditional MFN."[29] And it also (see below) led to serious fragmentation of an already weak legal structure.

Both these outcomes—the erosion of reciprocity and of MFN—were symptomatic of a more fundamental change demonstrated by the Tokyo Round, *viz.*, the much larger number of participants greatly increased the "transactions costs" of multilateral negotiations. As well, the larger number of "outsiders" also encouraged a shift in the *concept* of "rules," from *broad statements of principle,* drafted by members of a small club who understood that what was left unwritten was as important as the written words, to *detailed legalisms.* Perhaps this shift was inevitable since negotiating over rules does not lend itself to an exchange of "concessions," the mechanism underlying the GATT concept of liberalization.

But the increasing legalization of trade rules reflected other forces as well. The legalization of GATT reflected developments at the national level, led by the United States in the Trade Act of 1974 and in the Trade Agreements Act of 1979, which ratified the Tokyo Round. This trend to more tightly specified rules was designed to strengthen the contingent protection against unfair trade—dumping and subsidies. As the Canadian negotiator in the Tokyo Round, Rodney Grey notes:

> In part the determination by Congress to write detailed legalistic prescriptions was a reaction against what was perceived to be the unwillingness of the administration

. . . to administer the contingent protection provisions with due diligence. In part, it was a natural result of coming to rely more heavily on contingency measures than on a schedule of tariff rates. The draftsmen are driven by the logic of contingent protection to write down just when and where such protection is to be available—this is a field of law where it is all in the administration and in the procedures.[30]

But the U.S. Congress was not alone in wanting to make the use of contingent protection easier. The EU sided with those in U.S. industry who argued for a minimal legal definition of injury so as to make antidumping or countervailing duties easier to obtain. A seemingly arcane debate in Congress, which almost held up ratification of the round, concerned the adjective *material* to modify *injury*. The term *material injury* had been included in the antidumping and subsidy codes negotiated in Geneva. As Rodney Grey notes:

When the EEC Commission made an issue of the fact that the draft of the United States Trade Agreements Act did not use the adjective "material" to modify the concept "injury," although that word was in the Tokyo Round agreements, they must have known that if Congress agreed to use the word "material," they would define it in a way that would not indicate a high threshold of pain. The definition inserted by Congress is that the term "material injury" means harm that is not "inconsequential, immaterial, or unimportant." This definition is helpful to any group of officials proposing to make extensive use of the anti-dumping system to meet demands for protection. It seems to me that the Commission expects to be invoking their system more frequently in the future, and that they wanted a definition that would make it easier, not more difficult, to take anti-dumping action.[31]

If the Tokyo Round is to be judged by results, one consequence of the legalization was that by 1981 there was a marked increase in antidumping investigations and actions in both the EU and the United States and an explosion in countervailing cases in the United States (see tables 3.2 and 3.3).

Finally, in opting for the codes or separate agreements to sidestep the one-country one-vote consensus rule in the GATT (a rule that reflected the failure of the original ITO negotiations to secure the weighted voting of the Bretton Woods institutions), the Tokyo Round seriously fragmented the rules-based system. This "balkanization" stemmed from the fact that the codes were legally separate from the GATT and applied only to the signatories, who varied from code to code. A fragmentation of dispute settlement procedures developed as a consequence, creating legal and political difficulties and the opportunity for "forum shopping" to evade discipline. The failure to improve the main dispute-settlement mechanism of the GATT, the failure to come to grips with subsidies in agriculture, combined with fragmentation produced by the codes (especially EU forum shopping in the subsidies area) added to the declining credibility of the multilateral system in the United States in the 1980s.

Conclusion

The creation of the multilateral rule-based GATT system—termites and all—was a major achievement entirely due to U.S. leadership after the war. But, again, it's difficult to de-

Table 3.2 European Union and United States: Antidumping Investigations and Actions, 1981–1985

	1981 INVEST.	1981 ACTIONS	1982 INVEST.	1982 ACTIONS	1983 INVEST.	1983 ACTIONS	1984 INVEST.	1984 ACTIONS	1985 INVESTI.	1985 ACTIONS
European Union	49	28	77	47	80	58	56	36	63	30
Industrial countries	09	18	18	09	11	12	16	09	09	09
Developing countries	03	05	15	04	09	12	05	06	16	01
Centrally planned economies	35	03	22	29	16	21	27	16	20	02
United States	14	04	61	45	47	15	71	25	65	53
Industrial countries	07	03	47	41	27	09	32	08	19	19
Developing countries	04	—	13	03	19	06	23	17	41	20
Centrally planned economies	03	01	01	01	01	—	16	—	05	14

Source: Margaret Kelly et al., *Issues and Developments in International Trade Policy* (occasional paper 63, International Monetary Fund, Washington, D.C., 1988), appendix v, table A6, p. 120.

Table 3.3 European Union and United States: Countervailing Investigations and Actions, 1981–1985

	1981 INVEST.	1981 ACTIONS	1982 INVEST.	1982 ACTIONS	1983 INVEST.	1983 ACTIONS	1984 INVEST.	1984 ACTIONS	1985 INVEST.	1985 ACTIONS
European Union	0	01	03	—	02	03	01	01	—	—
Industrial countries	—	—	01	—	01	01	—	01	—	—
Developing countries	01	01	02	—	01	02	01	—	—	—
Centrally planned economies	—	—	—	—	—	—	—	—	—	—
United States	10	06	124	80	21	121	50	18	40	24
Industrial countries	06	01	85	61	03	03	14	02	12	06
Developing countries	04	05	39	19	16	18	34	16	27	17
Centrally planned economies	—	—	—	—	02	—	02	—	01	01

Source: Margaret Kelly et al., Issues and Developments in International Trade Policy (occasional paper 63, International Monetary Fund, Washington, D.C., 1988), appendix v, table A7, p. 121.

fend the mythology that it represented a transatlantic vision of "embedded liberalism" or, more precisely, a shared view about the nature and role of government in a mixed economy and the relationship between domestic and international policy objectives. The notion of a postwar consensus is usually presented in broad terms, as a compromise between domestic objectives and international rules, and at the highest level of generality it's difficult to reject. But, as always, there is a chasm between generalized rhetoric and the realities of actual implementation. Once subjected to shock and strain, both macro- and microeconomic in origin, the multilateral liberalizing norm underlying the GATT system began to erode. Furthermore, and in the longer run far more important, as the frayed edges of the fragile consensus became more visible and as the awareness of convergence grew, the builder of the system, the United States, began increasingly to question both the costs and the benefits of the system.

In the Tokyo Round of the 1970s, the trading system had become bipolar. There was an opportunity for shared leadership to reinforce and extend the rules-based system. But the Europeans declined to accept responsibility; indeed the EU, concentrating on internal matters, deliberately or inadvertently added to the strains engendered by stagflation. The Europeans assumed, "Uncle Sam would do it," as had been the case since the war.

By mid-1982—well before the full implementation of the liberalizing accomplishments of the Tokyo Round tariff negotiations—more than thirty bills had been introduced in the Ninety-seventh Congress to achieve "reciprocity in foreign trade" not in the GATT sense of an *overall* balance of reduction in protection, but in a new sense of *identical market shares on a sectoral basis*. Protectionism had become *export-oriented.* The proposed instrument to achieve reciprocity was U.S. *unilateral retaliation.* The main reason for the legislative blizzard was a profound sense of "unfairness." As the proponent of one of these bills put it, after the United States had led the world in trade liberalization "the result is an American market with comparatively few import barriers while foreign markets are protected by a variety of restrictions and thus it was essential to achieve the same degree of access to foreign markets for competitive U.S. exports, services and investment that we accord to other countries."[32]

In any event, none of the bills became law. But they were, as we now know, of course, important signals of things to come. Their main target was the growing bilateral trade deficit with Japan. The exclusive transatlantic focus of the postwar period was over, and the 1980s marked another major evolution in American trade policy and the multilateral trading system established under the GATT.

Four

The Eighties: Pacific Prelude

The Tokyo Round was for all intents and purposes a bipolar negotiation spanning the Atlantic. The unsolved issues— agriculture, in particular—remained a major source of friction between the United States and Europe and a central issue in the Uruguay Round negotiations. Chapter 6 will deal with the outcome of those negotiations, but here it is important to review the difficulties faced by the United States in launching them, in large degree because of the foot-dragging of the EU and the opposition of many developing countries. Once again, U.S. leadership was the essential ingredient in the mammoth effort to update, extend, and reinforce the multilateral system. However, by the time of the launch in Punta del Este in September 1986, an unstoppable momentum for major changes in U.S. trade policy was well under way. At the most elemental level, the United States abandoned its single, overriding commitment to multilateralism, by beginning the negotiation of preferential agreements under Article XXIV of the GATT and thus launching a twin-track trade policy. Perhaps more significantly, the active use of the almost forgotten Section 301 of the 1974 Trade Act added a third track—unilateralism—that became a trade instrument to achieve objectives outside the rules-based system altogether, objectives often related to other countries' domestic policies as well as to specific outcomes or results.

The most consequential long-run element in the evolution of unilateralism stemmed from the high-tech challenge from Japan, which was the least expected and least intended result of convergence. While there were also battles with the

EU in leading-edge sectors—the fight over Airbus subsidies, for example—the "Japan issue" better illustrates a more fundamental trend in American policy, a push to deeper integration in international economic relations, that is, the increasing intrusion of "trade" disputes inside the border. This has given rise to a new form of conflict, which at its most extreme could be called "system friction" or a clash between different market models. While system friction does cross the Atlantic, it is most vividly apparent in the economic relations between the United States and Japan and will extend into East Asia. For that reason the following chapter will review the dynamics of U.S.-Japanese relations in that area: the prelude followed by the intermezzo, with the finale, of course, unknown.

Post–Tokyo Round: New Protectionism Redux

While the Tokyo Round was not considered an outstanding success by trade-policy analysts, most assessments at the time judged that there was no serious threat to the system itself in the rise of the new protectionism of the 1970s, which had prompted the negotiations. Typical of such views was the argument that the sectoral pressures for such barriers arose in standardized, basic industries strongly subject to import competition. In high-tech sectors, where trade was mainly *intra-industry* (that is, where countries exchanged differentiated products in the same industry), there was little evidence of protectionist pressure and it was argued that such industries would serve to counterbalance the protectionist demands of the more traditional sectors.[1] Since trade among industrialized countries was increasingly intra-industry (and, as foreign direct investment flows increased, also intrafirm), the trading system would be sustained by a *built-in force for liberalization.* Thus, despite the flaws in the GATT, which the round had done little to eliminate, the basic liberalizing norm, buttressed by the demonstrated commitment of the U.S. executive branch, would sustain the postwar system. By and large, it was argued, the regime looked likely to survive hegemonic decline.[2] The round was a successful compromise "between incremental protectionism combined with the maintenance of a basic liberalism."[3] In other words, the postwar liberal consensus that underlay the GATT had weathered its first major challenge: the end of the golden age of growth and the emergence of the convergence club. Another romantic myth?

A more sober prediction by a practitioner rather than an expert policy analyst turned out to be more accurate. As noted in the previous chapter, a defining characteristic of the Tokyo Round was the increasing "legalization" of trade policy, most evident in the redrafting of the trade remedy rules for antidumping and countervailing subsidies. Thus Rodney Grey predicted that "the future work of the GATT will be policing these new agreements about contingency protection" because it was no longer clear that "the GATT is now about trade liberalization" rather than "trade policy regulation."[4]

Indeed, there was an explosion of antidumping and countervailing cases in the early 1980s, commencing as soon as the round was completed.[5] The unreformed safeguard clause fell into disuse (see figure 4.1) as a better substitute had been invented: protection against "unfair" trade. Antidumping was used most by the United States and the EU, with Canada and Australia catching up as the decade proceeded. Countervailing was almost exclusively American, reflecting *inter alia* the lesser use of subsidies in the United States, noted in the previous chapter, and the strongly held

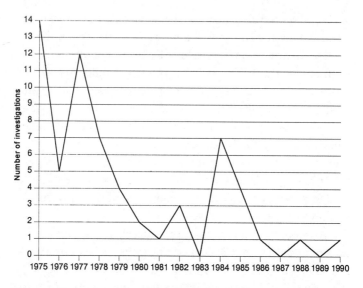

Figure 4.1 Escape clause investigations, 1975–1990

Source: I. M. Destler, *American Trade Politics,* 2d ed. (Washington, D.C.: Institute for International Economics with the Twentieth Century Fund, 1992), 151. Reprinted with permission of the Twentieth Century Fund, New York.

view that the actions of most other governments were basically "unfair." But over the 1980s antidumping became more popular with American business than countervail duties (see figure 4.2). Further, in the United States, nearly half (348 of 774) of the trade remedy cases in the period 1980 to 1988 were superseded by negotiated VERs.[6]

New Protectionism Redux

The increasing use of the trade remedy laws in the United States in the 1980s had a deeper significance than is recognized by those favoring trade liberalization who have strongly criticized the expanding use of such rules for pro-

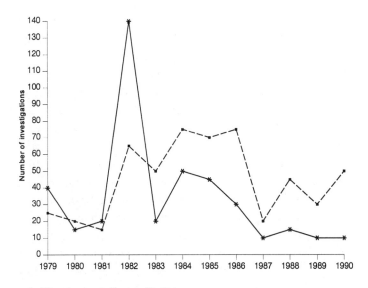

Anti-Dumping   Countervailing Duty

Figure 4.2 Countervailing duty and antidumping investigations, 1979–1990

Source: I. M. Destler, *American Trade Politics,* 2d ed. (Washington, D.C.: Institute for International Economics with the Twentieth Century Fund, 1992), 151. Reprinted with permission of the Twentieth Century Fund, New York.

tectionist purposes. They represented, in effect, a "privatization" of trade policy driven directly by business and often used as a strategic tool for business strategy.[7] They are "nondiscretionary" in the sense that a private party *cannot be overruled by a government agency*. As Gary Horlick notes, while countervail duties are also nondiscretionary, antidumping is much preferred by "sophisticated trade lawyers in Washington—in preference to any other form" as being more "winnable."[8]

Legalization and privatization of trade policy began to spread beyond the trade remedy laws in the 1980s. A rapidly rising trade deficit and an overvalued dollar, consequent on the impact of the ballooning fiscal deficit and tightening monetary policy of Reaganomics, unleashed a storm of protectionist pressures in the United States. While a key target of this ire was Japan (see below), the battle cry of unfairness struck a responsive chord in a growing array of beleaguered businesses. The macroeconomic *causes* of the deficit were largely ignored by those who were most seriously affected by the *consequences.* By 1985 more than three hundred trade bills had been sent to Congress proposing various forms of protectionist action. All reflected two basic themes: the United States was a more open economy than all others, and the trade policy of the executive branch was not protecting the national interest of the United States in tackling the "unfair" behavior of other countries (often because foreign policy concerns took precedence). Another way of expressing these two trade-policy themes was a growing demand for a new form of reciprocity and a new aspect of privatization of trade policy designed to prod the executive to retaliate, if necessary, when other countries refused to remedy their "unfair" or "unreasonable" practices—that is, Section 301.

Section 301 of the 1974 Trade Act not only sanctioned government retaliation against foreign barriers that violated U.S. rights under GATT or that the executive branch considered "unreasonable," it established a procedure allowing private citizens to petition the government directly to initiate action against foreign trade practices. As a U.S. trade policy practitioner has noted, "it goes against the grain of American political philosophy to leave decisions with respect to the exercise of rights and obligations entirely in the hands of government," reflecting a *"deeply held American distrust of governmental action that is not subject to full public scru-*

tiny"[9] (emphasis added). In the seventies this private channel was little used, but in the dramatically changed environment of the early 1980s, discontent with the Reagan
administration's benign neglect of 301 grew exponentially.
The result was the initiation of a profound change in American policy direction.

In September 1985 the Reagan administration, in an effort to staunch the mounting protectionist pressures, announced a new policy of dollar devaluation (the Plaza Accord of the major economic summit countries) followed by
a much-publicized speech emphasizing America's objective
of fair trade ("above all else free trade is, by definition, fair
trade"). To underline the commitment to fighting unfairness,
the president also announced his support for the first self-
initiation of Section 301 of the 1974 Trade Act.[10]

Prior to 1985, Section 301 had essentially been used to
strengthen the inadequate GATT dispute settlement process.
Beginning in 1985, Section 301 cases involved practices not
covered by GATT law but deemed "unreasonable" by the
United States.[11] (The force and scope of 301 was greatly expanded in 1988, as will shortly be described.)

There were many reasons for these changes in American
trade policy. Rising protectionist pressures stemming from
the overvalued dollar reflected a new aspect of increasing global interdependence, the increasing *linkages* among
countries by trade, financial flows, direct investment and
technology flows, and—a somewhat different aspect of the
same phenomenon—the increasing *inter-relationships* between major influences on the world economic system, with
monetary policy affecting trade policy and trade policy feed-
ing back into macropolicy, both monetary and fiscal.[12] The
Plaza Accord marked a rejection of the "hands off" policy
stance, both domestic and international, of the Reagan ad-

ministration. The link between macropolicy, more specifically between the growing fiscal and trade deficits and rising protectionism (*macrodumping* was the term used by
irate exporters), was underlined both by Treasury Secretary
James Baker and other members of the administration. International economic coordination to reduce growing structural imbalance in fiscal policies were stressed as fundamental to the preservation of the world trading system in major
speeches by Paul Volcker, chairman of the Federal Reserve
Board and Secretary of State George Schultz. But, given the
rising fury of protectionist cries in the United States, it was
also essential to launch a new round of multilateral negotiations.[13]

Frustration at the delay in launching the Uruguay
Round played a major role in the change in American trade
policy in the 1980s, both in the new track of bilateralism and
the emergence of unilateralism. Given the susceptibility of
Congress to special interest lobbies seeking import protection—reflecting the American system of governance with its
unique diffusion of power—the executive defense of the
liberal trading system since the Smoot-Hawley disaster
had essentially consisted of developing a range of "anti-
protectionist counterweights" designed to divert or at least
manage protectionist demands.[14] One important tried-and-
true counterweight in the postwar years had been a GATT
negotiation, based on the idea of the "bicycle theory" of
trade policy: keep liberalizing (moving) or you'll fall off the
bicycle (GATT). The major *medium* for the liberalizing *message* was the private-sector advisory committee structure established under the 1974 Trade Act to launch the Tokyo
Round. The top oversight committee, the Advisory Committee for Trade Negotiations (ACTN), was assigned a central
role by the U.S. Trade Representative (USTR) in the effort

to launch a new round with an agenda that would include items such as services, investment, and intellectual property, in which American comparative (or even absolute) advantage was strong but which were not included in the GATT because of their limited international relevance after the war. The push by the United States for these so-called "new issues" was essential to redress what was increasingly viewed as another aspect of "unfairness" in restricting GATT coverage essentially to manufacturing and also virtually excluding agriculture because of the distorting effects of the European CAP. Manufacturing imports, as a share of total U.S. imports, increased over the decade beginning in 1975 from nearly 54 to 72 percent. And the bulk of these imports came from the leading countries of the "convergence club," especially Japan (table 4.1).

The Americans had been trying to launch a new round since the early 1980s in recognition both of growing dissatisfaction with the results of the Tokyo Round among many business groups and among farmers outraged by the loss of not only the European market but of third-country markets because of massive European subsidies. But the EU was fearful of the inclusion of agriculture as a central item on the agenda of a new round. It was also initially opposed to negotiations on trade in services, a key U.S. priority. Thus the EU effectively blocked and then delayed the launch for four years after a near-catastrophic GATT ministerial meeting in November 1982 to which they had reluctantly agreed after strong American pressure. In this successful foot-dragging policy, they were greatly assisted by the strong opposition of a group of developing countries led by Brazil and India, who were fiercely opposed to the inclusion of the so-called new issues of services, trade-related intellectual property, and trade-related investment measures. It would, how-

Table 4.1 U.S. Imports by Country and Commodity (millions of U.S. dollars)

	1975				1985			
Total imports	96,941				358,895			
Manufacturing imports	52,108				258,374			
Share of total (%)	53.8				72.0			
	JAPAN	GERMANY	FRANCE	U.K.	JAPAN	GERMANY	FRANCE	U.K.
Imports by country	11,610	5,748	4,081	5,120	71,213	20,175	9,274	16,307
Share of total (%)	12.0	5.9	4.2	5.3	19.8	5.6	2.6	4.5
Manufacturing imports by country	11,025	4,983	1,808	3,040	70,891	19,801	8,296	10,412
Share of total (%)	11.4	5.1	1.9	3.1	19.8	5.5	2.3	2.9

Source: United Nations, *International Trade Statistics Yearbook*, various issues.

ever, have been impossible for these so-called hard-liners to prevent a GATT negotiation on their own. Only the skilled delaying tactics of the EU gave these countries the clout to block and, in this, it was believed by many other participants, they were ably assisted by EU officials behind the scenes.

Confronted by failure to budge the EU and the hard-line developing countries and in an effort to increase pressure for a launch, Ambassador William Brock (then the USTR) in January 1985 asked the official private sector advisory committees on trade negotiations to present their views on a new GATT round. The report, issued in May 1985, contained some unpleasant results.

The chairman's summary provided an interesting insight into the increasing ambivalence of American business attitudes to the GATT since the end of the Tokyo Round in 1979. Basically, it reflected mounting frustration with the Reagan administration's economic policies. After stressing that action was urgently required on the exchange rate and fiscal front, the report stated:

> While support for a new round among the groups contacted ranged from strong support to strong opposition, the broadest consensus on a new round can best be described as moderate support provided that parallel efforts, both domestic and international, are undertaken to address the cause of American trade problems. The broadest concern over entering a new round is that it would detract from or even replace efforts to develop a *national trade policy* [emphasis added].[15]

As the report points out, support for a new round was strong only among those groups advocating the inclusion of

the new issues of services, intellectual property, and investment. And the chairman emphasized that it was essential for
the administration to pursue a "tough U.S. trade policy."[16]
That "tough policy" was announced on September 23, immediately after the Plaza Accord in a report of the USTR. It
was a multitrack policy that included continuing efforts to
launch a new GATT round; "the possibility of achieving further liberalization through the negotiation of bilateral free
trade arrangements such as the one recently concluded with
Israel"; and the third track of Section 301.[17]

The intention to pursue Canadian-U.S. free-trade negotiations (track 2) was announced in the Canadian House of
Commons three days later, and formal negotiations began in
May 1986. During the lengthy and difficult process of securing agreement from the EU and the so-called "hard core" of
developing-country opponents to a GATT round, the United
States repeatedly stressed that bilateralism was a feasible alternative that would be actively pursued if the foot-dragging
continued. So the Free Trade Agreement was used as a "strategic threat," especially to the EU but also (because it would
include all the "new issues," so vigorously opposed especially by Brazil and India) to other opponents of the round.

Under the third track of the tough new policy, three
cases were filed in 1985 involving the "new issues": Brazil
Informatics, Korea Insurance, and Korea Intellectual Property. Brazil and India were also targeted under the expanded
Super 301 of 1988 (see below).

There are some who argue, quite plausibly, that the new
multitrack policy was designed to offset rising protectionist
pressure in the United States by the traditional means of
GATT negotiations. In using unilateralism, far from being a
break with past policy, the executive branch was simply being pragmatic in its defense of a system in need of updating,

especially because its overall coverage had created an unfair asymmetry of access for the United States by excluding the new issues. This interpretation—that is, that the change in policy was simply tactical and designed to strengthen the GATT—is also supported by the high priority placed on an improved dispute-settlement process as an agenda item in the negotiations. Growing dissatisfaction with the weakness of the process for enforcing GATT rules was indeed, as noted above, the original reason for including Section 301 in the 1974 Act. EU blockage of reform in the Tokyo Round only added to the diminishing credibility of the system, even though the United States itself was not blameless in evading rulings when domestic pressures proved too strong to resist.

The use of 301 by the executive, essentially as a "counterweight" to offset opposition to a new round, has been termed "justified obedience" by Robert Hudec.[18] While it may have violated GATT rules in some narrow technical sense, it was justified in terms of its broader aims. The U.S. administration, if not exactly Gandhi, was certainly not Rambo. Not yet.

The other tactic designed by the administration to offset the rise in protectionist pressure was to engage the support of U.S. export interests. The active engagement of the U.S. private sector in shaping the agenda for the Uruguay Round negotiations, especially the "new issues," was crucial in the launch and essential to overcoming resistance in both the EU and Japan.[19] But this *pluralist activist* model of policymaking, uniquely American, must strike a fine balance between *policy co-option* (rallying support for government objectives) and *policy capture* (using government policy instruments for private objectives). Of course, policy capture is simply another term for the privatization of trade policy. For the high-tech multinational oligopolies, export activism aimed mainly at the launch of a multilateral round was not an adequate "new tough policy." And the role of the multinational enterprises (MNEs) in setting the trade-policy agenda was increasingly enlarged by the surge of foreign direct investment that began in the mid-1980s.

Thus, instead of being a "built-in force for liberalization," as predicted by trade policy experts at the conclusion of the Tokyo Round, firms in sectors such as telecommunications, aircraft, and semiconductors favored a stronger brand of unilateralism that could deal with impediments to access arising from a range of "unfair" *domestic* practices rather than more traditional barriers. A major channel for complaint was the privatization element of Section 301. This newer objective—to extend the scope of *"unreasonable"* practices subject to retaliation and to *reduce executive discretion* in the use of the policy instrument—was achieved in the new Super 301 of the Omnibus Trade and Competitiveness Act of 1988. The target was Japan.

Why Japan?

Figure 4.3 presents a rough indicator of the rising American interest in bilateral economic issues with Japan starting at the end of the 1970s. Concern over Japanese competition in autos and electronics mounted in the early 1980s and reflected growing pressure on the administration for a new bilateral trade policy to deal with what was seen as a serious threat in capital- and technology-intensive sectors to American competitiveness.

In addition to this increasing press attention, a spate of books was published over the 1980s both decrying America's decline and spelling out the uniqueness of the Japanese market system: a different brand of capitalism that essentially

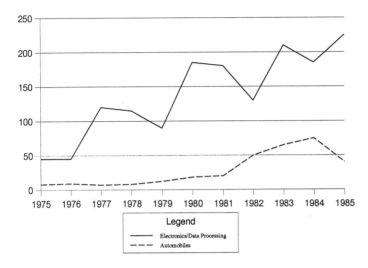

Figure 4.3 Number of articles on Japan appearing in the *New York Times*, 1975–1985

Source: *New York Times Indices: A Year in Review.*

created an unfair advantage for Japanese firms in international markets.[20] These two basic themes, one the product of the convergence club and hence the relative decline of the United States, the other the idea of different market models, were already apparent in the 1970s and in broad terms could also be applied to the European members of the club. So why the focus on Japan in the 1980s?

The answer comes in several pieces. One concerns a marked asymmetry in foreign investment access between Japan and the other members of the OECD. Since a major force affecting American policy evolution in the 1980s was the concern of the MNEs with barriers to market access, the enormous increase in foreign direct investment in the second half of the 1980s was an important independent factor in heightening high-tech friction and certainly added to the unilateralist thrust of U.S. policy vis-à-vis Japan by greatly magnifying the unique character of the Japanese postwar investment policy described above.

It was the investment surge of the 1980s that spawned the term *globalization,* first used in 1986. Growth of investment from 1985 to 1990 averaged nearly 30 percent per year, four times the rate of world output and three times the rate of trade. Most of it was in capital- and technology-intensive sectors. Technology flows (as captured from the very inadequate measure of royalties and fees) also exploded, increasing from an annual negative growth rate of 0.1 to 22 percent between the first and second half of the decade. While part of the "bulge" of the 1980s was due to one-off factors (e.g., protectionist actions and wide exchange rate swings), the outflows also reflected underlying structural forces, in particular the revolution in information and communication technologies (ICT), which was both an enabling factor and a driver, fostering innovation in products and processes and also in organization at the level of the firm and the industry. Thus, the traditional international rivalry among MNEs was greatly intensified by the ongoing technological revolution, as corporations sought to capture economies of scale and scope, customize products to satisfy consumer tastes, generate sophisticated high-quality inter- and intracorporate networks, and gain access to knowledge, both technological and "tacit," the latter being accessible only by continuing on-site learning. This rivalry intensified as fixed costs, including up-front R&D, mounted and time to market shortened. And, for the MNEs, market entry by means of trade *and* investment was essential: the two modes were complements rather than alternatives. And market presence was a two-way channel for both technology *diffusion* and technology *access*. Most importantly, impediments to effective access were no longer confined to overt border barriers to trade or explicit restrictions that limited foreign investment. Rather, impediments to effective access often arose from domestic regulatory policies, legal cultures or private sector actions—system differences—which had an *exclusionary* effect by accident or design.

Thus, international rivalry with Japan was greatly exacerbated by the marked asymmetry of investment access between Japan and other OECD countries, but especially the United States, resulting from the enormous outflow of Japanese investment in the second half of the 1980s, from $6.5 billion in 1980–85 to $36.5 billion in 1986–90. Much of this investment was in autos and electronics. Flows of investment into Japan over the same two periods, in striking contrast, were $500 million and $2.0 billion. The inflow figures did not significantly diverge from the postwar pattern; indeed the long-run trend was modestly rising, albeit from an extremely low base. But the outflow figures were strikingly different from the postwar pattern. Japan's share of the total outward stock of world foreign direct investment (FDI) tripled (from 3.8 percent to 12.2 percent) between 1980 and 1990 though it still lagged well behind that of the United States (26 percent) and the European Union (43.5 percent).[21]

The Japanese outflow can be attributed to several factors, including the marked increase in its current account surplus over the 1980s (see below), U.S. and European trade policies, relaxation of controls on capital exports, changes in the relative cost of capital in Japan and other countries, and the sharp drop in the value of the dollar against the yen after the 1985 Plaza Agreement. But whatever the complex causal nexus, the remarkable and sudden investment outflow added significantly to the friction with the United

States in the 1980s by highlighting the unique character of the Japanese economy in terms of foreign presence.

But there were also other answers to the "why Japan" question. Despite some heated rhetoric about "the buying of America," the asymmetry in investment access didn't evoke strong reaction from the public and the politicians; indeed, state governors eagerly solicited Japanese firms. More important as a widely publicized background factor was the burgeoning American bilateral trade deficit, which increased steadily from $12.2 billion in 1980 to nearly $60 billion in 1987 (see table 4.2). This was in marked contrast to the situation with respect to the EU, where a growing current account and trade surplus of Germany over the same period was increasingly oriented within Europe while the relatively small bilateral deficit with the United States began declining after mid-decade.

Indeed, the U.S. current account and trade balances, both overall and bilaterally with Japan were dramatically transformed in the 1980s (see table 4.3). As noted earlier, the consensus view among economists attributed the change to public sector dissaving in the United States due to the fiscal effects of Reaganomics. Indeed the issue was not only fiscal but also the uniquely low national savings as a whole including private savings in the United States. The Reagan "shock" pushed up real interest rates, attracted an inflow of foreign capital, and drove up the dollar. Japan, with far higher private savings and far lower fiscal deficits than the United States, was a major provider of this capital inflow.[22] These differences in savings behavior and macropolicies had nothing to do with a sudden rise in import or investment barriers in Japan in the 1980s. And while the savings surplus was a necessary condition for the investment outflow, it alone cannot explain why the form of export was FDI rather than port-

Table 4.2 United States: Geographic Composition of Merchandise Trade Balance, 1980–1992 (U.S. $ millions)

	1980	1981	1982	1983	1984	1985	1986	1987	1988	1989	1990
Total	−36,178	−39,612	−42,608	−69,352	−123,281	−148,474	−169,783	−171,184	−140,362	−129,517	−123,914
Japan	−12,182	−18,081	−18,965	−21,665	−36,797	−49,750	−58,575	−59,825	−55,508	−52,526	−44,485
Share of total (%)	33.7	45.6	44.5	31.2	29.8	33.5	34.5	34.9	39.5	40.6	35.9
Germany	−1,298	−1,641	−3,211	−4,493	−8,727	−12,182	−15,568	−16,281	−3,111	−8,790	−10,312
Share of total (%)	3.6	4.1	7.5	6.5	7.1	8.2	9.2	9.5	2.2	6.8	8.3
France	1,937	1,201	1,295	−346	−2,480	−3,864	−3,371	−3,233	−2,795	−1,923	59
Share of total (%)	−5.4	−3.0	−3.0	0.5	2.0	2.6	2.0	1.9	2.0	1.5	0
Italy	824	−190	−1,039	−1,912	−4,130	−5,755	−6,473	−6,169	−5,620	−5,519	−5,408
Share of total (%)	−2.3	0.5	2.4	2.8	3.4	3.9	3.8	3.6	4.0	4.3	4.4
United Kingdom	2,422	−876	−2,897	−2,279	−2,835	−4,301	−4,614	−3,884	−488	1,986	2,553
Share of total (%)	−6.7	2.2	6.8	3.3	2.3	2.9	2.7	2.3	0.3	−1.5	−2.1

Source: IMF, Direction of Trade Statistics Yearbook, various issues.

Table 4.3 Current Account and Trade Balances for the United States and Japan (annual averages, billions of U.S. dollars)

	1970–80	1981–85	1986–90
U.S. current account	−0.1	−54	−126
U.S. trade balance	−12	−73	−131
Japan current account	2	23	69
Japan trade balance	8	34	85
Bilateral U.S.-Japan trade balance	−4	−27	−53

Sources: IMF, *International Financial Statistics* and *Direction of Trade Statistics Yearbook,* various issues.

folio investment. But the impact of the overvalued dollar and the rising Japanese trade surplus certainly served to focus attention much more closely on the nature of barriers to access in the Japanese market. Workers and employers in high-wage mass production sectors such as autos and steel were battered by the increased import competition that continued the erosion of the "private social contract" that had been established in the postwar period. Firms in high-tech sectors such as electronics began to feel the heat of Japanese competition.

As well as the huge and growing bilateral deficit with Japan (table 4.4), Japan's import pattern stood out from other OECD countries in a number of respects: less intra-industry, less manufacturing, less foreign subsidiary sales because of the low level of foreign investment.[23] And, again in contrast to Europe, lower American investment in Japan meant a lower "voice" countering anti-Japanese sentiment in America.

Finally, the United States' "loss of competitiveness" in high tech does not show up in overall export performance as measured by comparative advantage, but rather in increasing *import penetration* in marked contrast to the situa-

Table 4.4 Selected Trade Indicators for Six Industrialized Countries

INDICATOR	JAPAN	UNITED STATES	GERMANY	GREAT BRITAIN	FRANCE	ITALY
Intra-industry trade index,[a] 1990	0.58	0.83	0.73	0.79	0.77	0.67
Import share of domestic consumption of manufactures, 1990 (%)	5.9	15.3	15.4	17.7	13.7	12.6
Foreign firms' share of domestic sales, 1986 (%)	1	10	18	20	27	N/A

Source: C. Fred Bergsten and Marcus Noland, *Reconcilable Differences?: United States–Japan Economic Conflict* (Washington, D.C.: IIE, 1993), 66.

[a] $\text{IIT}_i = \left[\dfrac{1 - [\Sigma_i \, | X_i - M_i \, |]}{\Sigma_i (X_i + M_i)} \right]$ where the subscript i refers to the ith industry and X and M refer to exports and imports.

tion in Japan (table 4.5). Thus the core of the unfairness argument really related to *asymmetry* of trade access both in total imports and especially in technology-intensive sectors. The asymmetry in both trade and investment evoked a long-familiar refrain: our market is open but yours is closed, and all these developments fed concern over the competitiveness of American firms in technology-intensive sectors and led to the high-tech battles of the 1980s. And to a strengthening of the unilateralist track. And to system friction.

Super 301

Although the Uruguay Round was launched in September 1986, the Reagan administration did not seek negotiating authority that year because of the rising protectionist fury in Congress. In 1988 the "price" paid for negotiating authority was the inclusion of Super 301. It was judged a price worth paying because the alternative, a proposal by Congressman Richard Gephardt targeted at countries with "excessive and unwarranted" trade surpluses (that is, Japan), was considered "too draconian to be effective."[24]

Super 301 differed in several respects from the original version, which was used mainly to support and strengthen the multilateral system: it reduced the room for executive discretion and it expanded the scope of "unreasonable" practices that could justify retaliation. These were intended to ensure that "tougher" policy could not be so easily circumvented in the interest of achieving broader liberalizing goals through multilateral negotiations. By requiring the USTR to list all "restrictions" by country and designating priority targets for removal and retaliation if necessary, Congress hoped to increase the pressure for action. By expanding the list of unreasonable to include many practices outside the GATT or outside what were generally considered "trade" practices, the door was open to include virtually any domestic policy or practice. By encouraging the use of trade barriers for retaliation against such practices, the Act sanctioned violation of GATT law.

This new version of unilateralism in the 1988 Trade Act was strongly criticized by other countries and by a number of eminent economists. There were dire warnings of trade wars and threats to the trading system. Yet some later assessments by American trade policy analysts were rather supportive of the unilateralist thrust generally, if not each and every detail of Super 301 itself.[25] In part, this view stemmed from the fact that no great tit for tat trade wars erupted. Up to 1995 there were only three cases of counter-retaliation, two from the EU and one from Canada.

The record of "success" (which would also include the relatively limited use of sanctions by the United States—fifteen out of ninety-one cases to mid-1995) stems from the effectiveness of a *unilateral* instrument used by a *powerful* country against *vulnerable* countries, that is, smaller countries highly dependent on the U.S. market. Indeed, this success record bears out Conybeare's analysis of the "mythology" of the RTAA. Smoot-Hawley was ineffective because it provoked retaliation. The Reciprocal Trade Agreements Act was effective because it maximized the advantage of "hegemonic asymmetry." If a large country can escape "coordinated or widespread retaliation, and direct (its) greater bargaining power toward smaller countries," the hegemon can choose a policy to maximize its own national income.[26] True, this advantage would be somewhat diluted by the MFN principle, so new theoretical arguments by American political

Table 4.5 Export Shares, Revealed Comparative Advantage and Import Penetration in the Developed Economies: 1970, 1980, and 1990

	EXPORT SHARES OF 13 OECD COUNTRIES[a]			RCA[b]			IMPORT PENETRATION[c]		
	1970	1980	1990	1970	1980	1990	1970	1980	1990
United States									
High technology[d]	31.1	30.3	26.3	1.59	1.60	1.61	4.2	7.2	18.4
Medium technology[e]	21.7	21.9	15.4	1.10	1.06	0.89	5.6	20.5	18.5
Low technology[f]	13.4	17.1	13.3	0.67	0.70	0.74	3.8	4.4	8.8
Japan									
High technology	13.2	14.1	21.1	1.24	1.30	1.49	5.2	4.1	5.4
Medium technology	8.5	14.8	16.9	0.78	1.06	1.13	4.5	9.3	5.9
Low technology	13.2	9.9	7.1	1.13	0.75	0.44	3.0	6.1	6.6
Germany									
High technology	17.7	14.9	16.2	0.97	0.95	0.83	14.9	18.2	37.0
Medium technology	23.1	19.8	24.7	1.25	1.17	1.21	17.2	37.6	29.5
Low technology	15.0	12.9	17.9	0.76	0.80	0.83	11.1	9.1	20.9

High technology	7.7	8.3	8.7	0.86	0.84	0.90	21.6	16.0	31.6
Medium technology	8.5	10.6	10.0	0.94	0.99	0.98	19.7	40.5	34.1
Low technology	10.7	11.0	12.1	1.12	1.09	1.12	10.7	9.1	21.4
Italy									
High technology	5.5	4.8	5.1	0.78	0.66	0.63	16.2	15.1	22.8
Medium technology	7.1	4.5	7.7	0.99	0.91	0.90	23.6	42.6	28.9
Low technology	8.5	7.4	12.8	1.09	1.28	1.40	11.6	10.2	15.7
United Kingdom									
High technology	10.5	13.7	10.2	1.05	1.27	1.23	17.4	23.7	42.4
Medium technology	11.9	12.3	8.5	1.17	1.09	0.97	N/A	46.1	39.4
Low technology	8.9	12.1	8.5	0.81	0.80	0.91	12.4	7.8	19.8

Sources: OECD, *Economic Surveys, United States 1993*, table 16, p. 87, *OECD Industrial Policy in OECD Countries, Annual Review, 1992*; and various UN sources.

[a] U.S., Japan, Germany, France, Italy, U.K., Canada, Netherlands, Australia, Finland, Norway, Sweden, Denmark.

[b] Country's exports in an industry divided by its total exports normalized by the same ratio for the 13 OECD countries considered.

[c] Imports divided by total domestic demand (production plus imports less exports).

[d] Drugs and medicines; electrical machinery; radio, TV, and communication equipment; aircraft; professional goods; office and computing equipment.

[e] Chemicals excluding drugs; rubber and plastic products; nonferrous metals; nonelectrical machinery; other transport equipment; motor vehicles; other manufacturing.

[f] Food, beverages, and tobacco; textiles, apparel, and leather; wood products and furniture; paper products and printing; petroleum refineries and products; nonmetallic mineral products; iron and steel; metal products; shipbuilding and repairing.

economists, extolling the benefits of predatory hegemony, update and strengthen a strategy for discriminatory bilateral bargaining.[27] The seductiveness of a predatory hegemon strategy with the end of the Cold War and the erosion of the broad milieu goals that created the convergence club, should not be underestimated.

Another reason for this benign view of Super 301 was that again, contrary to expectations, the executive branch of the American government stood firm in pursuit of its traditional commitment to a liberal trading system, using its albeit more limited discretion to avoid major damage and to further the progress of the Uruguay Round negotiations. Thus in the case of Japan, for example, the supercomputer, satellite, and forest products cases launched in 1989 were really another leg in the bilateral negotiations known as Market Opening Sector Specific (MOSS) talks of 1985–87 (see below). To avoid naming Japan as a "priority foreign country" because of the number and pervasiveness of its unfair and unreasonable practices, Ambassador Hills a few months later launched the separate Structural Impediments Initiative (SII), which we will turn to shortly. Again in 1990 no priority countries were named in order to prevent a disruption of the multilateral negotiations, which had reached a delicate stage.

But the most serious flaws in this rationalization of Super 301—or more broadly, unilateralism—as a price worth paying in the admittedly unique circumstances of the United States in the 1980s seem to have been overlooked by its defenders. One is the acceptance of a unique "right" of the United States to violate multilateral rules in defense of those rules—that is, doing the wrong thing for the right reasons. Essentially this implies that some countries are more "sovereign" than others, a view that seems to be growing in the

United States, as we shall discuss in connection with the WTO in the final chapter.

The second, perhaps in the long run more serious flaw is that the probabilities of "doing the right thing" are essentially *unpredictable*. They would depend on the nature of the executive and the circumstances. Ambassador Hills fought for the Uruguay Round. Will successors also do the "right thing" every time domestic pressures demand otherwise? The narrowly averted use of sanctions in the 1995 U.S.-Japanese auto dispute would suggest a justifiable doubt about an affirmative response. The notion of the executive as a barrier to protectionist pressures or local concerns and the concept of counterweights to offset these pressures on Congress is clearly eroding. And with the end of the Cold War, Congress is taking a much more active role in international economic policy, showing less and less deference to the president. Thus the essential problem with "benign" unilateralism is *uncertainty* and the further *politicization and privatization* of trade policy, which undermine the essential public good of a rules-based system.

High-Tech Issues: The Road to System Friction

While a full review of the high-tech U.S.-Japanese disputes of the 1980s would be inappropriate in the context of the present discussion,[28] it is important to highlight some of the main issues that emerged from the bilateral negotiations that shaped the longer-run evolution of U.S. trade policy. It should also be noted that there were trade disputes with the EU in high-tech sectors (Airbus and telecommunications equipment procurement, for example) so the growing concern over America's position as a technological leader was more than a "Japanese problem." Nonetheless, the conflict with Japan was far more intense than with Europe and far more significant in its longer-term effects on the international trade agenda.

Because of increasing Japanese competition in both the domestic and third-country markets in capital-and-technology-intensive sectors, the role of Japanese industrial policy—or, more broadly, innovation policy—hit the radar screen in the 1980s. This generated a spirited debate among economists (still going on) about the appropriate role of government in improving the competitiveness of their own multinational enterprises (MNEs) engaged in increasingly fierce rivalry in world markets. One effect of this debate was a modest change in American domestic innovation policies to encourage joint government-private R&D consortia in imitation of the Japanese and of the Europeans, who also borrowed this Japanese "invention" (who had, in turn, borrowed it from earlier, largely unsuccessful British efforts). In addition to these changes in American domestic policy, the debate about how to enhance the competitiveness of American MNEs in global markets had an important effect on trade policy vis-à-vis Japan. This discussion will concentrate on the latter, but as is increasingly the case in a globalizing international economy, domestic policies often have unintended international effects, and trade policies have important and unintended domestic consequences.[29]

In high tech, as in overall bilateral trade policy with Japan, trade deficits, in this case *sectoral*, were cited as emblematic of the unfairness/reciprocity issue. But there was an important variation in the assessment of asymmetry of access: our market is open, as evidenced by the rapid import penetration in a number of "high-tech" sectors, but yours is blocked and the blockage is devilishly difficult to pin down since it rarely takes the form of *transparent border barriers*.

The phrase "peeling an onion" became a popular metaphor to describe Japanese impediments to access in high-tech sectors.

A brief summary of five examples of the layers of the onion serve to illustrate the evolution of system friction as a guiding principle of a new trade agenda. These include: government procurement, in both the MOSS negotiations and the Super 301 cases on supercomputers and satellites; autos, featured both in the early MOSS talks and in the later bilaterals of Presidents Bush and Clinton; the semiconductor dispute; the bilateral Structural Impediments Initiative (SII); and finally, investment issues in the Clinton administration's Framework Negotiations.

In the mid-eighties the United States launched the MOSS negotiations with Japan, which included a number of high-tech products such as medical, pharmaceutical, and telecommunications equipment. The basic issue in these talks was government procurement and standard setting practices for high-tech products. The Super 301 supercomputer and satellite cases concerned essentially the same issues—that is, government practices as impediments to effective market access through trade. (In addition, access to technology through participation in publicly funded Japanese R&D consortia was raised for the first time on a trade agenda.)

Major barriers identified in the negotiations included the Japanese approach to standard setting and product testing (more focused on design than performance and less transparent), the relations between Japanese producers and government departments in regulatory procedures and in standards and certification, and the weak or nonenforcement of antitrust regulations in public procurement.

An American goal in these negotiations was to seek

harmonization of regulatory practices with the more *legalistic* American approach, which tends to favor more performance-orientation and an explicit statutory approach, which is inherently *transparent*. Transparency and legalism are basic characteristics of the American system so that regulatory barriers are precisely defined by statute. American legalism also emphasizes *due process* and *private rights of enforcement*, another defining characteristic of the American system. Design orientation, on the other hand, is more opaque, more intrusive and entails closer collaboration between government bodies and the private sector. Along the same lines, another objective of the Americans was to establish *independent agencies* for standards, testing, and certification and to include American representation on these agencies and boards to reduce the possibility of collusion between government agencies and domestic firms, which could result in using technical barriers to impede market access—that is, to increase *transparency*. This is a very important generic issue: system friction will be exacerbated when different legal and cultural practices result in significant differences in *transparency, due process, and private rights of enforcement.*

So the differences in government practices—that is, *what governments do*—can be considered one layer of the onion, or one component of system difference. And not only Japan was involved. It's important to note that the long-standing dispute between the United States and the EU over government procurement practices for telecommunications and heavy electrical equipment was the main reason for the inclusion in the 1988 Trade Act of a provision on sectoral reciprocity in telecommunications, and in 1989 the EU was identified. What was at issue were fundamental differences in government ownership of utilities, and in the respective roles of the commission and nation states in Europe, on the one hand, and the federal government and state and local governments in the United States on the other—that is, differences in the role of government and in governance arrangements.[30] (Parenthetically, the idea that system differences in Japan impeded market access was not an American invention. As will be discussed later, in 1982 the EU issued a complaint against Japan under a little-used GATT article concerning "nullification and impairment" of benefits because, in effect, of structural impediments to effective market access, although the term had not yet been coined. But later the EU withdrew the complaint. Further, the EU concept of sectoral reciprocity in banking aimed at opening the market in Japan—and hotly contested by the Americans—is also indicative of a similarity of view of structural barriers arising from differences in regulatory systems.)[31]

Another layer of the onion concerns not what governments *do* but what they *don't do* (for example not enforcing competition policy) or *what private actors do* (for example, establishing long-term reciprocal contractual relations). The competition policy issue arose in several high-tech sector-specific disputes with Japan including bid-rigging in public works projects, and in the ongoing debate about the exclusionary effects of vertical production and distribution keiretsu especially in autos. The example of the auto sector is also useful in illustrating the "law of unintended consequences" in a globalizing world economy.

The initial American response to growing imports of Japanese autos was the negotiation of VERs in the early 1980s. An unintended consequence of the VERs was to attract Japanese investment including assembly operations and parts suppliers, so the production keiretsus were transplanted. Although local content gradually increased, the bilateral deficit in auto parts continued to rise and this in turn spawned increasing U.S.-Japanese trade conflict under both the Bush and Clinton administrations. Despite the exclusionary consequences of the *production* keiretsu, which involve long-term reciprocal contractual relations between suppliers and assemblers, rather than vertical integration, most antitrust experts would question the relevance of competition policy as a "solution" so long as there is competition in end products. Yet the argument over the issue has continued and has been extended to the exclusionary impact of the vertical *distribution* keiretsu (exclusive dealing arrangements) in the auto sector in Japan. Indeed only a last-minute resolution of the 1995 battle over exclusive dealership averted major, perhaps terminal, damage to the infant WTO (see chapter 7).

Thus differences in the substantive and procedural aspects of competition policy and differences in private firm behavior or different "enterprise" forms have become part of the concept of structural impediments to market access. Furthermore, the U.S.-Japanese auto conflicts also reveal the increasingly close relationship between the Big Three auto companies and the auto parts producers and the American government in forming trade policy . . . another step in the policy privatization process.

Given the expanding and increasingly complex and contentious notion of structural impediments—so many layers of the onion to unpeel—a new twist in trade policy emerged in the 1980s. Rather than pursuing the tiring process of peeling, why not just divide up the onion by negotiating specific market shares for imports in a given sector, or voluntary import expansion (VIEs)? *Market shares,* or *results,* rather than rules-oriented negotiations seemed, in retrospect, an inevitable development. The first VIE was negotiated in the U.S.-Japanese semiconductor dispute.

The semiconductor dispute was important in several respects. Americans had been the unchallenged leaders in the semiconductor industry, which had originated in the Bell Laboratories after the Second World War. The growing power of the Japanese industry, in considerable part a result of Japanese industrial policy, challenged American dominance at home and in third-country markets. In addition, as economies of scale and scope are so important in this sector and R&D costs increasingly burdensome, access to the large and growing Japanese market was considered important in maintaining competitiveness, although the size of the U.S. and global markets makes this contention difficult to assess. The vertically integrated structure of the Japanese industry made exports by American firms extremely difficult, and access was also impeded by barriers to trade and investment. Finally, these entry barriers and the oligopolistic nature of the Japanese industry created the possibility of what would come to be called strategic dumping with monopolizing intent, which involves subsidizing exports through higher home prices sustained by collusive price behavior and a protected home market—or sanctuary market in the latest jargon.

The bilateral negotiations that culminated in the Semiconductor Trade Agreement (STA) in 1986 followed a Section 301 case and a series of antidumping actions by U.S. semiconductor firms. The agreement had a number of novel features and was modified over time, but from our vantage point the most important was the establishment of a numerical target for foreign market share. Moreover, although the target was defined in terms of foreign share, the definition of "foreign" was not the *country* of origin but the *nationality* of the company, reflecting, as in autos, the successful lobbying efforts of the American producers.

While the agreement has been both vigorously attacked and defended, the implicit argument in defense was that structural barriers to access in Japan are so complex that negotiation is both frustrating and fruitless and therefore the bilateral VIE may be the only practical and effective approach to counter dominance—that is, *the concept of structural impediments can imply a logic of results-oriented trade policy.* And this logic proved extremely attractive to the Clinton administration in its bilateral negotiations with Japan (see below).

At the end of the 1980s, the concept of "structural impediments" was officially adopted, although never defined, in the bilateral Structural Impediments Initiative launched by the United States to avoid naming Japan as a priority country under Super 301. The U.S. list of structural issues to be negotiated included the Japanese distribution system, land-use policies, investment policies, patent practices, antitrust enforcement, exclusionary buying practices by keiretsu, discriminatory pricing, and so on. (Japan's "list" was largely confined to macropolicy.) The final report of the SII was issued in June 1990, but under growing congressional pressure, a new round of talks was started in February 1992. In March Senator Max Baucus called the SII talks a failure and pressed for numerical targets.[32] The first report to the new Clinton administration of the Advisory Committee for Trade Policy and Negotiations (ACTPN) recommended "temporary quantitative indicators" in sectors where "invisible barriers" exist.[33]

The Clinton administration launched the U.S.-Japan Framework for a New Economic Partnership in July 1993.[34]

The Framework was a combination of MOSS, the SII, and results oriented "benchmarks" for measuring progress, hotly contested by the Japanese as a form of numerical targets. The Framework "sectoral and structural" negotiations included high-tech government procurement; autos and auto parts and financial services. The broad issue of regulatory reform in Japan was also included and defined as "reform of relevant government laws, regulation and guidance which have the effect of substantially impeding market access for competitive foreign goods and services."[35] In addition, a new heading, "Economic Harmonization," was specified to cover "foreign direct investment in Japan and the United States" as well as intellectual property rights, access to technology and long-term buyer-supplier relationships between companies in the two countries." In March 1994 President Clinton reinstated the lapsed Super 301 provision of the 1988 Trade Act by executive order.

In the high-tech field, the Clinton administration, in addition to launching a more activist industrial policy than its predecessors, endorsed the principle of "conditional national treatment" to govern access by foreign subsidiaries to U.S. government technology support programs. In a number of laws covering government–private sector research consortia, the participation of foreign subsidiaries would be conditional on, for example, both country policies and the behavior of the subsidiary in the United States, such as the extent and nature of its R&D activities.[36] The concept of conditional national treatment represents another means of dealing with asymmetry of access stemming from structural differences in both investment policies and innovation systems between the United States and Japan.

Given the scope of the Framework talks, only the term *system differences* seems appropriate to encompass the bilateral conflict. Furthermore, the inclusion of both investment and technology extends the concept of asymmetry/reciprocity beyond trade, *to investment and technology policies.* The inclusion of some form of "numerical indicators," however defined or redefined, continued the emphasis on *results* as an alternative (or in addition to) negotiations on *rules.* By the end of 1995, the Clinton administration had negotiated a record-setting twenty agreements that included "objective criteria" to allow monitoring of market share, and in January 1996 it established a new enforcement office in the USTR.

Finally, the new version of Super 301 allowed for greater flexibility in application so as to enhance the possibility that countries named would remove the "trade restrictive" practices without the need to use sanctions. Since the definition of "trade restrictive" practices is both vague and vast, among the most likely countries to be targeted would be those with significant differences in government and private practices with the United States—that is, with *systems* significantly different from the American. Many East Asian countries satisfy this condition: most of all, China. Furthermore, the unique dynamics of foreign investment as an engine of growth in East Asia not only adds a significant regional dimension to U.S.-Japanese conflict, but buttresses the push of trade-policy concerns inside the border.

Thus, coping with system friction is likely to be a significant challenge for American—and, *a fortiori,* global—trade policy in this region, the most rapidly growing area in the world. In the next chapter the main features of these developments will be reviewed.

Five

The East Asian Challenge: A New Convergence Club?

The term *East Asian Miracle*[1] was coined by the World Bank to capture the extraordinarily rapid growth rates of the Hong Kong, Singapore, Korea, and Taiwan NIEs; and Indonesia, Malaysia, and Thailand, the three countries of the Association of Southeast Asian Nations (ASEAN). Since the mid-1960s, their growth rates in gross national product have been more than twice the OECD average and real income per capita quadrupled in the Four Tigers and doubled in the ASEAN three. More recently, mainland China has been added to the miracle group, with growth rates outstripping even those of the NIEs.

While there is no single East Asian model—the countries vary widely in history, culture, and institutions—there are some common characteristics of the growth pattern. In addition to unusually high domestic savings and investment rates, all the East Asian countries assigned priority to improving the basic educational and skill level of the labor force. And in all these countries, growth was enhanced by rapid increases in exports. This education-led/export-fed growth improved efficiency and also provided for technology access from the advanced markets of the OECD. The scope and speed of East Asian penetration of world markets resembles that of Japan in the 1950s and 1960s, when her exports grew at double the rate of the OECD as a whole (tables 5.1, 5.2, and 5.3). Thus, their share of world exports more than tripled between 1965 and 1994, and the rise was even more dramatic for manufacturing: the export share ballooned from less than 2 percent in 1965 to nearly 20 percent in 1994 while the growth in import share during the

Table 5.1 Share of Global Trade (percentage)

	1965		1980		1990		1994	
	EXPORT	IMPORT	EXPORT	IMPORT	EXPORT	IMPORT	EXPORT	IMPORT
United States	15.9	12.8	11.7	13.2	11.6	14.8	12.2	15.9
Japan	4.9	4.5	6.9	7.3	8.5	6.7	9.4	6.5
OECD	77.4	78.0	66.8	72.4	73.5	75.0	69.5	68.7
Total East Asian[a]	5.0	5.2	7.5	7.5	12.3	11.9	16.9	16.9
China	1.5	1.2	1.0	1.0	1.8	1.5	2.9	2.6
Asian NIEs	1.6	2.1	4.0	4.5	7.9	7.6	10.4	10.4
ASEAN	1.9	1.9	2.5	2.0	2.6	2.8	3.6	3.9
World	100	100	100	100	100	100	100	100

Source: IMF, Direction of Trade Statistics, various issues.
[a]Asian NIEs: Hong Kong, Singapore, Taiwan, Korea, and ASEAN (Malaysia, Indonesia, Philippines, Thailand).

1980s failed to keep pace, so that trade surpluses emerged, especially in the NIEs. Furthermore, while the rapid climb in the NIEs share of exports in the low-technology sectors (such as textiles and clothing) began to slow in the 1980s, it has continued to rise in both medium- and high-tech products (table 5.3).

This export growth pattern resembles postwar Japanese development, but the East Asian growth miracle differs in a number of fundamental respects from the postwar catch-up of Japan and even more so from that of the other members of the convergence club. Thus, for example, the role of improvements in overall technology capability, as captured by total factor productivity, was far less important in fostering rising living standards in East Asia than it was for the OECD countries.[2] The growth of *inputs* rather than *overall productivity* accounted for most of the rise in living standards.

Another significant difference from the postwar catch-up model is that rapid *structural change* was a major force in increasing productivity in East Asia. Resources shif-

Table 5.2 Share of Global Manufacturing Trade (percentage)

	1965		1980		1990		1994	
	EXPORT	IMPORT	EXPORT	IMPORT	EXPORT	IMPORT	EXPORT	IMPORT
United States	15.70	11.90	13.36	11.38	12.15	15.72	13.12	17.74
Japan	5.50	1.30	11.24	2.29	11.51	4.18	12.43	4.44
OECD	90.00	70.90	81.52	65.0	80.85	75.22	76.96	69.25
Total East Asian[a]	1.60	3.00	6.76	7.39	13.51	12.66	19.87	18.29
China	0.30	0.50	0.79	1.16	1.86	1.77	3.28	3.18
Asian NIEs	1.20	0.80	5.44	4.49	13.51	8.19	13.03	11.26
ASEAN	0.20	1.70	0.53	1.74	1.78	2.69	3.55	3.85
World	100	100	100	100	100	100	100	100

Source: Calculations based on data from World Trade Organization, *International Trade: 1995 Trends and Statistics* (Geneva: WTO, 1995); 1965 data from OECD, Statistics Directorate, *Foreign Trade by Commodities*, various issues.
[a] Asian NIEs: Hong Kong, Singapore, Taiwan, Korea, and ASEAN (Malaysia, Indonesia, Philippines, Thailand).

ted out of relatively low-productivity sectors into higher-productivity manufacturing industries, which raised their efficiency through competition in export markets. This was not the pattern of postwar growth. Apart from the shrinkage of the agricultural sector after the war, structural change played a relatively minor role in the creation of the convergence club, with a modest exception for Japan.[3] (One reason may have been that the prewar industrial structures of these countries, as well as that of Japan in many respects, reflected a level of development closer to that of the more advanced United States.) Furthermore, once the postwar flow of low-wage agricultural labor in Europe began to slow, its moderating influence on real-wage growth dissipated and, by the end of the 1960s, a transcontinental strike wave was followed by a real-wage explosion.[4] But in East Asia as a region, the supply of lower-wage workers is more elastic because of rapid structural change *within* as well as *among* countries. The lesser role of unions and government

Table 5.3 Export Shares by Technological Category (percentage)

	TOTAL	LOW	MEDIUM	HIGH
United States				
1980	18.6	15.9	16.5	25.0
1985	17.4	13.0	17.5	25.2
1990	16.0	13.5	14.8	22.4
1993	17.1	14.2	10.4	22.7
Asian NIEs (Singapore, Hong Kong, Korea)				
1980	4.5	5.1	2.2	8.0
1985	6.4	7.7	3.4	11.9
1990	7.8	9.2	4.1	13.7
1993	10.3	11.4	3.9	16.7
Japan				
1980	10.7	6.7	11.7	16.4
1985	13.9	6.8	16.9	22.1
1990	11.4	4.7	13.5	18.0
1993	13.0	5.8	9.6	19.3

Source: United Nations, *International Trade Statistics Yearbook,* various issues; OECD, Foreign Trade by Commodities, various issues; OECD Technology Categories (see OECD, Industry and Technology, *Scoreboard of Indicators, 1995,* 114).
Note: Shares represent total OECD plus three Asian NIEs.

regulation than in Europe's labor markets facilitates rapid structural change in most of these countries. Indeed, government spending as a percent of gross domestic product averages about 20 percent in these countries compared with around 50 percent in Europe, 35 percent in the United States, and 25 percent in Japan. Further, *within the region as a whole,* foreign investors can, if necessary, shift parts of their production process to offset rising wages in the more advanced countries. Thus for this part of the world, unlike postwar Europe or Japan, the pace of convergence in pro-

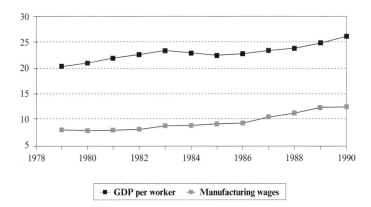

Figure 5.1 Weighted real GDP per worker and real manufacturing wages for East Asia Expressed as a percentage of real GDP per worker and real manufacturing wages of G7 countries

Source: Data from Robert Summers and Alan Heston, *Penn World Table 5.6*, 1995, World Bank, *World Bank World Table*, 1992.
Note: Real GDP per worker for Hong Kong, Singapore, Taiwan, Korea, Malaysia, Indonesia, Philippines, Thailand; real manufacturing wages for Hong Kong, Korea, Philippines, Singapore, Thailand.

ductivity may continue to outstrip that of real-wage convergence for some time (see figure 5.1).

But perhaps the most significant difference between the East Asian miracle and the building of the OECD convergence club is the role of foreign direct investment and its impact on trade and technology transfer. Although the degree of openness to FDI varies within the region, all countries have sought technology transfer either through welcoming, indeed soliciting, the establishment of foreign subsidiaries, or by contracts for manufacturing equipment (original equipment manufacture, or OEM), as well as by so-called new forms of investment such as strategic alliances of

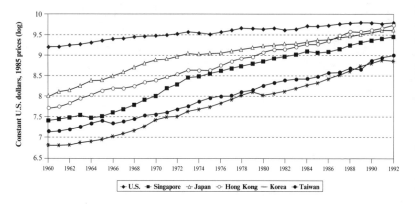

Figure 5.2 Real per capita GDP of selected countries

Source: Data from Robert Summers and Alan Heston, *Penn World Table 5.6,* 1995.

various types. But unlike the period after the war—when there was only one significant technology provider, the United States—there are now in East Asia three major foreign investors: the United States, Japan, and the Overseas Chinese (O/C) in Malaysia, Singapore, Taiwan, and Indonesia. European companies have fallen behind in the investment race, although more recently there are signs of changing priorities. In an effort to strengthen economic and political ties, the European Union and some East Asian countries held a first-ever summit (termed ASEM) in Bangkok in March 1996 to launch a regular series of regular intergovernmental and business meetings.[5] Hence, in sharp contrast with the postwar situation, the existence of multiple players in East Asia makes the game much more complex than one dominated and governed by a single hegemon (and dominant investor) with a broad and broadly shared vision of the desired economic template.

So the answer to the question of whether the creation of

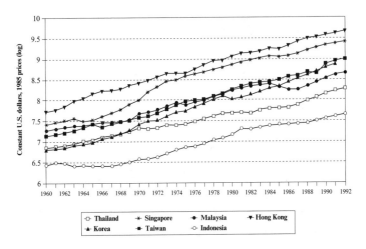

Figure 5.3 Real per capita GDP of selected countries

Source: Data from Robert Summers and Alan Heston, *Penn World Table 5.6*, 1995.

a new East Asian convergence club is under way is by no means a simple yes or no. For the NIEs (figure 5.2), Singapore and Hong Kong are already members of the old club (although the status of Hong Kong after 1997 cannot be taken for granted). While Korea and Taiwan have made remarkable gains since the 1960s, neither has yet closed the gap. And, as is apparent from figure 5.3, the gap between the leading NIEs and the three ASEAN countries has somewhat widened. To sustain further growth over the longer run will require higher levels of technology (or, more broadly, knowledge) since the returns to increasing inputs and to major structural transformation as well as the advantage of less expensive labor will inevitably diminish.

As was the case for the OECD countries, upgrading the knowledge base through improvement and expansion of higher education and investment in R&D is a necessary but not sufficient condition for catch-up. Liberalizing trade is also an important avenue for importing technology "embodied" in goods and services, and the East Asian countries have well understood this. But the key funnel for technology acquisition in this region overall has been foreign investment, which has not only transferred technological know-how but management expertise and access to export markets. Competition for "good" investment has become a key feature of industrial policy in many of these countries and especially in China. And these industrial policies will be the source of increasing friction as investment issues assume a higher profile in the global trade agenda (of which more below). Another question, also related to high-tech industrial policies, is whether East Asian, but more particularly Chinese, growing bilateral trade deficits with the United States will echo the "asymmetry problem," which has created a good deal of heat in U.S.-Japanese relations.

Finally, the role of Japanese investment in East Asia and its impact on regional and global trade has already begun to extend the bilateral conflict with the United States into the East Asian forum. One key question is whether Japanese firms are establishing exclusionary networks in the region that will seriously impede third-country access by trade and/ or investment in these rapidly growing countries. Another major concern to host countries is whether Japanese corporate strategies will restrict technology diffusion both to some NIEs as well as to ASEAN.

To consider these issues, the remainder of this chapter will review the role of foreign direct investment and the impact on trade and technology transfer of Japanese, American, and Overseas Chinese (O/C) multinationals in the region as a whole but also separately for China. Finally, the broader implications of this investment/technology focus for the global trading system will be considered briefly here and more fully in the concluding chapter.

FDI, Trade, and Technology Transfer: The Three Big Players

Investment flows into both the NIE's and the three ASEAN countries surged in the second half of the 1980s (figure 5.4). The inflow into China started later and began to take off at the beginning of the 1990s. Indeed in 1993 China was the largest recipient of investment worldwide. A sequencing is also observable in the later 1980s as some of the decline in flows to the NIEs reflects moves out of the higher cost countries into ASEAN and then China. The Japanese stock of FDI in the region is about twice that of the United States. But, while no stock figures are available (table 5.4), the cumulative flows from the NIEs between 1986 and 1994 dwarfed those from either Japan or the United States. The major portion of this investment was from companies owned by the O/C in Taiwan, Hong Kong, and the ASEAN. The O/C are now the dominant investors in China, far ahead of the United States, Japan or others (table 5.5).

While some of this investment was to serve local markets, an increasing proportion was for export both within and outside the region. This export orientation was particularly significant in some manufacturing sectors, especially electronics, which we will be discussing shortly. So, unlike Europe, where the major integrating force in trade was government policy—that is, the creation of the common market—an increasingly powerful force for regional trade integration in East Asia are MNEs. A good deal of the trade and investment liberalization since the mid-1980s has been unilateral rather than reciprocally negotiated within an institu-

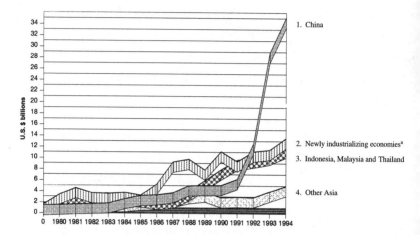

Figure 5.4 Foreign direct-investment inflows to South, East, and Southeast Asia, 1980–1994

Source: UNCTAD, Division on Transnational Corporations and Investment, based on International Monetary Fund, balance-of-payments tape, retrieved in April 1994; estimates of Organization for Economic Cooperation and Development; and national official sources.
[a]Hong Kong, Republic of Korea, Singapore, and Taiwan Province of China.

tional framework. For some countries in this region, East Asia is thus presented as an ideal model: a virtuous circle of liberalization to attract investment that generates trade and attracts more investment, thus sustaining the momentum of liberalization with no need for burdensome institutional mechanisms. (A favorite nightmare image about the institutional future of the Asia Pacific Economic Cooperation forum (APEC) is the "Brussels Bureaucracy.")

There has been a good deal of debate as to whether this "natural integration," as it's often called, is creating a regional bloc. Intraregional trade increased as a share of regional trade in all three regions of the Triad since the onset of the 1980s (table 5.6). But when account is taken of the growth of East Asian markets relative to world markets (as

Table 5.4 FDI Flows in Asian Economies by Origin (investing economy and region in millions of U.S. dollars)

RECIPIENTS	YEAR	UNITED STATES	JAPAN	NIEs	TOTAL
Malaysia	1986	7 (3.3)	23 (11.1)	48 (23.7)	203 (100)
	1988	96 (12.6)	214 (27.9)	271 (35.3)	763 (100)
	1990	69 (3.0)	657 (28.5)	1,100 (47.3)	2,302 (100)
	1993	676 (29.0)	609 (26.1)	1,451 (62.1)	2,335 (100)
	1994	478 (11.1)	672 (15.6)	1,989 (46.0)	4,321 (100)
Thailand	1986	41 (7.0)	251 (43.2)	91 (15.7)	579 (100)
	1988	673 (10.8)	3,063 (49.0)	1,709 (27.4)	6,249 (100)
	1990	1,091 (7.7)	2,706 (19.2)	3,794 (62.2)	14,128 (100)
	1993	306 (19.9)	366 (23.8)	473 (30.7)	1,540 (100)
	1994	1,309 (22.3)	2,556 (43.5)	1,282 (21.8)	5,875 (100)
Indonesia	1986	128 (16.0)	325 (40.6)	84 (10.5)	800 (100)
	1988	731 (16.6)	256 (5.8)	1,530 (34.7)	4,409 (100)
	1990	153 (1.7)	2,241 (25.6)	2,598 (29.7)	3,750 (100)
	1993	445 (5.5)	836 (10.3)	2,637 (32.4)	8,144 (100)
	1994	977 (4.1)	1,563 (6.6)	12,043 (50.8)	23,724 (100)
Republic of Korea	1986	125 (35.4)	138 (38.9)	16 (4.5)	354 (100)
	1988	284 (22.2)	698 (54.3)	15 (1.2)	1,283 (100)
	1990	317 (39.5)	235 (29.3)	21 (2.6)	803 (100)
	1993	341 (32.7)	286 (27.4)	86 (8.2)	1,044 (100)
	1994	311 (23.6)	428 (32.5)	128 (9.7)	1,317 (100)
Taiwan	1986	138 (19.5)	254 (36.0)	65 (9.2)	706 (100)
	1988	135 (12.7)	432 (40.7)	129 (12.2)	1,061 (100)
	1990	540 (25.9)	827 (39.7)	247 (11.9)	2,082 (100)
	1993	235 (19.4)	278 (22.9)	234 (19.3)	1,213 (100)
	1994	294 (18.0)	391 (23.9)	402 (24.6)	1,631 (100)
Singapore	1986	204 (37.3)	225 (41.3)	N/A	547 (100)
	1988	291 (35.3)	344 (41.7)	N/A	824 (100)
	1990	582 (47.6)	391 (32.0)	N/A	1,223 (100)
	1993	827 (30.1)	510 (18.5)	N/A	2,752 (100)
	1994	1,605 (56.7)	598 (21.1)	N/A	2,833 (100)

Table 5.4 *continued*

RECIPIENTS	YEAR	UNITED STATES	JAPAN	NIEs	TOTAL
China	1986	326 (14.5)	263 (11.7)	1,342 (59.8)	2,244 (100)
	1988	236 (7.4)	515 (16.1)	2,123 (66.5)	3,194 (100)
	1990	284 (8.4)	356 (10.5)	2,162 (63.7)	3,393 (100)
	1993	2,063 (7.5)	1,324 (4.8)	21,275 (77.3)	27,515 (100)
	1994	2,491 (7.4)	2,075 (6.1)	24,959 (73.9)	33,767 (100)
Total	1986	969 (17.8)	1,479 (27.2)	1,646 (30.3)	5,433 (100)
	1988	2,446 (13.8)	5,522 (31.0)	5,777 (32.5)	17,783 (100)
	1990	3,036 (11.0)	7,413 (26.8)	9,922 (35.8)	27,681 (100)
	1993	4,893 (11.0)	4,209 (9.4)	26,156 (58.7)	44,543 (100)
	1994	7,465 (10.2)	8,282 (11.3)	40,803 (55.1)	73,468 (100)

Source: Intra-Regional Investment and Technology Transfer in Asia (Tokyo: Asia Productivity Organization, 1994), 33. 1993 data from UNCTAD, Division on Transnational Corporations and Investment. 1994 data from JETRO, *JETRO White Paper on Foreign Direct Investment, 1996* (Tokyo: JETRO, 1996), 12.
Note: Figures in parentheses are percentages.

measured by the gravity coefficients), the intraregional share drops sharply in the first half of the 1980s and then begins to increase after 1985. The decline in intraregional bias in the first half of the decade reflects the growing penetration of world markets noted earlier: indeed half of East Asian exports still are directed to countries outside the region (see table 5.7). Moreover, over the 1980s the East Asian trade surplus with the United States grew very rapidly, but their deficit with Japan grew even more. This growing deficit is most marked in manufactured goods after the mid-1980s because of rising imports of capital goods from Japan, which were not matched by a concomitant rise in exports to Japan (see table 5.8). This dependence on Japan is evident in the pattern of trade for both the more advanced NIEs as well as for ASEAN (see table 5.9) and, for both, the United States is a major market for finished products, especially in

Table 5.5 Sources of Foreign Capital in China (cumulative 1979–1993)

SOURCE COUNTRY	NUMBER OF ENTERPRISES	PERCENT	FOREIGN INVESTMENT (BILLIONS OF US$)	PERCENT
Hong Kong	106,769	63.7	47.5	69.1
Taiwan	20,612	12.3	6.4	9.3
Macau	4,188	2.5	1.9	2.8
Singapore	3,037	1.8	1.5	2.2
Thailand	1,361	0.8	0.8	1.2
Subtotal	136,042	81.2	58.1	84.6
United States	11,554	6.9	3.7	5.4
Japan	7,096	4.2	3.3	4.8
Other	14,314	8.6	4.4	6.4
Total	167,500	100.0	68.7	100.0

Source: Department of Foreign Affairs and Trade, Australia, *Overseas Chinese Business Networks in Asia,* 198.
Note: The data, however, need to be interpreted with caution. Some of the investment has originated in China but has been reinvested through Hong Kong and back into China in order to take advantage of tax and other privileges accorded to "foreign" investment. Hong Kong is also likely to be overrepresented as a source of investment. Many Taiwanese companies route their investment in China through Hong Kong on account of past Taiwan government restrictions and to disguise the destination of their investment. Many Southeast Asian Chinese entrepreneurs also invest in China through Hong Kong. Taiwanese investment is likely to be closer to 25 percent than the official figure reported.

the electronics sector. Thus a pattern of triangular trade has emerged, manifested by growing surpluses with the United States and growing deficits with Japan.

Both the increase in intraregional intensity after 1985 and the triangular pattern of trade balances reflect in large part the impact of foreign direct investment as an engine of integration in East Asia. To explore this integration engine and the implications for policy more fully, it's essential to analyze the role of the MNEs of the three main players, Japan, the United States, and the O/C.

Table 5.6 Measures of Regional Interdependence, 1979–1993

	1979	1985	1990	1992	1994
Intraregional trade as a share of regional trade					
North America	0.287	0.330	0.313	0.314	0.365
European Union	0.535	0.542	0.607	0.611	0.565
East Asia	0.332	0.363	0.407	0.453	0.525
Gravity coefficients[a] of intraregional trade					
North America	1.95	1.71	1.84	1.86	1.87
Eurpoean Union	1.53	1.70	1.53	1.55	1.68
East Asia	2.64	2.05	2.09	2.13	2.24

Sources: Peter Petri, "Corporate Links and Direct Foreign Investment in Asia and the Pacific" (PAFTAD, Hong Kong, June 1/3, 1994, mimeographed), 7; figures for 1994 and for European Union calculated using data from International Monetary Fund. *Direction of Trade Statistics,* various issues.

[a]((Intraregional Trade) × (World Trade))/((Trade Exports of Region) × (Total Imports of Region)).

Japan's Investment in East Asia

Japan's foreign investment in East Asia grew dramatically in the second half of the 1980s. As may be inferred from table 5.10, outward flows slowed in the early 1990s because of serious domestic problems arising from the bursting of the 1980s asset price bubble, but the shift to East Asia as a location became more marked and flows picked up again after 1992. Most of this new investment in China and ASEAN was in manufacturing (see table 5.11), and of this about one-third was in the electronics sector. The shift in flows *within* the region from the NIEs to ASEAN and then to China may be seen in figure 5.5.[6]

Japan's postwar investment in East Asia has gone through several stages. Before the late 1970s, it was mainly in the resource sectors, and the products were exported to

Table 5.7 Trade Balance and Shares of Various Regions in Total Imports and Exports of East Asia

	1980			1985			1994		
	EXPORTS TO	IMPORTS FROM	BALANCE[a]	EXPORTS TO	IMPORTS FROM	BALANCE[a]	EXPORTS TO	IMPORTS FROM	BALANCE[a]
United States	22%	17%	6,467	29%	16%	28,084	22%	14%	53,783
Western Europe	14%	9%	6,936	10%	11%	-909	13%	13%	-798
Japan	21%	24%	-4,646	17%	26%	-12,622	13%	23%	-80,384
East Asia	21%	22%	0	25%	27%	0	38%	37%	0
Rest of world	22%	27%	-6,488	19%	20%	1,535	14%	13%	2,925
World	100%	100%	-2,269	100%	100%	16,089	100%	100%	-24,474

Source: Calculations based on data from United Nations, *International Trade Statistics Yearbook*, various issues; OECD, *Foreign Trade by Commodities*, various issues.
[a]Millions of U.S. dollars.

Table 5.8 Trade Balance and Shares of Various Regions in Manufactured Imports and Exports of East Asia

	1980			1985			1993		
	EXPORTS TO	IMPORTS FROM	BALANCE[a]	EXPORTS TO	IMPORTS FROM	BALANCE[a]	EXPORTS TO	IMPORTS FROM	BALANCE[a]
United States	27%	17%	6,860	40%	14%	3,161	25%	13%	62,983
Western Europe	19%	15%	1,212	12%	14%	-2,239	17%	17%	2,191
Japan	8%	35%	-25,316	7%	32%	-32,158	9%	25%	-82,700
East Asia	22%	19%	0	23%	23%	0	36%	38%	0
Rest of world	26%	13%	9,049	18%	18%	-209	14%	7%	35,135
World	100%	100%	-8,194	100%	100%	-2,995	100%	100%	17,609

Source: Calculations based on data from United Nations, *International Trade Statistics Yearbook*, various issues; OECD, *Foreign Trade by Commodities*, various issues.

Note: SITC: 6, 7, 8.

[a]Millions of U.S. dollars.

le 5.9 Balance of Trade of Japan with East Asia (billions of U.S. dollars)

	1984	1985	1986	1987	1988	1989	1990	1991	1992	1993	1994
st Asia											
'apital goods	16.7	17.8	21.4	26.6	33.4	35.5	39	46.4	52.4	62	73.9
'otal	9.7	9.2	15.5	14.7	18.4	17.8	22.5	32.4	41.9	54	62.2
an NIEs											
'apital goods	10.3	9.5	13.6	18.1	23	23.6	35	30.8	34.4	39	34.2[a]
'otal	14.3	12.7	17.5	20.6	24.8	25.6	30.7	39.5	46.5	54	62.4
ΞAN											
'apital goods	4.3	3.3	3.3	4.9	6.8	8.9	12.2	13.2	13.7	17	17.2[a]
'otal	−5.9	−9.4	−6.3	−6.8	−6	−5.1	−2.2	−1.5	0.5	4	8.6
.na											
'apital goods	2.2	5	4.5	3.5	3.6	2.9	1.8	2.4	4.3	7	6.7[a]
'otal	1.3	6	4.2	0.8	−0.4	−2.6	−5.9	−5.6	−5	−3	8.9
rld											
'apital goods	68.2	70.1	88.5	100.8	117.5	122.7	122.0	136.0	152.6	169.1	188.9
'otal	33.6	46.1	82.7	79.7	77.6	64.3	52.1	77.8	106.6	120.2	120.9

rce: Japan External Trade Organization, *JETRO White Paper on International Trade,* 1995, 1996
*alances estimated using data from Tariff Association, *Japan Exports and Imports,* 1994.

le 5.10 Japan's FDI Flows by Major Markets 1980–1994 (millions of U.S. dollars)

	1980	1985	1990	1991	1992	1993	1994
rth America	1,596	5,495	27,192	18,823	14,572	15,287	17,823
	34.0%	45.0%	47.8%	45.3%	42.7%	42.4%	43.4%
ited States	1,484	5,395	26,128	18,026	13,819	14,725	17,331
	31.6%	44.2%	45.9%	43.3%	40.5%	40.9%	42.2%
rope	578	1,930	14,294	9,371	7,061	7,940	6,230
	12.3%	15.8%	25.1%	22.5%	20.7%	22.0%	15.2%
st Asia[a]	1,186	1,435	7,054	5,936	6,425	6,637	9,699
	25.3%	11.7%	12.4%	14.3%	18.8%	18.4%	23.6%
al FDI	4,693	12,217	59,611	41,584	34,138	36,025	41,051

rce: Japan Economic Institute, *Statistical Profile,* various issues.
Hong Kong, Taiwan, South Korea, Singapore, Thailand, Malaysia, Indonesia, Philippines, China

Table 5.11 Japanese FDI Stock in Manufacturing as a Percentage of Total Japanese FDI Stock

	CHINA	TAIWAN	INDONESIA	SOUTH KOREA	MALAYSIA	PHILIPPINES	HONG KONG	THAILAND	SINGAPORE	ASEAN	4 NIEs	TOTAL EAST ASIA
1981	11.3	81.3	25.2	67.5	67.0	34.4	14.4	72.6	75.5	31.6	53.4	38.7
1982	13.3		25.8	64.1	67.4		11.8	74.8	76.6	30.0	42.3	34.3
1983	14.9	75.6	26.9	60.5	69.3	36.9	9.5	72.1	77.8	34.3	46.8	39.0
1984	16.8		26.8	58.7	70.8		8.3	71.2	72.6	32.0	36.7	33.7
1985	18.6	75.3	26.2	56.2	68.7	34.9	8.4	70.0	63.6	34.2	42.0	37.1
1986	14.9	54.4	25.8	51.4	65.3		8.7	70.1	60.2	31.5	38.2	34.0
1987	8.4	58.3	27.5	48.3	68.2	36.8	9.0	73.2	59.3	36.9	37.3	35.2
1988	17.2	60.9	28.9	48.9	72.7	40.4	8.0	73.1	52.2	41.2	34.4	36.4
1989	22.5	60.9	28.7	47.7	71.9	43.9	7.5	68.7	46.7	43.6	32.7	36.8
1990	25.4	61.0	31.5	48.0	73.8	49.1	7.3	66.9	44.8	47.0	31.4	38.0
1991	30.1	59.1	33.1	48.8	72.9	52.4	7.8	68.0	43.5	49.1	31.2	39.2
1992	37.5	57.7	35.8	48.3	71.9	53.5	8.1	65.4	41.5	50.0	30.6	40.0
1993	49.5	58.5	35.8	47.5	73.9	54.4	9.3	66.0	40.7	51.1	30.6	41.6
1994	56.2	68.7	36.9	45.9	74.4	54.4	10.1	67.1	39.7	52.1	31.7	43.6

Sources: Calculations based on data from Chia Siow Yue, *Foreign Direct Investment and Economic Integration in East Asia* (National University of Singapore Institute, 1995, mimeograph); Japan Economic Institute, *Statistical Profile,* various issues.

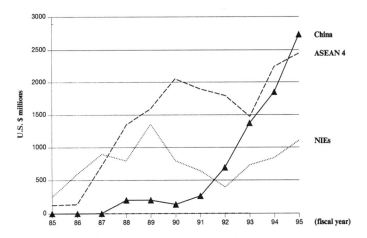

Figure 5.5 Trends in flow of Japanese direct investment in manufacturing industry to East Asia

Source: White Paper on International Trade, Japan (Tokyo: Ministry of International Trade and Industry, 1994); 1995 figures from JETRO, *JETRO White Paper on Foreign Direct Investment, 1996* (Tokyo: JETRO, 1996), 17.
Note: Figures for 1995 were obtained by doubling the figures from April 1 to September 30, 1995.

Japan. In manufacturing, it was for import substitution in domestic markets to evade high tariff barriers. From the late 1970s to the mid-1980s, investment in the NIEs by Japanese manufacturers was primarily motivated by the attraction of low-paid but educated labor for low-end consumer electronics assembly and labor-intensive products like textiles and clothing. Most of this production was for export to the United States and Europe. The third wave, which was prompted by the Plaza Accord yen shock, was the surge in the second half of the 1980s. The rise in costs in Japan pushed production—mainly for export—to lower-cost ASEAN countries and increased East Asian imports of components and equipment from Japan. Changes in the 1990s clearly involve more investment in China and a consolidation of intraregional production networks, especially in industrial and consumer electronics. Indeed, as noted above, it is the fear of exclusionary networks that could preempt American presence in this booming region and exacerbate the trade imbalance with the United States, which has worried a number of American officials and trade analysts.[7]

These new developments in the 1990s are driven by a number of factors, both domestic as well as external. One is clearly another yen shock, at first sparked by the bilateral trade conflicts with the United States but also reflecting more basic structural problems affecting savings behavior in both countries. With the higher yen shaving export profits, some shift to overseas production would be a likely response as it was after the Plaza Accord. But this time the response was more cautious. Although the yen had been rising steadily against the dollar since the onset of the decade, as late as August 1993 almost 70 percent of companies surveyed by the Industrial Bank of Japan indicated that they were not contemplating new offshore investment, a marked contrast between the immediate and rapid response to the Plaza shock.[8] So far as East Asia is the intended location, an important reason for this caution seemed to be that in the key manufacturing sectors, such as electronics and autos, planning for new offshore production has been more complex and time consuming than it was in the 1980s. (Indeed, a year later these plans were much clearer—of which more below). New corporate strategies had to take into account not just the rising costs of doing business in Japan because of exchange rate changes, but also the impact of ongoing structural changes in Japan and changing policies and circumstances in host countries.

The structural changes in Japan merit a brief digression.

The bursting of the 1980s asset price bubble in 1990 ushered in the longest recession of the postwar period. But it was no ordinary recession, and the bursting of the bubble exposed, rather than created, serious underlying structural weakness in the Japanese economy and the Japanese financial system, which had been masked in the 1980s by the growth push of an artificially low cost of capital. Indeed the overinvestment of the 1980s simply exaggerated a built-in propensity to overinvestment because Japanese firms, supported by an interventionist and uncompetitive financial system, were less subject to market discipline to produce high returns, less constrained from sliding down the yield curve, and more willing to live with far lower profit margins than firms in other countries. In part the weakness of market discipline stems from the corporate governance model acclaimed for its long-termism, which worked so well in the golden age of rapid export-led growth. Long overdue financial market deregulation and improved transparency will rationalize the financial system, increasingly force Japanese companies to pay competitive market rates for capital, and generate changes in the corporate governance model. In the period of transition, however, the greatly weakened financial sector will continue to act as a drag on the real economy. And Japan is likely to suffer a prolonged period of sluggish growth.

Moreover, the need for fundamental restructuring goes well beyond the financial markets and the corporate governance system. Japanese productivity is high mainly in capital-intensive manufacturing sectors, but productivity of white-collar workers or in service sectors is abysmally low, well below that of the United States.[9] An important aspect of the postwar "social contract" in Japan was the employment guarantee provided, in effect, by white-collar overemployment and inefficient domestic service sectors protected by myriad regulations and generating a wide "price gap" between Japan and other OECD economies. While both the Japanese government and Japanese business recognize the need for the regulatory reform advocated by the Americans, the radical restructuring it will engender (including erosion of lifetime employment and tenure-related wages) threatens these other fundamental aspects of the successful high-growth paradigm. And, indeed, the postwar political arrangements are also under assault, which adds to the difficulty of managing fundamental change. When the MITI Economic White Paper declared in 1956 that Japan was "no longer in the postwar era" they may have been forty years too early!

Parenthetically, by a curious paradox, the hand-wringing over Japanese declinism in the 1990s echoes that of the United States in the 1980s, but the massive restructuring of American manufacturing, aided by the decline in the dollar, as well as the much higher productivity of the American services industries, has greatly improved the competitiveness of American firms in international markets. And this has been another factor prompting a rethinking of Japanese corporate strategy.

It's far too soon to judge how effectively Japanese government and business will cope with these challenges of structural transformation. The adaptation will require change in domestic policy and politics. But major changes in *corporate strategy* will also be necessary. In the mass-production manufacturing sectors, which led the Japanese growth miracle and began investing abroad in the 1980s, one piece of the new corporate strategy will involve a new locational configuration. It is thus in this broader context that a "fourth wave" of Japanese investment in East Asia should be considered. And, in particular, its implications for the future development of the region.

Will the Geese Catch Up?

Japanese investment in East Asia has been characterized by the "flying geese" metaphor: as rich countries produce more technologically advanced new products, they shift production of lower value-added versions of the same product to less-developed, lower-cost countries, which helps generate a dynamic process of development based on shifting comparative advantage.[10] This was intended to depict Japanese investment behavior in East Asia especially in the two main manufacturing sectors, electronics and autos, from the late 1970s, first in the NIE's and then ASEAN and now China. The move to Asia of Japanese MNEs was sometimes accompanied, usually with a lag, by a move of small- and medium-scale enterprises (SMEs) with long-term supplier relationships with the main firm. Technology transfer, whether to subsidiaries or local firms, involved operational, maintenance, and inspection know-how. But technology-intensive components and capital equipment for these assembly industries, and the related R&D for design and development, were produced in and exported from Japan. To an increasing degree, this Asian production substituted for exports from Japan to the United States and the EU. Most of the trade flows were within the firm (see figure 5.6). Thus the host country "benefit," in terms of spillover to domestic firms and personnel, is not really analogous to the "flying geese" model. Moreover, the metaphor was inappropriate in another respect. These hierarchical regional intrafirm networks, which began in the 1980s, distribute different parts

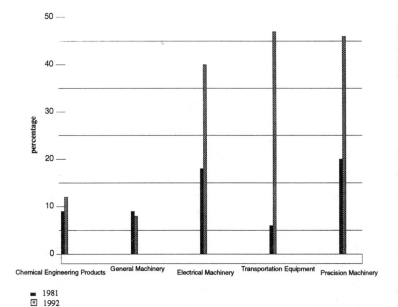

Figure 5.6 Intracompany trade ratio by major industries in Japan

Sources: Ministry of International Trade and Industry, "Overseas Business Activities of Japanese Corporations," "Survey of Japanese Corporation," *MITI White Paper on International Trade,* 1994.

of the production *process* (rather than different *products*) among countries in the region. The impact of this on technology diffusion is unclear since the host country operation is heavily dependent on imports of technology-intensive products from Japan. In sum, the lagging geese may have some difficulty catching up.

Some changes in these regional firm networks were already apparent in the early 1990s. In addition to Asian production substituting for exports from Japan, "reverse imports" into Japan from subsidiaries in East Asia began to increase. Some of these imports were of quite a sophisti-

cated nature because of the development of new highly auto-
mated production facilities installed in ASEAN countries
(see table 5.12). But these changes—and others, such as the
establishment of regional procurement centers in Singapore
and some increased localization of management, joint research ventures with NIE universities to produce applica-
tions software because of domestic shortages of software engineers—were insufficient to significantly change the basic
template of the Japan-centered hierarchical networks in the
two key industries of electronics and autos.[11]

However, in contrast with the hesitancy signaled in
1993, surveys in 1994 and 1995 do indicate that more significant changes in corporate strategies may be under way,
in response not only to the yen rise but also the ongoing
structural changes in Japan and the improving competitiveness of American firms.[12]

With respect to East Asia, these changes over the medium term include very significant increases in overseas production (in electronics, for example, increases in the range
of 50–100 percent); more local procurement both from unaf-
filiated firms and subsidiaries; and large increases in both
OEM and "reverse imports."[13] Again, all of these imply
some, but mainly incremental, adaptation of the current
networks and would be unlikely to significantly change either the triangular trade or the technology diffusion pat-
terns. But when questioned about longer-term global strategy, a more fundamental rethinking of corporate strategy is
clearly evident.

This change is best summarized by contrasting the medium term (defined as three years) with the longer term
(about ten years). In all industries, first priority in the medium term is increasing offshore production of what are
termed "commodity goods" and increasing somewhat R&D

Table 5.12 Development of Overseas Production by Foreign Affiliates of Japanese Firms for Export and Import Substitution of Electrical Machinery Products

	RATIO OF OVERSEAS PRODUCTION[a]		OVERSEAS PRODUCTION/ EXPORT RATIO		IMPORT/OVERSEAS PRODUCTION RATIO		JAPAN'S EXPORTS (IN 1,000 UNITS)		JAPAN'S IMPORTS (IN 1,000 UNITS)	
	1985	1992	1985	1992	1985	1992	1985	1992	1985	1992
Radio	55.2	61.1	153.1	649	30.1	37.7	5.6	1.6	2.6	4.0
Color TV	38.8	65.9	89.4	341	0.3	9.8	13.4	6.8	0	2.3
Electronic fan	32.9	59.1	121.2	111	15.7	57.5	2.1	0	0.4	3.0
Hi Fi speaker	31.9	77.0	45.0	144	12.7	64.8	4.4	4.7	0.3	4.7
Tape recorder	23.5	59.2	20.8	183	7.7	41.1	77.5	20.8	1.2	15.7
Electronic range	22.7	64.1	36.6	518	0	1.0	6.4	1.3	0	0.1
Refrigerator	18.7	40.8	64.6	680	0.8	11.3	1.9	0.4	0	0.3
Car stereophonic	8.3	28.3	9.0	46.5	8.7	7.7	16.3	15.6	0	0.6
VCR	6.3	31.4	8.1	56.9	2.3	4.6	25.5	18.8	0	0.5
Washing machine	5.9	20.2	15.0	152	1.3	11.0	2.1	0.9	0	0.2
Hi Fi amplifier	3.5	26.4	4.5	35.5	0	20.9	6.5	4.7	0	0.4
CD player	1.1	37.0	1.5	65.8	9.0	29.8	6.1	0.8	0	0.2

Source: Masaru Yoshitomi, "Main Issues of Macroeconomic Coordination: The Peso, Dollar and Yen Problems," in *The Halifax G-7 Summit: Issues on the Table,* ed. Sylvia Ostry and Gilbert R. Winham (Halifax: Centre for Foreign Policy Studies, Dalhousie University, 1995), table 6.

Note: Production, exports, and imports are all measured in terms of units of products.

[a]Overseas production divided by the sum of domestic and overseas production.

activity only in developed countries, especially the United States. But in the long term, focus shifts to the production of high-value-added goods in all regions. In electronics and autos, strategies focus on higher value-added production, more offshore R&D, greater reliance on local management, and more strategic alliances with foreign companies, not only in the United States and Canada and the EU but also in the NIEs and ASEAN.[14]

This long-term strategy is not regional but global and reflects a more pervasive concern by the corporations about the overall erosion of their competitiveness in key industries because of accelerating technological change and also the fear of being caught in a vice: squeezed at the low end (commodity goods) by Asian firms and at the high end by American firms.

Obviously, it's not possible at this time to evaluate the effects of these new global strategies or, indeed, even whether they will be fully implemented. In the context of the present discussion, however, one positive benefit for both the NIEs and ASEAN would be to increase technology diffusion both through the establishment of R&D centers (mainly for local market applied research and product development) and the upgrading of the production base in the host country. Whether or not these plans would be adequate to counter the mounting criticism by a number of East Asian countries of Japanese firms' technology transfer strategies is also an unanswerable question. This is worth briefly spelling out because it is also related to Japanese government technology policy.

Added to the forces *pushing* a change in Japanese corporate strategies in Asia, there is also a force *pulling* such a move. A number of Asian countries, most outspokenly Korea and Malaysia, have complained about Japanese unwillingness to transfer technology, not only by keeping the most advanced technology at home (which, by the way, is not unusual for all developed countries) but also by employing relatively few local managers and by limiting upstream and downstream linkages with domestic firms. But the Japanese have long argued that the overall level of technological capability in host countries is inadequate, and now government plans for such upgrading seem to be under way. More Japanese development aid is going into technology transfer and technical training, and the Asian Productivity Organization has launched a number of similar efforts.[15] The government has established a corporate tax credit for technology transfer in Asia to encourage more technology diffusion in host countries.[16] MITI recently announced plans to increase the number of technology experts for developing countries from one thousand to ten thousand by the year 2000 and to match that number with trainees from these countries coming to Japan.[17] In APEC a Japanese initiative has been a special program to promote technology transfer and joint R&D projects. And some East Asian firms are establishing R&D institutes in Japan.[18]

In summary, Japanese investment in East Asia has played a major role in regional integration through the creation and consolidation of hierarchical intrafirm industrial networks in key manufacturing sectors. While there are changes under way that could fundamentally change these networks, the triangular trade pattern that has emerged is likely to continue over the next several years to generate friction with the United States and also with many host countries. In the case of the latter, one sign of the increasing concern with catch-up is the proliferation of technology-related industrial policies, which we will discuss shortly. These policies will affect not only Japanese firms, because Japan is not the only player in the region.

American Investment in East Asia

While the stock of American FDI in East Asia is considerably less than that of Japan, American direct investment flows to East Asia increased significantly in the early 1990s (although it was far outweighed by Western Hemisphere flows) (see table 5.13). American investment in the region in the early postwar decades, like Japanese, was to supply manufacturing products in highly protected local markets or provide petroleum and other natural resources for use in the United States. More than a third of American foreign investment in the region was in the Philippines, largely because of historical linkages. Again, as was the case for Japan, wide exchange-rate swings (in this case the rapid rise in the dollar after the break-up of Bretton Woods and the first OPEC oil shock in the mid-1970s), prompted a surge in American direct investment in East Asia. Stocks quadrupled between 1966 and 1977 (see table 5.14). The share of manufacturing investment has remained at around one-third of the total, and within manufacturing, electronics has steadily increased, more than doubling between 1988 and 1994. A shift away from the Philippines to the NIEs (especially Hong Kong and Singapore), ASEAN, and China during the 1980s and into the 1990s is also evident.

In contrast to Japan, American corporations have more industrial as opposed to consumer electronics production in the region. (Under pressure from Japanese competition, the American consumer electronics industry virtually disappeared by the early 1980s.) But otherwise there are some

Table 5.13 United States Flows of FDI by Major Markets, 1980–1994 (millions of U.S. dollars)

	1980	1985	1990	1991	1992	1993	1994
Developed countries	14,108	13,366	17,971	21,601	24,005	46,845	24,217
	83.4%	77.4%	58.0%	66.1%	56.3%	65.7%	50.8%
Latin America (including Mexico)	2,655	3,838	10,141	7,194	12,751	16,859	15,724
	15.7%	22.2%	32.7%	22.0%	29.9%	23.6%	33.0%
East Asia[a]	210	165	2,913	3,180	4,604	5,700	6,853
	1.2%	1.0%	9.4%	9.7%	10.8%	8.0%	14.4%
Total FDI	16,918	17,267	30,982	32,696	42,647	71,349	47,698

Source: Survey of Current Business, various years.
[a]Hong Kong, Taiwan, South Korea, Singapore, Thailand, Malaysia, Indonesia, Philippines, China.

Table 5.14 U.S. FDI Stocks in East Asia by Country and Industry, 1966–1992 (millions of U.S. dollars)

	1966	1977	1988	1994
By Country				
Four NIEs				
Korea	42	395	1,501	3,612
Taiwan	58	259	1,622	3,882
Hong Kong	126	1,328	5,244	11,986
Singapore	30	516	2,290	10,972
ASEAN Four				
Thailand	51	237	1,132	3,762
Malaysia	57	464	1,135	2,382
Indonesia	106	984	2,925	5,015
Philippines	486	837	1,511	2,374
China	125[a]	175[a]	719[a]	1,699
Total	1,308	5,503	18,515	45,684
By Industry				
Manufacturing	405	1,496	5,957	16,104
Chemicals	83	494	1,481	2,450
Electronics	70	345	2,327	5,559
All Other	903	4,007	12,558	29,580
Petroleum	527	2,177	4,709	9,364
Wholesaling	145	677	2,954	7,649
Finance	25	638	2,049	4,291

Sources: Dennis J. Encarnation, "Bringing East Asia into the U.S.-Japan Rivalry: The Regional Evolution of American and Japanese Multinationals," in *Japanese Investment in Asia,* ed. Eileen M. Doherty (San Francisco: Asian Foundation and BRIE, 1994). 1994 data from *Survey of Current Business,* August 1995.

[a]China and other Asia not elsewhere specified.

similarities in the investment pattern of the two OECD players. The second wave of American investment, beginning in
the 1970s and pushed by another rise in the dollar in the
first half of the 1980s, was much more oriented to exports,
reflecting both the liberalization momentum in the region
and the pressure of Japanese competition, which spurred
the need for lower-cost production. But most of the exports
were to the United States. Low-cost assembly plants used
imported American components to produce low-end products for the American market. As noted, the Philippines lost
its predominance as American multinationals shifted to
other locations with an edge in costs and capabilities. Hong
Kong became a center for financial services and distribution
and Singapore became the regional center for American
electronics companies.

Nonequity forms of investment—contract assembly and
sourcing from local suppliers—were also established. While
no comprehensive data are available, a few case studies suggest American firms are more open—that is, more likely to
procure parts from local firms and sometimes from Japanese suppliers.[19]

But until the late 1980s, the dominant strategy of American corporations in manufacturing industries, such as industrial electronics, communication equipment, and capital
goods, helps explain the growing deficit with the region. In
other words, the triangular trade pattern does not only arise
from the pattern of Japanese networks. U.S. multinationals
continued to view most of East Asia (Hong Kong and Singapore being notable exceptions) as an inexpensive industrial
base for processing products to sell in the U.S. market. In
the shift away from investment to serve protected local markets, which characterized the earlier strategy of both Japanese and American firms, the Japanese began to focus on

both regional demand and third-country markets—especially the United States But a primary focus of the American firms remained the American market. (Another reason for this strategy could also be the low level of American investment in Japan, which made the extension of the American intrafirm networks into that market minimal.)[20] In manufacturing, and especially in electronics, "reverse imports" to the U.S. market—in stark contrast to the Japanese pattern—constituted nearly half the trade flows (see table 5.15). And they far outweighed the export of components and equipment from the U.S. headquarters of the firms (table 5.16). Thus, the industrial networks of Japanese firms are more regionally oriented (in both sourcing and sales), import far more from Japan in components and capital equipment, and export far less to Japan. The American networks are still strongly U.S.-centered, and East Asian markets for sales or exports still do not rank very high.

There are, however, some recent signs of changing strategy among a number of American companies, especially in industrial electronics (telecommunications equipment, computers, test and measuring instruments, office equipment, and so forth). Local share of sales is rising[21] as are strategic alliances with host country MNEs, especially in Taiwan and Korea, probably as a counter to similar Japanese moves.[22] And, as a reflection of growing Japanese fear of American preeminence in the new technology of the "digital revolution," there has been a spurt of Japanese-American alliances in the personal computer market, in software, and in multi-media consumer products.[23] And this American *tsunami* (tidal wave) has only just begun. Whether, having established a Japanese base, the tsunami will wash over the whole region is not yet clear. Nor is the effect it will have on American corporate strategy in penetrating Japanese net-

Table 5.15 Majority Owned Affiliate Sales by Destination, Manufacturing and Electronic Equipment, 1993 (percentages of sales to all destinations)

	SALES TO U.S.		SALES TO LOCAL		SALES TO OTHER FOREIGN COUNTRIES	
	MANUFACTURING	ELECTRONICS	MANUFACTURING	ELECTRONICS	MANUFACTURING	ELECTRONICS
All countries	13.86	22.70	59.71	50.04	26.43	27.26
Total East Asia	34.87	46.94	34.64	22.46	29.84	29.41
China	(D)	(D)	73.20	(D)	(D)	(D)
Hong Kong	21.04	10.66	44.96	51.64	34.03	37.76
Indonesia	(D)	(D)	87.08	(D)	(D)	(D)
South Korea	18.79	55.60	72.10	36.67	9.11	7.73
Malaysia	50.93	57.41	15.12	6.35	33.94	36.23
Philippines	14.67	44.20	62.66	10.69	22.67	45.11
Singapore	50.15	51.80	14.10	20.41	35.75	27.79
Thailand	27.09	75.08	38.79	(D)	34.15	(D)
Taiwan	16.49	33.72	61.17	39.63	22.33	26.59

Source: U.S. Department of Commerce, *U.S. Direct Investment Abroad: Operations of U.S. Parent Companies and Their Foreign Affiliates, Preliminary 1993 Estimates,* June 1995.

Note: (D)—Data suppressed to avoid disclosure of data of individual companies.

Table 5.16 Electrical and Electronic Equipment Shipped to and by U.S. Affiliates, 1993 (millions of U.S. dollars)

	EXPORTS	IMPORTS
All countries	10,654	14,084
Total East Asia	2,534	6,253
China	(D)	(D)
Hong Kong	5	(D)
Indonesia	1	0
South Korea	303	280
Malaysia	650	2,083
Philippines	(D)	353
Singapore	968	2,360
Thailand	221	494
Taiwan	386	683

Source: U.S. Department of Commerce, *U.S. Direct Investment Abroad: Operations of U.S. Parent Companies and their Foreign Affiliates, Preliminary 1993 Estimates,* June 1995.
Note: (D)—Data suppressed to avoid disclosure of data of individual companies.

works and gaining a better foothold in regional markets. Whatever the outcome of the American-Japanese game in East Asia, however, for both these players the highest stakes are in China. And that's where the third player counts—the Overseas Chinese.

The O/C Network

Some Korean and Taiwanese firms have already established market presence both in the East Asian region and world markets and compete with OECD firms in certain products in both consumer and industrial electronics. American and Japanese firms have formed alliances of various kinds with these firms for both defensive reasons and to gain share in host country markets. But the O/C networks are quite different from these new MNEs from the Asian NIEs. Their home

Table 5.17 Ethnic Chinese States' Investment in Selected Asian Countries (rank as foreign investor)

	CAMBODIA	INDONESIA	PHILIPPINES	THAILAND	VIETNAM
Taiwan	8th	3rd	8th	8th	1st
Hong Kong	3rd	2nd	5th	2nd	2nd
Singapore	2nd	7th	7th	4th	5th

Source: Department of Foreign Affairs and Trade, Australia, 179.
Note: Data for Cambodia relate to number of foreign invested project approvals given since 1989; for Indonesia, they relate to cumulative foreign investment between 1967 and 1994; for the Philippines, they relate to foreign investment between 1989 and 1993; and for Vietnam they relate to the existing stock of foreign investment. Information was derived from Department of Foreign Affairs and Trade, *Country Economic Briefs.*

base—whether it be Taiwan, Hong Kong, Singapore, Malaysia, Indonesia, or even Canada—is irrelevant. The networks are "international clan association based on dialect."[24]

Although no firm data are available, estimates of the O/C population in East Asia range from fifty to fifty-five million, half of whom are in ASEAN and the other half in the NIEs and Macau. They might be considered a prosperous mid-size country with a gross domestic product as large as or larger than that of the whole of mainland China.[25] They do not form a homogeneous community but rather a collection of tightly knit clans bonded by common roots and language in the original area of migration. The role of the family within each clan is, in economic terms, exemplified by family-owned or -controlled closed corporation° that dominate large businesses in Southeast Asia. While there is popular resentment against them in some countries, they have close ties with host country governments throughout the region. The potent combination of wealth, power, and influence are valuable assets everywhere.

The ethnic Chinese states are major players in a number of East Asian countries as well as, of course, China (table 5.17). With the opening up of mainland China, the asset value of the O/C family corporations was greatly amplified. Language, culture, and history are "capabilities" essential to navigate the labyrinth of the mainland. The Chinese term for this asset is *guanxi*, personal connections. The O/C use guanxi in China "to make up for the lack of the rule of law and transparency in rules and regulations."[26] With the gradual opening of the southern coastal provinces in the 1980s, the O/C corporations were the first to move in. Trade and investment links in the "Chinese Productivity Triangle" of Hong Kong, Taiwan, and southern China built up rapidly in the 1980s. The biggest spurt came after Tianammen, when Western companies stopped investing for several years and the O/C quickly took advantage of the void.

Many observers have commented on the remarkable entrepreneurial savvy of the Overseas Chinese and the rapid adaptive capacity of the networks. But, of course, the chief assets of the Japanese and American corporations in East Asian—capital, technology, and global distribution capabilities—are far greater than those of the O/C. Since the O/C networks are private and closed, equity purchase is impossible. That leaves only one possibility; mutually advantageous strategic alliances based on an exchange of complementary assets—that is, capital, technology, and third-country market access for O/C guanxi.

While data are scarce, press reports and other sources suggest that joint ventures with MNEs from the OECD are proliferating. These linkages are being fostered, in the case of Japan, by institutional backing from government and business associations.[27] Yet in the long run, if the liberalization of China continues and transparent rules for investment and trade are established, guanxi will depreciate in value and the O/C corporations will have to adapt their corporate behavior as they change from closed and exclusive family networks to public corporations in order to access capital for growth. Even now, since the ethnic Chinese links have been mainly at the local and provincial level in southeast China, as the focus of foreign interest shifts further north and to larger centers, O/C corporations are encountering many of the same problems as other MNEs.

But that's not the end of the story. By far the most elaborate and sophisticated example of guanxi is Singapore's undertaking to build industrial parks for foreign multinationals. The biggest undertaking in Suzhou will export a Singaporean "soft infrastructure" to China (legal, financial, and administrative arrangements) and serve as a base for attracting foreign multinationals.[28] This Singaporean effort is but one example of a major and significant shift in Chinese policy directed at increasing technology transfer.

China's open-door policy started by using tax and other incentives to bring investment to the special economic zones (SEZs). This investment was primarily low-cost assembly operations for export. But by the end of the 1980s a new industrial policy was developing, geared to technology transfer. Thus the government recently announced that its top priority is "a rapid upgrade of technology to the most advanced available in such fields as machinery, electronics and telecommunications."[29] A number of economic and technological development zones (ETDZs) were designated, and in these zones foreign investors are required to comply with specific technology-transfer conditions. In 1991 a new state-level program for industrial parks was launched. These industrial parks, located in principal cities with university research centers, are much more geared to high tech, and the performance requirements for foreign investors much more detailed. They may include, for example, the proportion of university graduates in total employment. Further, tax incentives are granted to Chinese companies as well as foreign corporations so that technology diffusion can be enhanced by building linkages among the foreign and domestic firms and the university research community.[30] In the contest to gain a foothold in the Chinese market, the Chinese authorities can play one MNE off against the other to secure the best deal. Since the Chinese foreign investment policies are rather opaque (to say the least), such deal-making is normal practice.

But China is not alone in this shift to high-tech industrial policy. Indeed, fear of investment diversion to China has added a new concern to the need for a policy geared to "catch up." Malaysia has recently announced a ten-year industrial plan to promote high tech, which will include foreign investment incentives geared to technology transfer. Korea has announced a Highly Advanced Nation (HAN) project to achieve technological parity with the G-7 countries by 2000.[31] And a number of other countries in the region are gearing both domestic and foreign investment policies to upgrading their industrial structure. These policies, whether successful or not in achieving their objectives, may often be in direct conflict with the investment negotiations, which are a key priority in the new trade agenda (see chapter 7).

Before concluding, it's worthwhile raising the question once again: will there be a new convergence club in East Asia? The dictum "those who do not learn from history are bound to repeat it" definitely does not apply in this instance. The comparison between Japan, as a technological power in East Asia in the past two decades, and the United States in the 1960s and 1970s is best captured by recalling the comment of the American official in 1978 who termed the technology strategy of American corporations a "disaster":

The cumulative cost to date for technology purchases by Japan from abroad—more than 25,000 contracts covering essentially all the technology the West had to offer and most from the United States—has been about $5 billion. That is a little more than 10 percent of the annual R&D expenditure of the United States. More to the point, that technology has nurtured competitors who now enter or threaten U.S. markets. And as a final irony, technology which might have been a lever to enter the Japanese market has been surrendered, and with it the advantage that might have made entry successful.

Japanese firms have well understood the lessons of history and are not likely to repeat them. Indeed, as the World Bank notes in its analysis of the East Asian miracle, there appears to be "a growing reluctance" on the part of companies and governments to transfer technology.[32] Moreover, the pace of technological change has accelerated and the complexity of all technologies has vastly increased, so catch-up (by reverse engineering, for example) is far more difficult in today's environment. The costs of running fast just to stay in the same place can be formidable. Indeed, this is a major reason for the proliferation of strategic corporate alliances in R&D as well as production. So the answer to the convergence question remains elusive. But the shift in policy in East Asia must be understood in the broader context of these technological developments.

Conclusions

The system friction that has increasingly characterized the U.S.-Japanese relationship may be exacerbated by the triangular trade pattern resulting from both Japanese and American investment in East Asia. While changes are under way in the corporate network strategies that created these trade flows, it's too soon to estimate their impact. Further, because of growing bilateral deficits with the United States, the issue of asymmetry of access, which fed the U.S.-Japanese conflict, is now influencing the American relationship with China.

But a more fundamental source of system friction will arise from the push by many of the East Asian countries to open the door of the convergence club. The key is seen to be the enhancement of technological capabilities. While East Asia includes a diversity of market models, in many of these countries governments have implemented a range of innovation policies[33] and, far from retreating, there is every sign that the role of government is becoming more intrusive in high-tech industrial policy. (There is an irony in this since one of the much-lauded features of the East Asian miracle has been "small government" when compared with most OECD countries: but the smaller governments are mainly due to a far smaller role in distribution policies.)

With the shift to high-tech industrial policies and growing trade imbalances, one should expect an increase in system friction that *aufond* stems from deeply embedded differences in government policies, institutions, and practices. The legal systems in these countries (with few exceptions, such as Hong Kong and perhaps Singapore) bear little resemblance to the common law tradition that has so influenced the legal aspects of international trade policy, in particular the importance of transparency. More broadly, history and culture, however diverse within the region, have established institutions and practices that vary widely from those of the United States, or, indeed, Western societies generally. While the idea of a "clash of civilizations" is a bit overstretched,[34] these fundamental differences with the American concept of a market economy—and, indeed, a democratic polity—are certain to cause conflict in the future, most of all with China.

While these difficulties are formidable, especially in the case of China, the full integration of this rapidly growing region into the global trading system also offers enormous opportunity for the OECD countries to enhance growth by increasing trade and investment. The concluding chapter will look at some of the policy options for tackling these challenges to the world trading system and thus enhancing the opportunities for global growth.

Six

The Uruguay Round: Renewing Multilateralism

The Tokyo Round was launched in September 1973 and formally concluded in November 1979 by ninety-nine countries. It was the longest and most difficult set of negotiations in the history of the GATT. Although the route from Havana to Tokyo was full of potholes and roadblocks and the steering rather difficult from time to time, the general direction was clear enough: expand the liberalization of trade by reducing border barriers. Thus the Tokyo Round was a traditional GATT negotiation, reflecting the "shallow integration" of the postwar international economy.

The Uruguay Round was launched in Punta del Este in September 1986. The formal conclusion, in Marrakesh, Morocco, in April 1994, involved 117 countries. A U.S. call for new negotiations had dated back to 1981. So the negotiations were not only much lengthier than any predecessor, but the negotiation to launch the negotiations took almost as long as the entire Tokyo Round. Why this extraordinary difficulty in both initiating and completing the Round? Many explanations have been and will be proffered in the many books and articles now proliferating on the negotiations. But two must be viewed as fundamental. The Uruguay Round in a sense consisted of a dual negotiation, and both parts were extraordinarily contentious and troublesome. The traditional negotiations concerned the "leftovers" of previous rounds—the potholes and roadblocks such as agriculture, textiles, trade remedy rules, some sensitive tariffs and a range of nontariff barriers. But the direction was clear—liberalization of trade by reducing or eliminating border barriers and the domestic proxies for these barriers.

Still, filling in the potholes and lifting the roadblocks wasn't easy, to put it mildly.

But the other part of the Uruguay Round, the so-called new issues of services, intellectual property, and investment, was anything but traditional. The inclusion of the new issues was demanded by the Americans to correct the basic structural asymmetry of the original GATT. The barriers to access are not at the border and are not necessarily transparent but mainly involved domestic regulatory policies or domestic legal systems. This is hardly the GATT world of shallow integration but a different world of ever deepening integration and globalization. For these negotiations the direction of the road ahead was shrouded in fog, and few negotiators fully agreed on the destination. Thus the Uruguay Round was so extraordinarily difficult because finishing unfinished business is tough by definition and also because it marked a watershed in the evolution of a new multilateral rules-based system. In addition, the experience of the endless and frustrating negotiations to launch the negotiations made it clear that the birth defects of the GATT needed some attention and consequently the negotiation agenda included the functioning of the GATT system (FOGS), although not the World Trade Organization (WTO), which was proposed while the round was under way (see below).

So how would one evaluate the results? An apt summary could be the Curate's Egg:

> Bishop: *How is your egg, my good man?*
> Curate: *Parts of it are excellent, m'Lord.*

In terms of traditional market access results, the Curate's evaluation would have to be excellent, even in "unfinished business" sectors such as agriculture and textiles.

Among other achievements, tariffs on goods were reduced
on average by nearly 40 percent. In agriculture both export and domestic subsidies will be cut; nontariff barriers
converted to transparent and declining tariffs; and negotiations on further reform are to recommence on January 1,
1999. The restrictive quotas of the Multi-Fiber Arrangement
(MFA) are to be phased out over an agreed transition period.
Various estimates suggest that this trade liberalization will
have permanent beneficial effects for the world economy.[1]
Of course all the models are based on an unwarranted premise, that the alternative to the successful conclusion of the
round would be maintenance of the *status quo,* instead of
serious erosion. If compared with the latter and more likely
alternative, the impact of the liberalization would be considerably higher. But the models have other inherent limitations that further reduce their relevance. None take into account the changed trade rules—safeguards and the trade
remedy laws, also unfinished traditional round business.
Most importantly, none of the models can estimate the full
implications of deepening integration or the heart of the
new system, the WTO. These parts of the Curate's Egg are
not so easily captured by econometric estimates or conventional trade policy analysis.

Trade Rules

After the Tokyo Round—itself a response to the rise of the
"new protectionism"—the renewed new protectionism was
spurred by use and abuse of the trade remedy laws against
unfair trade, especially against dumping. These developments have been attributed to the failure of the Tokyo
Round to reform either the safeguard rule, which sanctioned trade restrictions for the temporary protection of

threatened domestic industry, or the rules for contingent protection against unfair trade.

Hence under the unfinished business agenda, the reform of Article XIX of the GATT—the safeguard clause—was a high priority at the outset of the Uruguay Round. Indeed, the objective of reform was to *encourage* the use of safeguards, under carefully prescribed circumstances, as a temporary protection against imports that were causing or threatening serious injury to a domestic industry. By encouraging the use of a reformed safeguards remedy, both VERs and antidumping measures might be constrained.

The reform of Article XIX contains a number of positive elements. Existing VERs are to be phased out within four years, although each member may maintain one exception until December 31, 1999, and an annex lists one example, *viz.* the VER on Japanese autos to the EU. An effort is also made to discourage any more voluntary agreements by encouraging greater transparency through notification to a Committee on Safeguards by either the exporting country or third parties. And while it may not be possible to ban VERs altogether (especially arrangements between industries informally sanctioned by governments), the reforms also seek to encourage the use of safeguards as an alternative by providing such incentives as a relatively long time period for relief against imports, relaxed conditions for compensation, and the use of selectivity under certain conditions. These incentives are balanced by a substantial increase in transparency, including a completely new condition that Article XIX may be applied only after public hearings and the publication of a report assessing whether the proposed measure is in the public interest. The report must demonstrate that "serious injury" to the domestic industry has occurred or is threatened, while other new provisions spell out in considerable detail the conditions required to validate this determination. The appropriate level of initial restrictions is also specified. And finally, a formal limit on duration and progressive liberalization of the safeguard measures are required.

These reforms represent an effort to remedy the limitations of GATT safeguards as safety valves in the face of structural adjustment pressures. Unfortunately, they do not include a provision obliging countries to adopt an adjustment program. But by providing incentives, which include the possibility of as much as eight years of relief to the domestic industry, and by emphasizing the importance of transparency, the new provisions go some distance in that direction and are likely to reduce the use of VERs, which proliferated in the 1970s as a response to structural change. But whether or not safeguards will prove more attractive than the remedies against "unfair" trade, especially antidumping, is much more problematic. Since antidumping became the chief mechanism for *de facto* VERs in the 1980s, the results of the Uruguay Round reform of Article VI merits close consideration.

Article VI specifies that dumping occurs when the "normal value" of a product—the price of the product in the home market of the exporter or its cost of production—is higher than its export price. When a product is dumped and the dumped imports have caused injury to the domestic industry producing a "like product," a government may impose a duty no greater than the dumping margin—that is, the difference between the product's "normal value" and export price. The explosion of antidumping cases in the 1980s, the spread of actions to countries beyond the OECD, and the use of antidumping as a form of trade harassment or even, in the EU, as a disguised investment policy,[2] all ensured that reform of the antidumping code would be a major issue in the Uruguay Round. Not only did it outlaw price behavior that was perfectly legal within a country—so that if competition policy standards were applied to foreign firms far fewer cases would survive legal scrutiny—but also the GATT rules scarcely restrained the exercise of discretion by national authorities. A determined government and a clever lawyer could find dumping and injury for virtually any import or industry.

So the battle between governments seeking much more restrictive conditions on antidumping actions and those fighting to maintain or even expand their scope was very intense. There was also, especially in the United States, a battle between lawyers representing export interests, or domestic users of imported components, and the lawyers for large import-competing industries such as steel.

Although many aspects of reform were contentious, the heart of the debate over constraining discretion and reducing abuse of the basic objective of the code concerned the calculation of dumping margins. Attention centered specifically on techniques related to *averaging,* since prices vary over time and with the characteristics of the sale, and also on the method of *constructing costs* either for production or exports. In both these instances, biased procedures employed by both the EU and the United States had been repeatedly shown to produce inflated dumping margins. Yet the combined efforts of these two trading powers forestalled any significant change. On the whole, as one expert has noted, "de facto, the Agreement comes very close to authorizing (these) procedures."[3]

There is, however, one restriction included in the new code: if a case is brought before a dispute panel, governments must explain why they have chosen a particular method of estimation. But near the close of the negotiations, the United States secured a potentially significant constraint on the freedom of panels in antidumping disputes:

> Where the panel finds that a relevant provision of the Agreement admits of more than one permissible interpretation, the panel shall find the authorities measure to be in conformity with the Agreement if it rests upon one of these permissible interpretations.

This new "standard of review" suggests that in practice it will be very difficult to overturn a domestic antidumping determination.

Finally, the new rules codify agreements by exporters to raise prices as a means of avoiding antidumping duties. These agreements—often called price undertakings—can also include quantitative restraints. These price undertakings, or suspension agreements as they are termed in the United States, bear a marked resemblance to VERs.

In sum, the Uruguay Round failed in an effort to reform the "weapon of choice," antidumping. Moreover, the code adds new layers of detailed and arcane legal language. And because of improvement in the subsidies code, antidumping will be even more popular. As the use of antidumping continues to spread to new users, there should be plenty of work for both plaintiff and defense lawyers. Hence, the basic reform required to eliminate the protectionist threat of antidumping is to replace it with competition policy rules in the WTO (see chapter 7).

Another leftover from the Tokyo Round was the unsettled dispute between the European Union and the United States on reform of the subsidies code. Here considerable change is apparent. The new agreement on subsidies and countervailing measures (SCM) contains strengthened disciplines on both subsidies and countervailing procedures. Subsidies are classified as prohibited, actionable, and nonactionable (or red, yellow, and green in the traffic light metaphor). The definitions of each category are precisely specified and an injury test is spelled out in painstakingly detailed procedural rules. Indeed the SCM itself is the largest part of the entire Final Act of the Uruguay Round, reflecting the imprint of the American and European negotiators for whom the new agreement represented a major victory on subsidies for the former and on countervail for the latter.

The general definition of subsidies is very broad in order to keep loopholes to a minimum. This is followed by a definition of "specific" subsidies—limited to some economic entities—which can be subject to countervailing measures. Specific subsidies are prohibited when they are contingent on export performance or the use of domestic over imported goods. Within the group of specific nonprohibited subsidies, the possibility of antisubsidy measures is open when adverse trade effects result. Finally, a "positive" list names specific subsidies, including research activities, regional development, and environmental requirements, which are nonactionable within specified limits. The addition of much more generous research and development exemptions was pushed by the American negotiators at the eleventh hour in order to accommodate planned new programs of the Clinton administration.[4]

The SCM puts in place a different remedy for each type of subsidy. Remedies differ by time constraint, the bodies involved, and a number of procedural details. For prohibited subsidies the WTO dispute-settlement panel will be assisted by a Permanent Group of Experts, which is a most useful innovation to avoid unnecessary wrangling over the analysis of evidence. The much more stringent dispute settlement procedure of the WTO ensures compliance—that is, withdrawal of the measure—in the case of a positive finding or sanctions for noncompliance (see discussion of the WTO later in this chapter). Furthermore, the more comprehensive scope of the new institution is reflected in the reduction of the number of countries exempted from the new disciplines. All developing countries (except the least developed) will come under the SCM agreement after a specified transition period.

Thus real progress was made on subsidies and countervailing measures, in part because two of the most contentious issues dividing the Americans and the Europeans, agricultural subsidies and aircraft subsidies, were handled in other negotiating groups. At the same time, the changed approach to subsidies reflected underlying trends in domestic policy. Rising fiscal deficits in the 1980s increasingly constrained all forms of government spending and encouraged the European reform of the Common Agricultural Policy. These trends facilitated the essential rapprochement between the Americans and Europeans who, as in the Tokyo Round, dominated the negotiations. When international rules can reinforce domestic policy, it is obviously easier to achieve reform. With the possible exception of the high-tech sectors and national security exemptions,[5] future disputes over subsidies are likely to be mainly between the OECD and non-OECD countries, rather than transatlantic as in previous decades.

The "New Issues": Toward Deeper Integration

The "new issues," as they were called in the lengthy and often acrimonious debate leading up to the launch of the Uruguay Round, were new in two fundamental ways. The original GATT covered only trade in goods and primary products. Trade in services would have been termed an oxymoron in 1950, so it is hardly surprising that it was not included. The ITO did have a much broader scope that would have covered investments but not intellectual property rights (IPRs), which were the domain of a UN institution, the World Intellectual Property Organization (WIPO).[6] So the new issues were almost wholly new to the GATT and, indeed, to many member countries seemed quite out of place in any multilateral *trade* negotiations.

As we have stressed, the new issues were new in a fundamentally radical sense: they would involve negotiations centered entirely on what were considered domestic policies of GATT tradition. While the trade rule negotiations were an echo of the past, the new issues were a signal of the future—the ongoing trend to deeper integration. The coalition of developing countries opposed to this innovation (nicknamed the G-10 hard-liners by those countries supportin the negotiations) was led by Brazil and India, and the inclusion of the new issues was regarded as a direct assault on the role of government since both these countries were pursuing highly interventionist (and protectionist) industrial development policies. Inclusion of the new issues was at first also opposed—or at least not vigorously supported—by the European Commission as part of a foot-dragging strategy to stave off the negotiations on agriculture.

The United States saw the question very differently. Trade in services grew much more rapidly over the 1980s than did merchandise trade, and the United States was the leading exporter by a considerable margin. The same lead status was evident in investment and technology. U.S. multinationals controlled 43 percent of the world stock of foreign investment at the outset of the 1980s and the American technology balance of payments surplus was well over $6 billion, while every other OECD country was in deficit. Without a fundamental rebalancing of the GATT, it seems highly improbable that the American business community or politicians would have continued to support the multilateral system for much longer. More broadly, the new issues are also illustrative of the wider and ongoing trend to deeper integration, including the push to regulatory convergence and harmonization of legal systems in an increasingly legalistic global trade regime. Seen in this light, the results of the Uruguay Round negotiations, especially in services and TRIPS, are of considerable significance. In contrast the negotiations on TRIMS were very restricted in scope, a last-minute victory of Brazil and India in Punta del Este. (As a result, the issue of negotiating new rules for investment could be described as part of the unfinished business of the Uruguay Round.)

In this larger context, the success of the Uruguay Round in establishing a General Agreement on Trade in Services (GATS) should be seen as a historic achievement, one that went well beyond the expectations of many of the negotiators who fought for the inclusion of the new issues at Punta del Este. The GATS provides a comprehensive set of rules for preserving and expanding market access for internationally traded services under the institutional framework of the WTO. It also includes an initial set, albeit limited, of market access commitments. These include standstill agreements in many sectors, which bind existing levels of liberalization and constrain future barriers. Less was achieved in the way of reduction of barriers, but the GATS includes a provision mandating future negotiations to begin by January 2000 with the goal of increasing the scope of commitments already undertaken by member countries.

The GATS comprises three main components: a set of general obligations intended in principle to apply to all services; sectoral annexes that detail how the rules apply to specific sectors; and annexes detailing schedules of specific commitments of member countries by specific sectors. The set of general obligations or framework agreement illustrate the move to deeper integration, while the annexes reveal the extent and nature of exceptions to the basic principles as well as the degree of market access achieved by the negotiations.

The GATS defines trade in services to include all possible modes of supply: cross-border, movement of customers to the location of the suppliers, provision by an established presence by investment, and provision by temporary cross-border movement of persons. Although the extent to which specific modes can be used by a foreign supplier is determined by a country's schedule of commitments contained in the annexes, the acceptance in principle of this exhaustive definition of modes of market entry is highly significant in reflecting the needs of the MNEs in organizing their global production and distribution chains, a key aspect of the push to deeper integration.

Indicative of the same impetus is the telecommunications annex, which requires each country to provide access to public telecommunications networks on nondiscriminatory terms for intracorporate communications and for the supply of any service included in that country's schedule of commitments. As has been noted by one of the negotiators of the GATS:

This telecommunications annex is one of the most important achievements of the services negotiations, since the most troublesome barriers to the expansion of cross-border trade in information-based services have been government regulations that limit access to state of the art telecommunication facilities at competitive prices.[7]

Most services—and indeed most industries—are increasingly information-based, so this provision is rightly viewed as essential to the further evolution of the GATS. However, the GATS did not deal with the *provision* of basic telecommunications services; this issue was left to continuing negotiations with a specific completion date. (The same approach was also applied to several other key service sectors, of which more later.)

As comprehensive as the *definition* of trade in services is the definition of the *scope* of the agreement that applies to all government actions, including sub-national governments such as state, provincial, and local authorities, or even to nongovernmental bodies acting on behalf of any public authority. All services are included with the exception of those supplied in the exercise of governmental functions. This inherent intrusiveness into domestic regulatory regimes is significantly circumscribed by the country schedules of commitments in the annexes, but once again, a key principle of deeper integration has been established. When combined with the obligation for transparency of all laws and regulations affecting trade in services—an *across-the-board* obligation *not* conditional on specific sectoral commitments by member countries—the essence of the services negotiations can be seen as domestic regulatory and institutional reform.

While this principle has been established, there's still

a long way to go in implementation because the GATS agreement provided a number of avenues for derogation from core principles, including MFN. Thus, for example, the ministerial decisions appended to the GATS, reflecting American concerns about reciprocity, defined implicitly as asymmetry of access, mandated continued negotiations for six months in financial services. If the results were unsatisfactory to some member countries, they would be allowed to withdraw unconditional MFN for a specified period. This last-minute compromise over a fundamental disagreement on the extent and nature of liberalization failed its first test when, despite an extension of the six-month deadline, the United States rejected the financial services agreement as inadequate, especially in the case of a number of Asian countries. The serious threat to the credibility of the WTO represented by the American action was somewhat mitigated by the role of the EU in salvaging the agreement.[8] The negative effects of failure to meet the deadline of April 30, 1996, for the negotiations on basic telecommunications because of a last minute American rejection of the results as inadequate were dodged (or postponed) by agreeing to establish a new deadline. In maritime transport the United States sank the talks by refusing to make an offer before the June 30, 1996, deadline. In these sectoral negotiations the basic complaint of the United States related to reciprocity, but not in the traditional GATT sense of an overall balance of benefits or an exchange of comparable reduction of barriers as a negotiating modality. Sectoral reciprocity in financial or telecommunications services must rest on regulatory reform, a very different and more complex negotiating modality that will be discussed in the following chapter.

Sectoral negotiations aside, the constraints on what GATS could achieve are most apparent overall in its relatively limited market access results, which to a large degree stemmed from the nature of the negotiating process. This took a *positive-list* approach to sectoral coverage—that is, sectors for which liberalization commitments are made must be listed in the annexes.[9] This approach, which as noted reflects the basic compromise essential to overcome the strong opposition to the inclusion of services in the round, contrasts sharply with the NAFTA *negative-list* approach, which implies full liberalization as an objective unless *specifically excluded*. And, along the same lines, and again unlike NAFTA, in the GATS national treatment applies only to those service sectors listed in a country's schedule of commitments because where regulations on services have the effect of protecting domestic industry, national treatment would be equivalent to full liberalization.

As with the services negotiations, the American demand to include intellectual property issues in the Uruguay Round was strongly opposed by a number of developing countries, not only because it would involve higher costs of technology acquisition, but also because it would limit the use of industrial policy instruments such as compulsory licensing or technology transfer conditions on foreign investment. Like the services agreement, the TRIPS outcome represents a significant breakthrough by establishing comprehensive standards for domestic intellectual property laws (substantially higher than those in current international conventions administered by WIPO) and, most significantly, rigorous provisions for enforcement and dispute settlement, which WIPO lacked.

Transparency and other characteristics of legal systems whose importance was noted in connection with the services negotiations were also key in the TRIPS debate. To highlight this issue and garner support from other OECD countries, the U.S. Trade Representative (USTR) commissioned a special study on the extent and nature of foreign protection of IPRs by the International Trade Commission.[10] This study of nearly eight hundred American firms reported huge worldwide losses of $23.8 billion and named the countries with "inadequate protection" of IPRs. The aspect of "inadequacy" cited most often was lack of effective enforcement. This became a key priority in the negotiations, and it is, indeed, the enforcement provisions that best exemplify the legal harmonization aspect of deeper integration. As an expert on the TRIPS agreement has noted, with regard to enforcement, the outcome reflects a significant gain for the American negotiators since

> the enforcement procedures largely mirror the administrative and judicial mechanisms in the United States, with requirements for transparency, evidentiary collection, judicial injunctions, domestic and border provisional measures, access to civil judicial procedures, monetary damages and compensation of the rightholder (or of the accused infringer if the accusation is false), and criminal proceedings in the event of willful counterfeiting.[11]

Compliance with these extremely detailed obligations will be very demanding for countries with legal systems or traditions that differ significantly from the American model. In this respect, it is also important to note the highly significant feature of TRIPS, which permits a domestic challenge procedure and thus an avenue for extensive and expensive litigation. This new and significant concept of "direct effect," to use the legal term for domestic challenge of WTO rules (which is also included in the government procurement agreement), thus reinforces the legalization aspect of the "new issues." Further along this line, the TRIPS agreement stresses transparency of rules by establishing a council for TRIPS to which notifications of regulations and administrative arrangements must be made by member countries (with transition periods allowed for developing countries). This council will also monitor compliance with all the terms of the agreement. Dispute settlement will come under the procedures of the WTO, a responsibility that will represent a formidable challenge to the understaffed WTO.

This brief review of the "new issues" in the Uruguay Round stresses both the remarkable breakthroughs made and the equally important fact that the process of liberalization of services and ensuring protection of intellectual property rights has only just begun. The GATS in particular represents the beginning of a fundamental rebalancing of the GATT, essential to correct the mismatch between its inherited scope and the transformation of the global trading system. Much remains to be done, nor is this surprising. GATS must be evaluated in two ways: as the first exemplar of deeper integration in a multilateral forum, and as a groundbreaking market access negotiation for internationally traded services. The intrusion of trade negotiations inside the border was not only strongly resisted by a number of countries but also represents a fundamental change in the central principle of the GATT. The compromise on financial services, along with a similar compromise on basic telecommunications in the last days of the negotiations, can be seen as the outcome of the deep-seated disagreement over the inclusion of services that so delayed the launch of the entire round. Further, it is worth remembering that it took forty years of GATT negotiations on border barriers for trade in goods to achieve the current state of market access commitments. It is hardly surprising, then, that the GATS—like the original GATT, but negotiated under far more difficult conditions—suffers some shortcomings.

But, as repeatedly stressed, the GATS and TRIPS represent more than rebalancing. They exemplify—perhaps more than the drafters of the Punta del Este declaration realized—key parameters of deeper integration, a much more intrusive concept than traditional liberalization. Should future multilateral negotiations prove too difficult an avenue for such an intrusive agenda, unilateralism or, as the contrast with NAFTA suggests, regionalism may prove more attractive alternatives. The question of unilateralism (301 variants) was handled in the round via the WTO, but the question of regionalism, and its relation to multilateralism, was not discussed in the negotiations and thus remains as an important item on the emerging post-Uruguay agenda.

The WTO

Because of the circumstances at the time of its birth, GATT, unlike the Bretton Woods institutions, was an "institutional" anomaly, a temporary arrangement of murky if not dubious legal status. It functioned amazingly well during the golden age of growth, but since the 1970s GATT's credibility had seriously eroded and the difficulty of launching the Uruguay Round only served to highlight its weakness. In the Punta declaration there was recognition of these problems in the establishment of the FOGS negotiating group, pushed by a coalition of middle powers, both developed and developing, since FOGS was not a priority for either the United States or the EU. The middle powers recognized that the alternative to a rule-based system would be a power-based system and, lacking power, they had the most to lose. It was also clearly understood that a rule-based system without a strong dispute-settlement mechanism was unlikely to be sustainable over the long haul.

Nonetheless, the goals of FOGS were relatively modest: to improve the adaptability of GATT in order to respond to accelerating change in the global economy; to improve the coherence of international policies by establishing better linkages between the GATT and the Bretton Woods institutions; and to strengthen the enforcement of the trading system's rules of the road by improving dispute-settlement arrangements. The creation of a new institution was not included among these objectives, and the proposal by Canada for a new institution—the World Trade Organization—was not put forward until April 1990. It was soon endorsed by the EU. The main reason for this change was growing concern about American unilateralism. The EU, which had opposed a strengthening of dispute settlement in the Tokyo Round, and took a position of benign neglect with respect to FOGS, became an active supporter of a new institution that could house a single, strong dispute-settlement mechanism.

The Canadian proposal was couched in terms of the substantive aspects of the Uruguay Round negotiations. The Tokyo Round had begun a process of fragmentation since the Tokyo Codes were legally separate from the GATT and applied only among the signatories, who varied from code to code. A fragmentation of dispute settlement procedures developed as a consequence, creating a myriad of legal and political difficulties and the opportunity for "forum shopping" to evade discipline. It was feared that further fragmentation by a separate GATS, an Agreement on Intellectual Property, Investments etc., by overburdening the ramshackle system, could well negate the results of the entire negotiations. As the press release announcing the Canadian proposal stated:

> Developments in the substantive negotiations are now demonstrating that the Uruguay Round results cannot be effectively housed in a provisional shelter. It is also becoming clear that the post-Uruguay trade policy agenda will be complex and may not be adequately managed within the confines of the GATT system as it now exists. (Ottawa, April 1990)

The World Trade Organization turns the GATT from a trade agreement into a membership organization. It establishes a legal framework that brings together all the various pacts and codes and other arrangements that were negotiated under the GATT. Members of the WTO must abide by the rules of all these agreements as well as the rules of the GATT as a "single undertaking."[12] Apart from the new Dispute Settlement Body, which will be discussed shortly, the WTO also includes two institutional innovations proposed under FOGS: a Trade Policy Review Body, designed to highlight changes in the policies of member countries through published analytical studies, and a biannual ministerial conference, designed to raise the public and political profile of trade policy trends. The FOGS group was acutely aware of the costs of delay in launching the Uruguay Round and wanted to enhance the adaptiveness of trade policymaking to continuing change in the international economy. As to the objective of greater coherence, the Final Act includes only a hortatory declaration encouraging the director general of the WTO to review possible cooperative mechanisms with the heads of the IMF and World Bank.

What the FOGS group failed to do—and the WTO reflects this failure—was to establish a smaller executive body, like the Interim Committee of the IMF, to steer the institution. The GATT operated by consensus because the failure to create the ITO, which would have had weighted voting like the Bretton Woods institutions, left no other feasible option. But achieving consensus among forty-plus "like minded" members is far easier than achieving consensus among 120 members of widely different views. Thus the cumbersome decision-making of the GATT will be even more difficult in the WTO unless a steering committee can be agreed. And the more cumbersome it is, the more other alternatives will prove attractive. There is now, especially in the United States, a growing view that deeper integration policies are better pursued regionally, where the United States has more clout, than in the larger and more unwieldy WTO.

But the absence of weighted voting (or some proxy such as a steering committee) carries another danger, which was highlighted by the debate over the Uruguay Round implementation in the United States (and was a basic reason for U.S. wariness about endorsing the WTO until the very end of the negotiations). The uproar about loss of sovereignty (do we want the United States overruled by Botswana?) was due at least in part to this basic flaw in the WTO as an institution. But only in part. Growing antipathy to international institutions in Congress could not have been assuaged simply by weighted voting or a steering committee.[13] In a paper prepared for the Republican Research Committee on the Uruguay Round, it was noted that "President Harry Truman withdrew the ITO from consideration when it became apparent that Congress was not going to accept the transfer of authority over U.S. economic and trade policy from itself to the ITO."[14]

Congressional views on the international role of the United States of course affect more than trade negotiations. What Robert Paarlberg terms "lack of congressional deference" to the president in foreign policy has been rising, as the reference to Truman suggests, virtually since the end of the war.[15] In 1991, when President Bush needed fast-track authority to negotiate NAFTA, "he had to empty his pockets and tie his hands with promises" to buy enough votes for passage.[16] The lack of deference was even more striking in 1994, with the congressional debate over the Uruguay Round. The heated rhetoric over sovereignty was nearly matched by the wrangling over the impact of tariff cuts on the domestic budget.

To mitigate the "sovereignty problem," the United States negotiated a number of procedural rules to constrain "the tyranny of the majority."[17] Nonetheless, strong opposition to the WTO by the newly elected Republican Congress required a last-minute deal by President Clinton and Senate Majority Leader Robert Dole to avoid derailing congressional approval of the Uruguay Round implementing legislation. The deal was to placate concern over alleged challenges to U.S. sovereignty, particularly through the operation of its dispute resolution panels, whereby member nations will not have the power to block approval of unfavorable panel findings. Thus the U.S. implementing legislation provides for the establishment of a board to review WTO panel findings over a specified period and recommend to Congress whether the United States should withdraw from the institution.

The sovereignty uproar really centers on the issue of the

extent and nature of the constraints imposed on the use of U.S. unilateralist trade policy by the new dispute-settlement procedures of the WTO. The Uruguay Round established a unified system whereby all disputes will be handled by the Dispute Settlement Body (DSB). The new disciplines provide more automaticity in the adoption of panel reports, strict deadlines, binding arbitration, and final appeals through a new appellate body. If a solution to a dispute cannot be achieved through mutual agreement, a panel is established unless the DSB decided by consensus against it. The panel proceedings and findings, issued in a report, are subject to strict time limits, as is the process of appeal by parties to the Appellate Body. The Appellate Body report will be deemed adopted unless there is a consensus *against* adoption. A panel report, if not appealed, is to be adopted within thirty days unless *rejected* by consensus.

Thus, compared with previous procedures that required positive consensus, and could therefore be blocked by one of the parties to the dispute, this new negative-consensus approach involves automatic adoption.[18] The new dispute settlement procedure also explicitly addressed the question of implementation of a panel report, by requiring timely implementation, compensation, or retaliatory type actions in either the same sector as that subject to the dispute or in a different sector ("cross-retaliation"). Finally, an interesting new provision of the dispute settlement procedures deal with so-called nonviolation cases, which will be discussed below in connection with the post-Uruguay agenda.

Strengthening the dispute settlement procedures of the GATT was one of the priorities of the United States in the launch of the Uruguay Round. But by the conclusion of the round—delayed well beyond the 1990 target in the Punta declaration—the question of whether the Uruguay

Round results would require fundamental changes in Section 301 and other similar statutory provisions had dramatically changed the terms of the debate. Back to the Curate's Egg analogy: what would have been excellent in 1986 was inedible by 1994.

So what do the new WTO dispute-settlement procedures mean for the exercise of U.S. trade policy? The answer is that an array of legal experts in the United States and abroad will be debating the question for some considerable length of time! There is, of course, agreement on some parts of the puzzle. The provisions for tight procedural time limits were included so as to satisfy the criteria of Section 301 and allow the United States to go first to the WTO before undertaking action. As another inducement to ensure use of the multilateral arrangement, the increased "legalization" of the procedure, especially via the new appellate body, was included to allay American concern about the possibility of legal error, given the automaticity aspect of the new mechanism. So, since the basic structure of Section 301 and like instruments "provides for cases to be taken to the international dispute settlement process that pertains to the case—and does not *require* the Executive Branch to ignore the results of the international dispute settlement process" (emphasis in original) no *fundamental* changes in Section 301 statutes are required.[19] In recognition of this situation, Uruguay Round negotiators (especially the EU) insisted on the inclusion of Article 23(1) of the agreement, which provides: "When members seek the redress of a violation of obligations or other nullification and impairment, they shall have recourse to, and abide by, the rules and procedures of this Understanding."

So it's all okay? Well, not quite. At least it's not quite clear. The only way to escape this very broad commitment would be to admit that a complaint has no GATT-legal basis at all. Thus if regular or Super 301 were to be used without first going to the WTO, the United States would be violating a binding commitment. Equally, if the United States argues that there is no GATT legal basis to its complaint, it could not take any GATT-type trade retaliation.[20] Given this dilemma, the U.S. administration stressed that it would continue to use 301 "aggressively" by finding "new" ways to retaliate. To this end the implementing legislation "specifically grants the Administration the authority to take any retaliatory action it chooses." Further, "services would continue to be considered for retaliation because of the large 'carve-outs' where countries made no commitments in the Uruguay Round Agreement."[21] Of course, in many instances, especially for vulnerable countries, and possibly even for Japan, the threat of 301 could still be effective without the use of retaliation, as noted in our earlier discussion on unilateralism.

In sum, it is not clear whether the intent of the strengthened dispute-settlement procedures of the WTO will or will not effectively constrain U.S. unilateralism. In the auto dispute with Japan, which might have provided a test case (see below), the dispute was settled bilaterally, and perhaps this marked a turning point in the long-established Japanese acceptance of bilateral arrangements negotiated under American pressure. But in general, as is usually the case, domestic politics will likely be the determining condition of U.S. acceptance of the multilateral rules, and not the 128 numbered paragraphs comprising the twenty-seven articles of the Understanding on Rules and Procedures Governing the Settlement of Disputes in the Final Act of the Uruguay Round. While the Uruguay Round did seek to rebalance the structural asymmetry of the GATT coverage, and did fundamentally change the domain of trade policy by moving inside the border to tackle domestic policy impediments to market access, American ambivalence about the "legitimacy" of the rule-based system remains. A pessimistic view from one distinguished international legal scholar asserts: "Those who want the new GATT legal regime are going to have to wage a rather nasty and messy fight for it."[22]

Seven

Building the Post–Cold War Trading System

If the WTO is to provide an effective foundation for a rules-based global system, the first order of business is to complete the Uruguay Round. There is indeed a very extensive "built-in agenda" that was included in the negotiations that commit the WTO members to continuing monitoring and negotiations. As may be seen from the appendix to this chapter, this built-in agenda includes broad negotiations on agriculture to begin on January 1, 1999, and on services by January 1, 2000. These negotiations and the extensive monitoring provisions for all the fundamental rules of the WTO system will help to ensure that the gains of the round are not dissipated and the bicycle continues to move forward.

This bicycle mechanism is reinforced by another, the Trade Policy Review Mechanism (TPRM), an innovation included in the FOGS negotiations purposely to sustain the momentum of liberalization.

The idea of surveillance was strongly recommended by trade experts during the 1980s as a means of counteracting the new protectionism by improving the understanding of policymakers and the public of the full economy-wide impact of trade measures. International surveillance also creates peer group pressure that can assist domestic policymakers in resisting protectionist lobbies and provide a means of monitoring the impact of trade-related policies on the international economy. While the TPRM was adopted on an interim basis at the midterm ministerial meeting in December 1988, it is now established as a Trade Policy Review Body under the General Council of the WTO. Unfortunately, limited secretariat resources have seriously constrained the analytic and informational content of the reports as well as the effectiveness of the mechanism for generating public debate in the country under surveillance or debate on international implication within the GATT. This resource constraint is unlikely to be eased in the near future. If we drop the bicycle metaphor, because in today's world a more powerful vehicle is required, the WTO has been termed a Mercedes Benz without gas. More broadly, it will be argued below that the lack of analytic resources in the WTO constitutes a serious handicap for its effective functioning in new areas.

While completing the negotiations and establishing effective monitoring and surveillance mechanisms for the Uruguay agreement are essential building blocks, they are not sufficient to create a firm foundation for a new trading system of deeper integration. If the commitments to continuing negotiations and effective monitoring that were included in the final agreement are not honored by, at a minimum, all the major countries, there is a distinct danger that the WTO will become marginalized. The United States torpedo of the sectoral negotiations on services raises a warning signal in this regard.

The danger of marginalization arises from three main sources: increasing resort to regional arrangements that appear to offer a faster route to deeper integration; continuing system friction, with its incentives for bilateral or unilateral action, especially on the part of the United States; and failure to extend the WTO to include all major trading countries, especially China. Each will be discussed in turn in this chapter, with policy options recommended where appropriate. The chapter will conclude with a discussion of how the scope of the WTO rules could be still further expanded, and with a review of the outlook for the world trading order as we enter a new millennium.

The Regional Option

The view that regionalism is complementary to multilateralism is widely held. Proponents argue that the advantages of regional free-trade agreements (FTAs) are that they are quick to establish, they can provide an intermediate and more manageable structure in the international trade system (like the role of states in a federal political system), and they can produce negotiation results (for example, the NAFTA investment chapter) that help to advance multilateral processes. As is clear from the earlier discussion, the push to deeper integration is especially evident in NAFTA, both with respect to the "new issues," especially in the investment area where relatively little was accomplished in the Uruguay Round and the built-in agenda provides for a review of investment policy and competition policy, which would only begin at the end of this decade. In Asia the Americans have put a high priority on negotiating a trade and investment agreement under APEC. And, as will be discussed shortly, in 1995 negotiations of a multilateral investment agreement were launched in the OECD to be completed in 1997. All these developments are proffered as initiatives that will prepare the way for, and indeed catalyze, global negotiations in the WTO.

While this all sounds plausible and no doubt has some validity under certain circumstances, serious concerns about the present regionalism "fad" are now growing. Indeed, it may be time to rethink the regionalism issue and remember its inherent dangers. One reason is that the process has gotten out of hand. For example, the EU has launched negotiations with Mercosur (a custom union that includes Brazil, Argentina, Uruguay, and Paraguay) while the United States proclaims a vision for a free-trade agreement of the Americas. APEC has stimulated ASEM (EU and ASEAN) discussions. And so on and on. Today nearly every member of the WTO belongs to one or more regional trading arrangements.

Moreover, regional FTAs will increasingly place countries in a conflict of trade rules resulting from membership in overlapping agreements; or, more seriously, FTAs might even promote trade-bloc conflict if preferences extended on a less-than-MFN basis by one FTA were to stimulate a fearful or competitive response by another FTA. Thus the "world" trading system could become increasingly diffuse, or more accurately, increasingly messy. At a minimum, if the renewed core is not to wither, it is essential to establish some mechanism for ensuring that the multilateralization option is not *excluded*. All regional, plurilateral and bilateral agreements or arrangements should be tabled in the WTO as part of an overall monitoring process. This would provide an opportunity for WTO members not only to keep abreast of policy evolution but also to discuss whether and how these policy initiatives should be multilateralized and perhaps linked.

Beyond monitoring, it would be desirable to establish a mechanism for ultimate *convergence* of regionalism and multilateralism. The new WTO Committee on Regional Trading Agreements will be considering various options in this respect, including an application of the MFN principle, with perhaps some delay, to nonmembers.[1] This would likely meet strong resistance from the United States because of the growing emphasis on reciprocity, especially in the services sectors. It might be easier to revive the old idea of a "super GATT"—that is, plurilateral agreements in specific functional areas such as competition policy, for example, that would be housed in the WTO and that could, over time, embrace the full membership. If nothing is done there is a real danger that regionalism will undermine, not energize, the global rules-based system.

System Friction: Structural Barriers Inside the Border

The issue of domestic impediments to market access won't go away. As the domain of trade policy has extended inside the border, a new definition of market access is emerging, borrowed from the Structural Impediments Initiative (SII) of the 1980s: *effective access* involves reduction not only of border barriers but also of "structural impediments," which include both government regulations as well as private sector actions. A similar concept—*effective presence*—is applied to investment.[2] As noted above, the risk inherent in these imprecise definitions is that they are unilaterally determined and virtually open-ended, as the SII and subsequent U.S.-Japanese framework talks illustrate.

The WTO, perhaps in cooperation with the OECD, should establish a working group to prepare a comprehensive listing of government regulatory practices that member countries consider structural impediments to effective market access. The practice of country notification of trade barriers was well established under the GATT and in the OECD trade committee, so there is precedence for the concept of notification, which should now be updated to recognize the move of international negotiations inside the border. However, simply listing barriers would not provide a definition of government-related structural impediments. Rather, the purpose of the exercise would be to initiate discussions on an agreed definition of these impediments as a basis for subsequent multilateral negotiations.

Thus parallel with these efforts, a research project should be undertaken to develop an *impediments index,* in the form of price differentials between domestic prices of traded goods in member countries to assess the openness to market competition or "market contestability" (see below). The overall objective of "market contestability" is an elusive concept and reaching agreement on definition and measurement will take considerable time and effort (as did, for example, the production of an index of agriculture protection, the Producer Subsidy Equivalent or PSE, which helped launch the Uruguay Round negotiations). So while these would obviously not be easy tasks, the alternative approach—unilateral definitions or quantitative targets—represents a threat to the system perhaps serious enough to energize WTO member countries.

In addition to government policies and practices, business practices can also impede effective access or presence to some markets. Thus, for example, vertical upstream or downstream long-term agreements may have the unintended effect of impeding imports, while bank-centered corporate governance arrangements may, again unintentionally, impede foreign direct investment by means of mergers acquisitions. Some have argued that these impediments stem from inadequate enforcement of competition policy.[3] In any case, while discussions on harmonizing competition policy have been under way for some years in the OECD and elsewhere, progress has been limited and international agreement will be a long and difficult process, even among the OECD countries, let alone the much larger number of WTO members. Furthermore, since neither vertical nor horizontal agreements (except those involving price collusion) are per se offenses in any current competition policy regime, negotiating new international rules for removing private sector structural impediments would require reconciling conflicts between competition-policy and trade-policy objectives, possibly on a case-by-case basis.

The new WTO dispute-settlement agreement provides an opportunity to begin a discussion of this issue and also to promote more consultation and discussion between competition policy and trade-policy authorities in national capitals. The mechanism would be to bring a complaint about structural impediments (in this instance involving private-sector practices) under the so-called nonviolation nullification and impairment provisions of the new Dispute Settlement Understanding (DSU). The GATT language on disputes always contained the phrase "nullification and impairment" in a little-used and rather vague section, Article XXIII:1(b). The term implied that a member country had an imbalance with another country in overall benefits, not through violation of a specific GATT rule but through "the application by another contracting party of any measure whether or not it conflicts with the provisions of the Agreement." The EU issued a complaint against Japan in 1983 under this broad and vague rubric, which in effect charged that structural impediments blocked effective market access, but subsequently withdrew the request for a panel. Under the new DSU, an additional provision has been added to the so-called nonviolation cases, which allows the panel to provide a remedy in cases where a perfectly legal action nonetheless impairs the "reasonable expectations" of the overall balance of benefits of a member country.

The inclusion of nonviolation cases in the strict new procedures was to replicate the Section 301 concept of "unreasonable" measures, which were nonetheless GATT legal. To constrain U.S. unilateralism, the Uruguay negotiations brought 301 into the WTO, thus providing an opportunity for panel consideration of a "test case." A panel ruling cannot mandate removal of the disputed measures but can make a recommendation for ways and means of reaching "a mutually satisfactory adjustment." Under the new WTO provisions, it is possible to seek expert advice from "any relevant source" or "request an advisory report—from an expert review group." Thus the views of experts in competition policy and industrial organization could be integrated into the process to begin the multilateralization of the definition of structural impediments. In this regard, the 1995 auto dispute between the United States and Japan was a lost opportunity to launch that process.

There were two aspects of the auto dispute that could have been brought to the WTO, either under Section XXIII:1(b) or other articles of the GATT that deal with aspects of domestic regulation.[4] The alleged exclusionary impact of the agreements between the Japanese automakers and dealers (exclusive dealerships) could have been reviewed by a dispute panel assisted by competition policy experts. In neither the United States nor the EU are such arrangements illegal. In the United States, they lie in the "grey area of antitrust permissibility," and manufacturers risk legal action if their market share is very large so that new entry is difficult.[5] The EU, however, has provided a "block exemption" from competition policy law to permit exclusive distribution contracts between manufacturers and distributors (an exemption strongly supported by the Big Three American car subsidiaries in Europe). Nonetheless, there is a good case to be made that such arrangements should be reviewed in terms both of their impact on consumers and on market access by imports—that is, contestability of the market. A review in the WTO could serve two purposes: to establish a foothold for consideration of international rules for competition policy (see below) and, equally important, to launch a review of such vertical arrangements in national capitals.

The other complaint by the Americans concerned regulation of the aftermarket for parts, a much more complex issue than the vertical distribution keiretsu. The heavily regulated market for replacement parts in Japan, ostensibly designed to improve auto safety and satisfy environmental standards, ensures that most vehicle servicing and repair work goes to "designated garages" that exclusively stock parts made by Japanese suppliers. The issue here is not whether safety and environmental regulation is desirable— clearly it is—but whether intentionally or not the mode of regulation has a serious impact on market access by imports or, indeed, by new entrants generally. Ironically, in Europe the major car makers, including General Motors and Ford subsidiaries, have been lobbying for arrangements similar to those in Japan.[6] Whether brought under the "nullification and impairment" or some other article, a discussion could have been initiated on issues such as how to achieve regulatory objectives (in this instance, related to safety and environment) by the least trade-restrictive means.

Unfortunately, the Americans and the Japanese preferred a bilateral "deal" rather than a lengthy and possibly inconclusive WTO dispute-settlement process. The Japanese chose not to exercise leadership by taking a test case to the WTO and seeking the support of other countries who opposed unilateralism. This was a double lost opportunity for Japan, since an international discussion of domestic regulation would have assisted those in the country who recognize the need for pervasive and radical regulatory reform to improve Japan's domestic economic health. Both business groups and even consumers have criticized the hesitancy of Japanese politicians and bureaucrats to launch such reform and multilateral discussions plus peer group pressure could have helped their cause.

These examples by no means exhaust the opportunities for innovative initiatives designed to build on the new WTO system by incremental adaptation.[7] This adaptive approach could serve two purposes: to entrench the gains of the Uruguay Round by containing system friction and also to prepare the ground for launching a new agenda, which would certainly include competition, investment, and regulatory policy issues. Further, since the most acrimonious disputes of the 1980s and early 1990s reflected differences in regulatory and legal systems between the United States and Japan, this adaptive process in the WTO would be facilitated by growing domestic pressures for reform in Japan. Most of the domestic impediments to market access in Japan stem from the postwar development model, which restricted foreign investment and utilized regulation for both economic and political management. There is growing disillusionment in Japan with the postwar development model and growing agreement for domestic change as a means of effective international integration.

Perhaps the waning of system friction with Japan is now a real possibility. But this is hardly the situation in China, and the problem of integrating China into the global trading system is much more formidable than has ever been true of Japan. It is also increasingly urgent, as China's sheer size and explosive economic growth makes it an ever more important participant in world trade.

China: The Long March to the WTO

No day passes without an item of news, whether economic or political, about China. This is understandable, of course, since without doubt the emergence on the global stage of the world's largest country, which for most of the past two millennia has been essentially closed, represents the most formidable challenge the Western powers have ever faced. Both because of China's isolation and the West's ignorance stemming from that lack of historical relationship as well as from profound differences in culture and institutions, the need to understand the likely development path of China over the coming decades has become a matter of increasing concern. And the single most important policy instrument available to influence that development path in a positive fashion is China's accession to the WTO.

The economic reform model of decentralized gradualism launched in December 1978 has been unique in a number of respects. There's been no economic big bang, no official privatization, and very little glasnost. The marketization has proceeded alongside the state-owned enterprises (SOEs) so that well over half of industrial output today and virtually all the growth in gross domestic product since the mid-1980s comes from "spontaneous" privatization. There have been no overall plans of transformation provided but rather an ad hoc, pragmatic evolution, first concentrating on reform of the agricultural sector, then import-substitution industrialization and, by the mid-1980s, export-led growth fueled increasingly by foreign direct investment first in the coastal special economic zones (SEZs) and then more widely across the mainland. The latest phase of this evolutionary process is designed to upgrade the technology base.

And China has increasingly used the lure of its market to extract concessions from competing MNEs. And to score political points.

Both Chinese economic growth and Chinese export performance since 1978 has been impressive, and because the decentralized gradualism has defied all conventional economic doctrine, the Chinese experience has generated considerable debate. Both economic and political factors have been proffered as explanations.[8] On the economic side, high rates of domestic savings have been extremely important. But the politics of reform have also been essential to the effectiveness of the process—at least thus far. In the prolonged post-Mao struggle for party leadership, the need to build constituencies of support in the vast and uncontrollable party structure made pragmatic, decentralized incrementalism an attractive strategy. Payment for political support increasingly took the form of "entrepreneurship"—the opportunity for state officials and the military to "earn" money either in the state sector or by moving to the private sector to earn profits.[9] A new form of what economists might call "dynamic rent seeking" in exchange for political support has been a key element in explaining the high rate of Chinese growth, especially since the mid-1980s.[10]

There are many reasons to doubt the sustainability of dynamic rent seeking as an engine of growth. The corruption intrinsic to the system is generating increasing concern both domestically and internationally, and the central government will be forced to take action to control it. The decentralized ad hocery has greatly reduced the central government share of fiscal revenue and ability to implement comprehensive price reform and effective monetary policy. And, in addition to these mainly domestic reasons for change in the market-reform approach, China's full integration into the international economy will also require fundamental change in the model.

The decentralized rent-seeking model has generated a maze of often contradictory regulations. States and local governments competing for investment were unconstrained in the use of tax incentives. No central rules on trading rights exist—indeed no outside observer knows how many SEZs actually exist. There are estimated to be five hundred laws governing foreign investment at various levels of government, as well as fifty bilateral agreements and an unknown number of codes on property rights.[11] If one word were chosen to describe the essential characteristic of the Chinese legal system from an international perspective it would be *opaque*. Furthermore, even when the laws are transparent, as for example those recently adopted to guarantee intellectual property rights, the enforcement capability of the central government is inherently weak because of the intrinsic nature of the rent-seeking development process. Since *transparency* and the *enforcement of rules* are integral to the world trading system today, an effective accession of China to the WTO is bound to fail in the absence of major internal reforms, including a rebalancing of power between Beijing and the provinces and the establishment of a transparent, enforceable and enforced rule of law.

China first applied for "re-admission" to the GATT (it was a founding member but withdrew in 1949) in 1986. Negotiations for accession were suspended after the Tiananmen Square events and did not recommence until 1992, but were again suspended because of the dispute with the United States over lack of enforcement of a 301-based bilateral agreement on intellectual property rights. They recommenced in early 1995 after a new bilateral agreement on intellectual property was reached under threat of United States 301 sanctions and stalled again a year later because of the same dispute. No serious negotiations are likely until well after the 1996 American presidential elections. As the negotiations stall, both the political and economic stakes of Chinese accession are escalating.

If China had joined the GATT in the 1980s the negotiations would have centered on traditional trade issues or border barriers. They might still have been difficult, given China's size and concern by the OECD countries about the domestic adjustment costs that would have been generated by growing Chinese exports. But this traditional concern could be offset by the traditional "balance of benefits" from the prospects offered by liberalization of the potentially huge Chinese market. Negotiating accession to the WTO after the Uruguay Round and in a world of deepening integration is quite another matter. While concern about adjustment pressures have surfaced (for example, in demands for special safeguards or refusal to grant China developing-country status), the "balance of benefits" paradigm now extends well beyond the border. China has resisted a number of proposals detailing, for example, elements of transparency in regulatory matters, as well as other procedural and administrative provisions of a similar nature, on the grounds that these go beyond long-standing GATT rules and constitute an intrusion on Chinese sovereignty. This is, of course, in a very profound sense quite true since full integration into the global economy will require fundamental changes in Chinese institutions and her economic development model. On the other hand, sustained economic growth in China will not be assured if these fundamental changes are not undertaken.[12]

How will these disputes be resolved? It's not possible at present to hazard an answer, but if they are "fudged" by the usual GATT-type diplomatese rather than tackled in a more constructive manner, the underlying problems will threaten the longer-term viability of the WTO through continuing conflict between China and her trading partners. China must be persuaded that the benefits provided by WTO membership include not only secure access to world markets but also a set of international rules that could greatly facilitate the process of China's domestic reform by providing an external counterweight to the domestic bureaucracy blocking reform and strengthening the domestic interests that would benefit from reform.

A successful deal with China would also require that the leading members of the WTO recognize that gradualism is a deeply ingrained priority for the Chinese, especially in a period of political uncertainty. Thus the Protocol of Accession should establish a transitional review mechanism over a reasonable medium-term time frame, with regular monitoring arrangements and provision for technical assistance and consultative mechanisms with other UN agencies, especially in the field of international law and dispute arbitration. When one considers that in Japan the Administrative Procedures Law of 1946 promoted by the American Occupation Powers to ensure transparency of regulatory procedures was only revised, because of domestic and international pressure, in 1994, a medium-term time frame is hardly unreasonable. But given American impatience and Chinese fear of change precipitating political chaos, reason may not prevail if the negotiations for accession are mainly a bilateral or regional affair colored by a clash of cultures and infected by political tensions.

Expanding the WTO System: The Road Ahead

At least some part of the road ahead can be easily mapped. The WTO built-in agenda includes negotiations in the two key areas that were the most difficult in the Uruguay Round, agriculture and services, the unfinished business and the new territory of deeper integration. In addition to these undoubtedly difficult negotiations, there is a lot of work to do in eliminating the remaining border barriers, perhaps by a combination of accelerating the Uruguay Round commitments and launching new negotiations. Replicating regional targets for border-free trade, say 2010 for industrialized countries and 2020 for all the others, as in APEC, could be an attractive and feasible agenda item to broaden the scope of a new round to commence before the end of the decade. Finally, it would not be necessary to wait for a new round to begin negotiations on unglamorous but very useful trade facilitation measures such as improving customs clearance procedures, harmonization of tariff nomenclatures, harmonization or mutual recognition of product standards and certification procedures, and so on. Such work is proceeding in many of the regional arrangements and this could serve as an exemplar for similar WTO activity.

But services apart, a new round confined to traditional issues would be unlikely to garner sufficient political support, especially in the United States. If it is not to be marginalized, the WTO agenda must include the high-priority issues of deeper integration: investment, competition policy, and regulatory reform. In addition, at the ministerial meeting in Marrakesh, which formally concluded the Uruguay Round, the Committee on Trade and the Environment was established and ordered to report to the first biennial WTO ministerial conference in 1996. And there is considerable pressure from some countries to include labor and social standards in the WTO mandate but opposition, especially from the non-OECD countries, is very strong, so negotiations in this area are unlikely over the foreseeable future.

Analysis of all these agenda items has been under way for some time, and it's not necessary to duplicate these studies at length.[13] Presented below are brief highlights of the main issues of deeper integration in order to illustrate why these issues will be more difficult to negotiate, and thus why the road ahead could be long and not-so-easily mapped.

Investment

As noted in the previous chapter, the progress the Uruguay Round made in the investment field, contained in the agreement on Trade-Related Investment Measures (TRIMS), was relatively modest. The agreement is a valuable start toward a more far-reaching accord, but in substance it is not seen as an important arrangement. The agreement deals exclusively with national rules on performance requirements, and it largely codifies GATT law as it has been interpreted in GATT dispute-settlement panels. The agreement does put into play certain valuable concepts that have potentially wider significance, such as notification and transparency, but it is limited when measured against the range of concerns expressed by private investors, host countries, and FDI exporting countries. In addition to TRIMS, the two other significant investment-related contributions of the round concern the progress on investment protection in intellectual property rights and the GATS rule that establishes trade and investment as complementary modes of market access.

Thus there have been many calls for a multilateral

agreement on investment, especially from the United States and the EU. The hundreds of bilateral investment treaties, mostly between OECD and non-OECD countries, have produced a complex and uneven basis of regulation for international investors. What is needed is a more uniform set of rules with broader application, and particularly rules that will limit the frequent exclusions taken in investment treaties for "domestic laws, regulations and policies."

What should a general investment agreement provide? Most lists would start with the right to locate and then include nondiscrimination (both between investors of different nationality and between foreign investors, once established, and national companies). Transparency of government regulation is another desideratum. Freedom from unreasonable and uncompensated expropriation and the right to repatriate profits are also important, as are assurances against the application of unduly onerous performance requirements. Finally, a fair and effective dispute settlement system rounds out the traditional list of concerns on investment.

A proposed model for a multilateral agreement suggested by the United States is the far-reaching chapter on investment contained in the NAFTA. This chapter established a broader definition of investment by including not only FDI (that is, an investment made by and under the control of a foreign head office) but also equity and debt securities, loan and interest, real estate, and capital commitments—in other words, virtually all investments that are made across national boundaries.

The NAFTA provides for MFN and national treatment, repatriation of profits, and limits on expropriation. It reduces the screening on incoming investment, which both

Canada and Mexico practice, and it disciplines performance requirements. The NAFTA provides numerous exceptions for sensitive sectors, such as culture in Canada or petroleum in Mexico (which the United States would prefer eliminated or greatly constrained in the Multilateral Agreement on Investment, or MAI), and it establishes the illegitimacy of attracting investment through derogating from environmental requirements. Finally, and perhaps most important, the NAFTA provides a mechanism for dispute settlement and arbitration between private investors and host states in addition to state-to-state dispute settlement provisions. Investors have the right to request an arbitral tribunal if host governments (including subnational governments) violate obligations under the investment agreement. This provides important increased security for foreign investment, resulting in greater security for international transactions, although it opens up the danger that excessive litigation could become a means of economic harassment. Of course, that danger is inherent in the essential legalization and privatization of American trade policy that established the NAFTA template.

Negotiations on an MAI were launched by OECD ministers at their May 1995 annual meeting. The MAI was to be concluded in two years. Although reference was made to future discussions in the WTO and the OECD was "encouraged" to cooperate with the WTO, given the weak infrastructure of the institution it seems likely that the MAI will be concluded before any significant global discussions begin unless concrete action is taken by WTO members to remedy the situation. Given the facts that the share of FDI received by non-OECD countries more than doubled between the years 1987 and 1994, that nearly 50 percent of world investment now goes to developing countries, and that some of these countries are also increasingly important sources of investment outflow, the role of the WTO will be crucial.

And the task of undertaking global investment negotiations in the WTO will be far more difficult than in either the NAFTA, where the United States is the dominant partner, or in the OECD, where differences in policy objectives are marginal and where institutional regimes are very similar. In many of the non-OECD countries, and especially in East Asia, western legal tradition is nonexistent or, at best, superficial, having been imposed by a former colonial power but later indigenized. This will create problems with respect to transparency and enforcement. Moreover, the widespread use of various types of industrial policy, now increasingly targeted at enriching the technology base, will run head-on into the need to limit exclusions, exceptions, performance requirements, technology transfer, investment incentives, and so on. Thus, the OECD agreement and the OECD analysis of investment policy will have only limited relevance to the broader global negotiations. If the WTO negotiations are to be successful, the analytic base as well as the technical assistance and training resources of the institution will have to be greatly strengthened so that broader negotiations can be launched with some hope of success. Special attention will have to be paid to the technology issue and the technology-targeted investment policies, since for most non-OECD countries FDI is a major funnel for technology diffusion both directly and through externalities or spillovers. Perhaps the rather dismal experience with strategic industry policies and national champions of many of the OECD countries now advocating their elimination in non-OECD countries might be especially informative in advancing fruitful discussions in the WTO.

Competition Policy

There is a broad intersect between competition policy and trade policy, and a number of proposals have been put forward to bring competition-policy rules into the WTO. Some examples of trade issues that relate to competition policy are the inadequacy or nonenforcement of national competition policy, which may restrict access to markets through imports or investment, distort trade through exemptions for export cartels, provide loopholes for market dominance at the global level because of mergers beyond the reach of national jurisdictions, and permit different standards for predatory pricing as between domestic and foreign firms (antidumping). And trade policy in the form of voluntary export restraints or voluntary import expansion may well encourage anticompetitive collusive behavior and reduce the contestability of markets.

But none of the growing number of studies that have explored options for international competition rules suggest that it will be an easy task. Less than half of the WTO member countries possess antitrust or competition codes, many only recently adopted. Moreover, overall objectives of competition policy vary from country to country, and indeed, have varied in the same country over time. But even substantive convergence would be only half the battle. The variation in the enforcement of both the structural and behavioral instruments of competition policy is probably even greater than that in objectives. American pressure has certainly helped strengthen the Japanese Fair Trade Commission (FTC) (which undertook its first prosecution of a price cartel in November 1991), but the FTC has some way to go if reasonable convergence in enforcement is to be achieved among most other OECD countries. Differing legal traditions among countries are also an important factor in divergence, and the United States is unique in its emphasis on private avenues of enforcement, triple damage suits, and a greater predisposition to extraterritorial application. Differences in legal traditions among the three participants of the NAFTA may well impede progress in the harmonization of competition policy in order to eliminate antidumping laws. Only in the European Union has convergence been achieved, but it has taken a very long time. Based on the European experience, it would be foolhardy to assume rapid progress in East Asia.

Thus, an incremental approach to incorporating competition policy within the multilateral trading system is likely the only feasible tack. (This would not, of course, preclude bilateral agreements to facilitate greater cooperation and procedural harmonization, especially in the area of mergers and joint ventures.) In such a step-by-step approach, it would be best to start off with rules on cartels, since in all jurisdictions horizontal price-fixing arrangements are, at least in principle, per se offenses and thus it might be easier to reach a consensus with countries now establishing competition policy laws. There are many exceptions, however, including export cartels, which are legal in a number of countries. So even in this area, reaching agreement on an international rule would take time. Other issues, such as mergers, price discrimination, and predatory pricing (to replace antidumping laws) and rules on subsidies (to replace subsidy/countervail laws) are also on the "wish list" but are likely to be more difficult to harmonize. Finally, the WTO would have to house an international authority to gather information, investigate anticompetitive behavior, settle disputes, and enforce penalties.

Many of these topics have been under active discussion for the past few years in special committees of the OECD. As in the instance of the MAI, it is essential to involve the WTO and to upgrade its analytical and training resources, since the ultimate objective is the establishment of transparent and enforceable global competition rules. And that is likely to be a far more difficult task in developing countries than in the OECD. But, as noted above, even for OECD countries, since competition-policy legal issues are exceedingly information-intensive, the challenge of building institutional capacity in the WTO should not be underestimated.

Finally, just as there is a broad intersect between competition and trade policies, albeit with many differences and difficulties remaining before coherence is established, there is also growing recognition in trade-policy discussion that domestic regulatory policies can impede the international flow of goods, services, capital, and business personnel. And, indeed, there is also a broad intersect between competition and regulatory policies. One way of capturing this convergence of policies is through the overall concept of "contestability," which defines a market that has very low barriers to entry. The negotiations on telecommunications services provide a useful illustration of the implications of regulatory policy in the new trade agenda. While the telecommunications negotiations are in a sense unique, because the basic regulatory issues are sector-specific and therefore would be different in, say, financial services, the generic issue of radical change in the political-economic model of the negotiating dynamic is the same.

Regulatory Reform

The first effort to reach agreement on telecommunications services in the Uruguay Round was unsuccessful, and so it was agreed to continue the negotiations for a specified period after the completion of the round. This also failed and so another extension was agreed. In both instances the Americans were unwilling to sign up because the offers on the table did not satisfy the basic principle governing their policy in the sectoral negotiations, which was reciprocity.

In the services negotiations—both financial and telecommunications—the principle of reciprocity as a bargaining modality is profoundly different from the basic GATT concept of an overall balance of benefits or even sectoral reciprocity in a particular manufacturing industry because those negotiations involved measurable border barriers. In telecommunications services, however, the barriers to entry are domestic regulatory policies. Identical market-access offers do not imply a comparable exchange of benefits if regulatory regimes are different. Effective market access will be limited where monopoly providers of basic services exist and regulatory regimes inhibit provision of services by foreign firms through, for example, vague rules on interconnection to the public telecommunications network or cross-subsidization of competitive services from public network revenues.

Since the United States undertook major regulatory reform in 1984 with the breakup of the monopoly service provider AT&T, a massive structural transformation has taken place, which unleashed competition, reduced government cross-subsidies for local and long-distance calls and significantly reduced costs. An even more pervasive and fundamental reform in early 1996 set the stage for a new era of competition and restructuring among different telecommunication carriers as well as cable, broadcast, and information-technology industries. Hence the United States is unwilling to improve access by reducing its restrictions on foreign investment or provision of international services from the American market unless regulatory reform provides similar access in other markets. This reciprocity concept was reinforced by new rules adopted by the Federal Communications Commission at the end of 1995, which permit the FCC to keep foreign companies out of the United States telephone market unless there are "effective competitive opportunities" in markets dominated by the foreign carrier.

So negotiation in this sector really rests on trading access to the American market for regulatory reform in other markets. But, since the major American companies have an absolute (not comparative) advantage, largely because of their "first mover" advantage in regulatory reform, the trade-off might not be very appealing to those countries whose own companies (often protected state monopolies) would have little to gain from entry into the American market and whose own markets would be serviced by a small number of globally dominant foreign providers. Of course, the true benefit to the country would be access to leading-edge telecommunications services, which is an essential part of "soft infrastructure" and therefore of continuing growth.

Thus the negotiations on basic telecommunications services involve not only offers on improved access, but also principles of procompetitive regulatory reform spelled out in the United States submission and incorporated in a "reference" paper issued by the chairman of the negotiating group. The regulatory disciplines, based on the American experience "in moving its domestic regime from monopoly to the competitive supply of basic telecommunications services, include commitments to set disciplines for interconnection of competing basic telecommunications suppliers; provide competition safeguards to ensure non-discriminatory behaviour on the part of the dominant network operator; assure transparency of regulatory processes; [and] guarantee the independence of regulators."[14]

This new concept of reciprocity—access for regulatory reform—will not be easy to sell to a number of countries, not least in East Asia, as was clear in the initial negotiations where, apart from Singapore, the "critical mass" of offers (as the Americans phrased it) were unsatisfactory. While regulatory reform, privatization and liberalization of investment in the telecommunications sector has been launched in many countries, there is still considerable government control designed to protect and nurture dominant providers as well as to achieve a range of social policy objectives. The final stages of "reforming regulatory reform" are thus likely to be the most difficult and most prolonged. The suggestion that the negotiations would be easier if conducted within a broader agenda, which would permit cross-sectoral trade-offs, seems dubious. Is it really possible to equate textiles or grain with fundamental structural transformation and five hundred TV channels?

It may well be that locational competition, perhaps prodded by bilateral pressure, will prove a stronger force for regulatory reform than multilateral negotiations. But if these sectoral negotiations fail, or the United States chooses a bilateral or unilateral route, the credibility of the WTO would be severely damaged. A much better alternative would be to recognize that these are radically new forms of negotiations and that they will require considerable effort and time to achieve a consensus on the benefits of regulatory reform and the boundaries of domestic sovereignty.

The interrelated issues of investment, competition policy, and regulatory policies largely reflect the new agenda of the global corporations. But there are also other new global actors with their own policy agenda and at present the most visible and influential are the greens.

Trade and the Environment

The GATT activated a Working Group on Environmental Measures and International Trade in November 1991 to consider three issues: (1) trade provisions in multilateral environmental agreements (for example, the Montreal Protocol on the Ozone Layer); (2) transparency of national environmental regulations; and (3) trade effects of packaging and labeling requirements. In July 1993 the group expanded its agenda to include issues in Agenda 21 of the UN Conference on Environment and Development (UNCED), which would make trade and environmental policies mutually supportive. At the ministerial meeting in Marrakesh in April 1994, which formally concluded the Uruguay Round, the working group was upgraded to a Committee on Trade and Environment and ordered to report to the first biennial WTO Ministerial Conference in 1996. The agenda was further expanded to include issues such as the impact of environmental measures on market access, especially for developing countries; exports of domestically produced goods; and the trade effects of environmental standards, technical regulations, and recycling.

By 1996 the GATT/WTO agenda will have included environmental concerns for five years. After that length of time, it can no longer claim that it is still analyzing the issue. However, consensus is not near. The main lines of cleavage are between the environmental policies of the United States and the EU, and the conflicting concerns of the smaller industrialized countries and the developing countries. The cleavage focuses on the use of trade restrictions to achieve environmental goals. Environmentalists claim that such restrictions are necessary to prevent international trade from diluting high product standards that have been achieved in domestic economies. They also claim that restrictions are necessary—as included in the Montreal Protocol—to prevent "free riders" from taking advantage of, but not paying for, the benefits of international environmental agreements. Developing countries especially oppose these claims on the grounds that they may be used to reduce export access to developed country markets bought and paid for in the Uruguay Round negotiations.

The more extreme environmental proposals are motivated by the concept of "greening the GATT." They would seek, possibly through amendments to Article XX, prior approval to apply unilateral trade restrictions against products produced by "non-environmental" processing methods in exporting countries, or against products benefiting from "sub-standard" environmental regimes (eco-dumping). There is little chance that these proposals will find consensus in the WTO, nor should they. They represent mainly the attempt by an importing country to force its assumed higher environmental standards on an exporting country. It should also be remembered that there is a wide range of processing methods and environmental regulations in the world, and if countries are to look over each others' shoulders on these matters, there is no assurance that the larger WTO members will be the least blameworthy. The GATT/WTO remains at base a contractual arrangement, intended to ensure nondiscrimination and national treatment between trading countries; it is not an environmental organization. Attempts to make it serve a perceived environmental function will only lessen the valuable role it plays in promoting an open trading system, and the resulting discord will produce little gain for the environment.

There may, however, be grounds for near-term consensus around the issue of trade restrictions in international environmental agreements (IEAs). There are more than 150 IEAs. Only a few contain trade restrictions, and none has been challenged in the GATT. However, there conceivably could be a GATT challenge to some IEAs in the future, and the environmental community wishes to resolve this uncertainty. There is assumed to be no problem of inconsistency between an IEA and WTO rights for the countries participating in an IEA: therefore one solution is to achieve broad participation in any IEAs that are established. But that leaves a problem—namely, should a WTO member in an IEA seek to apply trade restrictions to a WTO member not participating in the IEA? Proposals for reconciling this situation include negotiating a general waiver (an "environmental window" from GATT rules for IEAs) or less expansively, negotiating waivers or exceptions on a case-by-case basis. The former is clearly more acceptable to the environmental community, but it attracts more opposition from developing countries, which view it as a potential uncompensated loss of GATT rights of nondiscrimination. It may be possible to form a package by incorporating proposals dealing with issues like transparency and domestically prohibited goods. Some developed countries, however, have not been eager to publicize environmental regulations arising in subfederal authorities or in the private sector, and the United States government, due to pressure from domestic industry, has resisted a proposal requiring prior informed consent (PIC) from governments importing goods such as hazardous wastes that are prohibited for sale in the United States.

In the long term, the prospects for agreement could be favorable since new trade liberalization might provide a quid pro quo for the costs of environmentally based trade restrictions. The first step should be to begin a negotiation to achieve border-free trade at a given date. The fact is that the WTO operates on consensus, and proposals that carry differential costs in the name of environmental protection are unlikely to find support. The flip side of this argument, however, is that when the environmental community does achieve consensus on proposals, as it did on the Montreal Protocol, the GATT/WTO is unlikely to stand in the way.

That said, it is not likely that the conflict between the WTO and environmentalists, especially environmental nongovernmental organizations (NGOs), will dissipate quickly. The NGOs are linked globally by e-mail and act as "transformational coalitions" that are less concerned with traditional interest-group concerns like the *division* of the pie than with the *recipe* for making it. They are skilled in dealing with the media, especially television, and have also demonstrated considerable ability to raise significant amounts of money from direct memberships and private foundations. Environmental NGOs are best viewed as another aspect of globalization of the world economy. Although it is difficult to bridge the gap between free-trade purists and radical environmentalists, the more pragmatic NGOs are eager to engage in dialogue and to search for pragmatic policy initiatives involving compromise on both sides. Such dialogue is to be encouraged.

This brief review of the new agenda to extend the scope

of the WTO rules—the road ahead—leaves unanswered two fundamental questions: what is the destination of the voyage and who will navigate the trip?

Deeper Integration: A Global Single Market?

There's an ancient Chinese saying: "If we don't plan where we want to go we'll end up in the direction we're going." The direction of deeper integration ends up in a global single market. But no country has a plan for steering such an ambitious voyage and even if such a plan existed most members of the WTO at present would not share it.

The logic of the single market stems from globalization itself and, in particular, the role of the dominant transnational actors, the MNEs. As noted, however, new transnational players, the greens, have a somewhat different vision of a single market, which will have to be accommodated in some fashion, as will that of newer global players, the human rights (labor standards) transformational coalitions. So even if all governments, who are still the negotiators sitting at the table, could agree on the destination, the road ahead would be long and bumpy.

The compelling arguments for a global single market are economic. Consumers would be able to buy the best products at the lowest prices anywhere and everywhere. The gains stem not only from the static, once-and-for-all efficiency gains from eliminating trade barriers but also, and more importantly, from dynamic efficiencies that would increase growth and create new jobs as global competition forced firms to restructure, reinvent, and innovate. In many sectors—for example, financial services, telecommunications, multi-media—restructuring will involve transnational alliances or mergers. Global oligopolies of only OECD transnationals will be unacceptable to many non-OECD countries who will want a presence in the global market for their own firms and will be prepared to nurture their own "national champions" for that purpose. This clash between "efficiency" and "sovereignty" is already visible, especially in China.

The clash will not be easy to resolve. To reap the economic benefits of a global market would require a truly "level playing field." All impediments to market entry by trade or investment would have to be removed so that globally integrated production and distribution processes could be established. Globally integrated production would also require access to equivalent "soft infrastructure" not only in the form of state-of-the-art financial and telecommunication services but also transparent and enforceable legal regimes.

A global single market would unlink the economic optic of the nation state and the global corporations. Global distribution of production would blur the national identity of any particular product. "Global" growth would increase, "global" consumers would benefit, but the distributional effects of these gains, the distribution of winners and losers both among and within countries, would affect the immobile factors of production, the land, and most of the labor of the nation state. While it would be possible to design compensatory mechanisms to mitigate the effects on the losers, the task of achieving such policy coherence, both domestic and international, would be formidable. The present institutional and political underpinnings of a global single market are virtually nonexistent.

The European experience in launching the "1992 program" to complete the single market and the subsequent efforts to strengthen political and monetary union is the only example of "deeper integration" in the world. It has taken half a century so far, and the process is still ongoing. While a great deal of progress has been made, the complex institutional infrastructure and the extraordinary political difficulties of maintaining momentum should serve to underline the need for prudence and patience in launching a similar global initiative. The European countries, whatever their differences, share a common cultural legacy and were motivated to pursue deeper integration by a vision of the past, the vision of "never again." Finally it must be emphasized that the choice today is not between doing nothing or enunciating grand visions of the future. The new agenda must include the full liberalization of trade as well as the main priorities for deepening global integration. But the ultimate destination must be agreed, the WTO must be strengthened, and the main drivers must all be on board or the road ahead will turn out to be a dead end.

It remains, then, only to ask, who will lead the voyage?

Who's on First?

Previous chapters have traced the evolution of trade policy from the shallow integration of the postwar, Cold War era to the deeper integration of the post–Cold War world of the 1990s and beyond. The primary role of the United States in reshaping the policy template from border barriers to ever more intrusive domestic policy and institutional issues, it is argued, stemmed from a growing resentment of structural differences in market systems, which have created marked asymmetries of access. The root of this resentment has been the erosion of the overwhelming postwar lead of the United States, which was, ironically, largely a consequence of its success in building the postwar system. More recently, the push to this new policy paradigm is not only reinforced, but increasingly led by the global enterprises, among which the

American companies are the most ubiquitous, powerful, and assertive.

In a framework of deeper integration, the more marked the structural asymmetries of access, the more intrusive will be the policy content of liberalization: hence the emergence of a new, broad, and constantly evolving *system friction*. As described in this book, there are significant differences in market systems between the United States, the EU, and most of all, Japan. And these differences affect access in the new dimension of domestic barriers, again, most of all in Japan. But the differences with China are of a different order of magnitude. And the system friction, most visible in American-Japanese negotiations, will also be of a different order of magnitude vis-à-vis China. Because these systems are deeply entrenched in the historical and cultural roots of societies, the intrusiveness of deeper integration policies can threaten the fundamental human value of diversity among nations. Thus the boundary line between pressures for harmonization and some form of cooperation or coordination designed to reduce marked asymmetries in access will be difficult to define as well as implement.

System friction has been aggravated because the United States, for profound cultural and historical reasons, is far less tolerant of system differences than either the Europeans or the Japanese, and far more impatient. At the same time, American perceptions of asymmetry have a strong basis in fact. The American system is structurally the most porous and transparent in the triad. The relative ease of access is particularly striking in the case of investment, because of the primacy of equity markets as markets for corporate control, and in the case of access to scientific and advanced technological knowledge, because of the primacy of universities in the innovation system. Further, with the shift in technology trajectory from hard to soft—from manufacturing to services—American leadership in software and services has reinforced the importance of global access and the propensity to bilateralism or unilateralism. In services and intellectual property negotiations, the WTO is less and less likely to be the primary forum for ongoing American negotiations.

But the American system is unique in other respects as well, and its special character is of special significance in the transition to the next century. The contrast between the United States and Europe has been characterized as a contrast between a system premised on Exit versus a system centered on Voice. In a period of ongoing and pervasive structural change, which impacts not only on business but also on governments as well, an Exit paradigm—fluid, flexible, and disposable—is far more adaptive: in Exit social change is ensured through a decentralized and anonymous mechanism that secures victory for the most efficient. Through a largely anonymous process, winners are rewarded—and losers appear to disappear. Of course there are costs in the decline in social cohesion, but they can be hidden for longer than when expressed through Voice.

Thus the ongoing redesign of the postwar welfare state in all OECD countries may be less difficult in the United States, in part because of the smaller role of government in the provision of public goods and equity than in Europe, but also because Europeans must engage in a political renegotiation of the redistributive impact of change. This difficult and painful task is likely to increase protectionist pressures, even though ongoing liberalization and deregulation would indeed enhance the adjustment process. Furthermore, in both Europe and the United States, the politics of radical restructuring, difficult enough in democracies in the best of times, are made more rancorous by rising structural unemployment in Europe and stagnant real income of the average family in addition to widening income disparities in the United States. Thus in the industrialized democracies, the "permissive consensus" of the postwar decades, which allowed the elites to govern, has all but disappeared. While economists debate the complex mix of underlying causes for these developments, politicians round up the usual suspects, and foreign competitors often get the highest ratings as Public Enemy Number One.

In the case of Japan, the market model of managed capitalism and the governance model are closely intertwined and were remarkably successful in the earlier postwar decades. Now, both are under severe strain, and the angst of declinism has shifted from the United States to Japan. The postwar social contract was constructed not primarily through extensive government expenditure and redistributive mechanisms but through extensive regulation and protection, which guaranteed jobs for farmers, mom-and-pop stores and other service sectors, and layers of white-collar workers. Thus the need for restructuring of Japanese industry and the ongoing pressure from the United States for greater liberalization will require profound changes in the nature and role of government. Indeed, there is now growing demand in Japan both by business and even consumers for such change, especially for major regulatory reform and a diminished role for bureaucratic "administrative guidance." But this process too will be difficult and lengthy and it is impossible to predict whether continuing American pressure will accelerate reform or foster a new assertiveness in Japan and hasten the "Asianization" of Japanese foreign economic policy. In either case, while bilateral disputes between the United States and Japan may decline over the long run, system friction in East Asia will certainly be with us for a very long time.

Because systemic differences are real and often intractable, they do much to explain the attractiveness of unilateralism for the powerful. Yet this is a deeply disturbing trend, however understandable. If the new rules-based global trading system established by the Uruguay Round—a negotiation launched and led by the United States—is to cope with a new trade agenda of deeper integration, this fundamental challenge of unilateralism, an option only for the powerful, will have to be tackled. While regionalism is compatible with such a system—although it may fortify or diminish the scope of the multilateralism, depending on the circumstances—over the long run, unilateralism may well prove incompatible with any rules-based system. That danger is heightened by the end of the Cold War.

The glue of the Cold War that held the Western Alliance together is gone. The focus on a single threat to collective security was a powerful fount for cohesive purpose, in both the economic and political arena. Indeed there was perfect congruence between the institutional structure of the OEEC and the Marshall Plan so that overall economic and security objectives reinforced cohesion of policy and purpose. And although the notion of shared values—"embedded liberalism"—was part romantic myth, the postwar elites did share enough basic ideas to serve as a context for policy dialogue. In East Asia, perhaps APEC will become an economic forum comparable to the OECD, but there is no congruence of policy or purpose between APEC and the hub and spoke security arrangements under American leadership. More to the point, what are the shared ideas that will provide the context for dialogue with China? As the convergence club widens and diversifies, agreement on basics will be increasingly difficult to achieve. This is the essential challenge of the geo-economic shift to Asia, where systems diversity is far greater than in the Euro-Atlantic alliance, which governed the post-war system.

In such an uncertain world, there is a certain irony in the fact that the WTO, a descendant of the ill-fated ITO, is the first construct in a new post–Cold War architecture of international cooperation. Fundamental changes in the template of global trade policy amplified and highlighted the inadequacies of the original postwar institution, the GATT. Yet, flaws and all, the institution survived and so did the multilateral rules-based trading system. And both the survival of the system and the most ambitious effort at reform and adaptation—the Uruguay Round—were entirely due to American leadership, despite the change in policy purpose and ambience. Without U.S. leadership, the Uruguay Round would simply not have happened. Equally, to sustain and reinforce the multilateral trading system and to reform the other postwar institutions will require that the United States play an active role. But the WTO would also not exist without the cooperative efforts of a number of middle powers and, in particular, the major power of the EU. Broader engagement is now essential, and if the United States is unable or unwilling to take the lead, the EU and Japan, the two other great trading powers, must assume greater international responsibilities and work with consensual coalitions of smaller countries both to strengthen the WTO as an institution and to constrain threats to the rules-based system. The leadership of the EU, in rescuing the financial services agreement, was an impressive example of what could and should be a new pluralist system of global governance. This is desirable in itself as power, both economic and political, is diffusing, and this diffusion will accelerate in the next century. But it is not only *desirable,* it is *essential* to sustaining and extending the rules-based system. The experience of the Europeans in building the EU has made them well aware of the significant variations that exist in both economic and political systems and the need, however difficult and tedious, to work out ways of adapting to divergence. Thus the high "transactions costs" of EU decision-making delayed the launch of the Uruguay Round. But the experience of taking time to deal with diversity is a most valuable asset in a new world of deeper integration and could be especially so in dealing with Chinese integration into that world.

Japanese cultural affinity in Asia also opens up an important venue for Japanese leadership both in the evolution of APEC, the integration of China, and the building of a new Consensus Club of middle powers in Asia. But the paralysis of decision-making in Japan and the unwillingness or inability to confront the radical domestic reforms essential for renewed growth and effective democratic governance has also constrained Japan from accepting a larger international responsibility both in Asia and in global terms. It is to be hoped that the shock of "declinism" will provide a spur to new domestic and international initiatives.

So the answer to who's on first must certainly be the United States, but just as certainly, it must sometimes be partnerships of many others, sometimes including the United States and sometimes not. That pattern was already evident in the Uruguay Round, and it should be even more effective in the post-Uruguay era. And for whoever is on first at any given time, the objective should always be not to force countries to act in unison, but to encourage them to work in harmony for the common good.

Appendix: The Built-in Agenda and the Singapore Ministerial Conference Australian Paper

The Built-in Agenda is one of the major achievements of the Uruguay Round. It is an integral part of the WTO legal framework; and ministers should give political emphasis to its full implementation as a centerpiece of the Singapore WTO Ministerial Conference in December.

The built-in commitments to monitor and review the Uruguay Round agreements and to negotiations on further liberalization for some important issues provide the basis for a WTO "road map" to improve the effectiveness of the multilateral rules and expand global market access. It is important that ministers demonstrate to the international community that the WTO has such a road map. This paper demonstrates the scope of the Built-in Agenda to provide this, and that the implementation, reviews, and further negotiations contained in it are integrally related to the WTO's central mandate: trade liberalization.

This paper also illustrates the extent to which the Built-in Agenda is a framework for most of the agenda items already under consideration for the Singapore Ministerial Conference: implementation and monitoring of the Uruguay Round Agreements, ongoing work on Trade and the Environment and on Services, additional work to strengthen the rules and further liberalization.

With Singapore Trade Minister Yeo's Set of Principles, the Built-in Agenda should be central to the preparations for Singapore. In this paper, we set out an organizational approach to the Built-in Agenda for Singapore and beyond. We have set out its component parts clearly and in chrono-

Department of Foreign Affairs and Trade (draft working paper, June 1996).

logical groupings, in plain language but without changing the intent of any of the provisions.

The attached listing sets out the Built-in Agenda as follows:

- Issues for which there are built-in commitments to deadlines before the end of 1996;
- Issues for which, although there are not specific or one-off deadline commitments, built-in work is already under way and will continue; and
- Issues for which there are specific built-in commitments due from 1997 onward for work programs, reviews, and improvements to agreements and negotiations on further liberalization.

Recommendations to Ministers at Singapore

As the Built-in Agenda is an integral part of the WTO legal framework, the Ministerial Conference has overall responsibility for its oversight and development. We therefore believe that a set of recommendations on this should be put to ministers in Singapore. The General Council could take the overall responsibility for preparing the report to ministers, based on input from committees and the work of the heads of delegation in considering additions to the agenda of any new issues and new trade liberalization initiatives.

The challenges of globalization and of assuring the WTO's primary role as the engine for trade liberalization require that the multilateral trading system demonstrate that it can make progress on a broad and balanced front, with wide participation, according to efficient timetables. Giving the Built-in Agenda a strong ministerial profile will send a clear message that the WTO has a dynamic and vigorous forward agenda of relevance and importance to international business.

As shown in the attached listing, the Built-in Agenda provides the starting points and basic objectives for a great deal of this forward-oriented work; and it can be seen that each stage of implementation leads to further activity, from unfinished business and monitoring of implementation, to the scheduled reviews of the effectiveness of many of the rules, and on to the programs for continuation of reform through renewed negotiations on some issues. It will be important to manage this as a dynamic process of continuous improvement on specific issues within a broader framework, to avoid the approach becoming too ad hoc or sectorally focused.

- We should recommend to ministers that the Built-in Agenda represents the strong and coherent framework, within which all parts are integrally related, for strengthening the WTO through improving the rules and further liberalization; and that ministers give political direction for its further implementation by providing an overall goal, based on the WTO's central mandate, and end dates for completing it.
- We should recommend to ministers that a clause be added on industrial tariff liberalization negotiations in 1999 to provide for a balance of key issues to be addressed by negotiations in the final phase of the implementation of the Built-in Agenda. Progressive tariff liberalization has been a cornerstone of the multilateral trading system for fifty years, and its omission from the Built-in Agenda was a technical rather than substantive oversight in the finalization

of Uruguay Round texts because there was no "Market Access text," as such, besides the implementing protocol.

- We should recommend to ministers how the built-in work could be carried forward effectively from Singapore:
  - The outcomes and next steps for the built-in work with specific deadlines to the end of 1996;
  - Reports on progress to date and recommendations for further steps on that part of the built-in work that, although not containing specific built-in deadline commitments, is already under way and will continue into 1997 and in some cases beyond. Further work should build on that undertaken so far and include recommendations on indicative principles and deadlines to guide further work in these areas;
  - Recommendations related to the implementation of the built-in specific commitments for the post-Singapore period, based on the implementation experience and other relevant work to date. The effectiveness of the work programs, reviews, and negotiations scheduled under various agreements will rely upon such good groundwork, including to take account of developments in the trading environment; and this preliminary work will need to be commenced from Singapore across the board. Such work should be carried out in the respective WTO committees in conjunction with implementation and ongoing work, under the direction of the General Council.
- We should recommend to ministers that the Built-in Agenda represents the framework for conducting an-

other comprehensive set of multilateral trade negotiations from 1999/2000.
- We should report to ministers the possibility that implementation of the Built-in Agenda will reveal substantive or timetable overlaps or linkages between
some elements of the built-in work. It may be possible to make recommendations on this aspect also.

Notes

It will be obvious that one important element of the Built-in
Agenda relates to the comprehensive stocktake of Uruguay
Round implementation already agreed as one of the major
agenda items for the Singapore Meeting. That item is important in its own right, both for identification of existing
difficulties or nonimplementation and indications of how to
address any such issues. The Implementation Stocktake can
also be seen as a very useful basis for undertaking the next
stages of the Built-in Agenda.

The Built-in Agenda framework outlined in this paper
would not close out the prospect of also making progress
where possible on other issues. For example, there could be
opportunities to do so on issues such as unilateral accelera-
tion of Uruguay Round bindings, improvement of the zero-
for-zero and harmonization tariff outcomes, and identification through reviews of provisions that could be updated by
consensus without negotiation.

*Issues for which deadlines fall due in 1996, on which the
outcomes and next steps should be reported to Ministers
at Singapore:*

Services

Negotiations

Arising from the Ministerial Decisions at Marrakesh to conduct the four post–Uruguay Round services sectoral negotiations, there would be a report on these to ministers at Singapore. This would cover the conclusion of the negotiations on the movement of natural persons, the interim agreement on financial services, the extension of the negotiations (to February 1997) on basic telecoms and the outcome of the negotiations on maritime transport. At Singapore, ministers will need to consider the approach they wish to set down for 1997 on these issues.

- For example, on Financial Services, the interim agreement concluded on 28 July 1995 will enter into force from 1 August 1996 to 31 December 1997. From 1 November 1997, participants may, for a period of sixty days, modify or withdraw all or part of their specific commitments and/or list MFN exemptions relating to financial services. The Committee on Trade in Financial Services will oversee any negotiations that take place prior to 1 November 1997.
  - There will of course also need to be appropriate reports and recommendations to ministers on the other three sectoral negotiations.

Trade and Environment

The Marrakesh Decision requires the Committee on Trade and the Environment (CTE) to report to the first meeting of the Ministerial Conference, when the work and terms of reference of the CTE will be reviewed. Arising from the CTE's report to ministers on its 1994–96 work, some recommendations could be put for decision or further specific work. The review of the work and of the terms of reference may see refinement or new aspects added. It could also be asked whether there is any need for closer alignment of other committees' work to support that of the CTE.

Agriculture

At Singapore, ministers are to review the Trade Negotiations Committee's (TNC) Decision on Measures Concerning the Possible Negative Effects of the Reform Program on Least-developed and Net Food Importing Developing Countries. The Committee on Agriculture, which monitors the implementation of this decision, will report to the Ministerial Conference.

Market Access Commitments

The Market Access Committee's terms of reference require it to report at least once a year on its activities, which include supervision of implementation of concessions, keeping GATT schedules up to date, analysis of Quantitative Restrictions, and oversight of the application of Article XXVIII rules and procedures for renegotiation of tariff concessions.

TRIPS (Agreement on Trade-related Aspects of Intellectual Property Rights)

The first review of geographical indications issues under Article XXIV:2 of the agreement shall take place within two years of the entry into force of the WTO agreement (that is, by the end of 1996).

GATT 1994 Rules

Subsidies and Countervailing Duties Agreement

As well as the annual review of the operation and implementation of the agreement, Article VIII:2, footnote 25, of the agreement provides for a review of provisions on nonactionable subsidies for research and development by June 1996.

Import Licensing Agreement

Article VII of the agreement provides for a biennial review by the committee of the implementation and operation of the agreement (that is, the first review by the end of 1996). In addition, Article VII:2 provides for this to be based on a secretariat report based on notifications, responses to the annual questionnaire, and other reliable available information.

Preshipment Inspection Agreement

Under Article VI of the agreement, the provisions, operation and implementation of the agreement are to be reviewed by the Ministerial Conference at the end of the first two years of operation (that is, by the end of 1996).

Rules of Origin Agreement

There is to be an annual review by the Rules of Origin Committee, reporting to the Council for Trade in Goods, on the implementation and operation of Parts II and III of the agreement.

Anti-dumping Agreement

Under Article XVIII:6, there is to be an annual review of the implementation and operation of the agreement.

TRIMS Agreement (Trade-Related Investment Measures)

Under Article VII:3, the TRIMS Committee is to monitor the operation and implementation of the agreement and report annually thereon to the Council for Trade in Goods. (The main review of this agreement is to be undertaken no later than five years after entry into force of the WTO (that is, by the end of 1999) by the Council for Trade in Goods, which may propose amendments to the text. Under this latter review, issues such as investment and competition policy are to be considered—see Category Four below.)

Waivers

GATT 1994 paragraph 1(b)(iii), footnote 7 provides for the Ministerial Conference at its first session to establish a revised list of waivers, covered by this provision, that adds any waivers granted under the GATT 1947 after 15 December 1993 and before the entry into force of the WTO and deletes those waivers that will have expired by that time.

GATT 1994 paragraph 3(c) provides for an annual submission of notifications regarding measures maintained under GATT 1994 paragraph 3(a) (the remaining special grandfather waiver). Two such notifications would thus be due by the end of 1996.

Institutional Issues

The Notifications Working Party is to make recommendations to the Council for Trade in Goods no later than two years after the entry into force of the WTO (that is, by the end of 1996).

> *Issues for which there are not specific or one-off deadline commitments but on which work is already under way and will continue; and issues for which there are specific commitments due from 1997 onward for work programs, reviews and improvements of Agreements and negotiations on further liberalization:*

Ongoing Built-in Work

Services

The Decision on Professional Services establishes a Working Party on Professional Services to put into effect the work program foreseen in Article VI:4 of the GATS on Domestic Regulation in the field of professional services. The decision provides for no deadline or specific reporting arrangements on the Working Party's activities. GATS Article VI:4 provides for the Council for Trade in Services or through appropriate bodies that it may establish, to develop any necessary disciplines to ensure that measures relating to qualification requirements and procedures, technical standards and licensing requirements do not constitute unnecessary barriers to trade in services. At Singapore, further action on this could be taken up.

GATS Article XV provides for members to enter into negotiations with a view to developing the necessary disciplines to avoid the trade-distortive effects that subsidies may have on trade in services. Work commenced in 1996.

TRIPS Agreement

Article XXIII:4 of the agreement provides for ongoing negotiations in the TRIPS Council to establish a multilateral system of notification and registration to facilitate protection of geographic indications for wines.

Agriculture

Article XVIII of the agreement provides for the committee to monitor, on an ongoing basis, the progress of implementation of the commitments negotiated under the Uruguay Round.

Article XVI of the agreement provides for the committee to monitor the follow-up to the Decision on Measures Concerning the Possible Negative Effects of the Reform Program on Least-Developed and Net Food Importing Developing Countries.

Rules

Sanitary and Phytosanitary Measures Agreement. Article XII:4 provides for ongoing work to develop a procedure to monitor and coordinate the harmonization of Sanitary and Phytosanitary measures; and Article V:5 for the development of guidelines for consistency in the application of risk assessment provisions.

Anti-dumping. The Marrakesh Decision on Anti-circumvention refers this issue to the Anti-dumping Committee. The committee would thus report on its work to date.

State Trading Working Party. Paragraph 5 of the GATT 1994 Understanding on the Interpretation of Article XVII established a working party to review notifications, the adequacy of the questionnaire and to develop an illustrative list of enterprises and activities relevant to Article XVII. The Working Party is to meet at least annually and to report annually to the Council for Trade in Goods. While this is under way, there are no specific timetables for review or completion of this work.

Institutional Issues

The TNC Declaration on the Contribution of the WTO to Achieving Greater Coherence in Global Economic Policymaking provides for the WTO to pursue and develop cooperation with the IMF and World Bank under certain conditions and for the director-general to review with his counterparts the implications and forms of cooperation. There are no reporting or review requirements or timetables in this declaration.

Specific Built-in Commitments

Services

GATS Article XIII provides for multilateral negotiations on government procurement in services under the GATS within two years from the entry into force of the WTO agreement (that is, to commence before the end of 1996). At Singapore the start of and progress on this should be assessed and preferably an end date set.

GATS Article X provides for conclusion of multilateral negotiations on emergency safeguards, the results of which shall enter into force three years from the date of entry into force of the WTO agreement (that is, by the end of 1997).

GATS Article XIX:1 provides for successive rounds of liberalization negotiations, the first of which is to begin not later than five years after the entry into force of the WTO (that is, by the end of 1999).

Regarding MFN Exemptions, the GATS Annex on Article II Exemptions in paragraph 3 provides for the Council for Trade in Services to review, no more than five years after the entry into force of the WTO (that is, by the end of 1999), all such exemptions that were inscribed for a period greater than five years.

The GATS Annex on Air Transport Services provides for a review at least every five years of developments in air transport services and of the operation of this annex, with a view to considering the possible further application of the GATS to this sector.

Institutional Issues

Dispute Settlement Understanding. The Decision on the Application and Review of the Understanding on Rules and Procedures Governing the Settlement of Disputes (DSU) provides for a full review by the ministerial conference of dispute-settlement rules and procedures under the WTO (note: this is somewhat broader than the DSU alone) within four years after the entry into force of the WTO (that is, by the end of 1998), including consideration of whether to continue, modify or withdraw such rules and procedures.

Trade Policy Review Mechanism. An appraisal of the mechanism is to be completed after five years (that is, by the end of 1999) and the results submitted to the ministerial conference.

Agriculture

The continuation of reform commitment in Article 20 of the Agriculture Agreement provides for the initiation of negotiations for further liberalization one year before the end of the implementation period (that is, by 1999).

Rules

Anti-dumping Agreement. The Decision on the Review of Article XVII:6 of the Anti-dumping Agreement provides for the standard of review in Article XVII:6 of the Agreement to be reviewed after a period of three years (that is, by the end of 1997), with a view to considering whether it is capable of general application. The issue of possible extension to the Agreement on Subsidies and Countervailing Duties also arises.

This question may be relevant to the general review of the Understanding on Rules and Procedures Governing the Settlement of Disputes, which is due to commence by the end of 1998.

Technical Barriers to Trade Agreement (TBT). Article XV:4 provides for a review, no later than three years from the entry into force of the WTO (that is, to commence by the end of 1997) of the implementation and operation of the agreement.

Sanitary and Phytosanitary Measures Agreement (SPS). Article XII:7 of the agreement provides for a review, no later than three years after the entry into force of the WTO (that is, by the end of 1997), of the operation and implementation of the Agreement. There may be some substantive policy linkages between the TBT and SPS reviews.

Textiles and Clothing Agreement. The first stage of integration to the GATT 1994 is to be completed by 1 January 1998. The second stage of integration of this sector into the GATT 1994 is due to be completed by 1 January 2002 and the final stage by 1 January 2005.

Rules of Origin Agreement. Article IX of the agreement provides for the Work Program on harmonization of nonpreferential Rules of Origin to be completed within three years (that is, by the end of 1997).

Agreement on Trade-Related Investment Measures (TRIMS). The agreement provides that the Council for Trade in Goods will review the operations of the Agreement and as appropriate propose amendments to the ministerial conference. This is to be conducted within five years (that is, by the end of 1999) and should include examination of whether provisions relating to investment policy and competition policy are needed.

Waivers. The ministerial conference is to undertake a review of the exemption provided in paragraph 3(a) of the GATT 1994 (the remaining special grandfather waiver), not later than five years after the entry into force of the WTO (that is, by the end of 1999), for the purpose of examining whether the conditions that had created the need for the exemption still existed.

Subsidies Agreement. The agreement provides, in Article XXXI, for the commencement, not later than 180 days before the end of the five-year period for the application of the provisions of Articles VI:1, VIII, and IX* (that is, by mid-1999), of the review of the operation of those provisions, with a view to determining whether to extend their application, as presently drafted or in a modified form, for a further period.

The operation of the provisions of Article XXVII:6 (export competitiveness provisions for developing countries) of the agreement are to be reviewed five years from the entry into force of the WTO (that is, by the end of 1999).

Article XXVIII Negotiating Rights. Paragraph 1 of the Understanding on Article XXVIII in GATT 1994 provides for a review by the Council for Trade in Goods, five years after the entry into force of the WTO (that is, by the end of 1999) to decide whether the criteria† for determination of additional negotiating rights has worked satisfactorily in securing a redistribution of negotiating rights in favor of small and medium-sized exporters.

TRIPS Agreement

Article LXXI of the agreement provides for review of the agreement, by the TRIPS Council, within five years of the entry into force of the WTO agreement (that is, by the end of 1999). There is also a standing provision for review in

---

*Article VI:1 presumption of serious prejudice; Article VIII identification of nonactionable subsidies; Article IX consultations and authorized remedies for nonactionable subsidies.

†Granting of an additional principal supplier's right to the member with the highest ration of exports affected by the withdrawn concession to its total exports.

light of any new developments that might warrant modification or amendment of the agreement.

A year earlier, after four years' operation, Article XXVII:3(b) on Patentability of Plants and Animals is to be reviewed.

The provision in Article LXIV of the TRIPS agreement regarding the nonapplication to TRIPS of GATT Article XXIII:2(b) and (c) non-violation situations for five years is to expire on 1 January 2000, and a review of the necessity of the provision is to be carried out prior to the expiry date (that is, no later than 1999). This particular aspect of TRIPS would appear closely related to the overall Dispute-settlement Understanding review due in 1998, as well as the overall review of the TRIPS agreement listed above and due in 1999.

Plurilateral Agreements

The Civil Aircraft Agreement provides for further negotiations to broaden and improve the agreement, based on mutual reciprocity, by the end of 1997.

The Agreement on Government Procurement (Article XXIV:7(b)) provides for further negotiations to improve the agreement and achieve the greatest possible extension of its coverage among all WTO members on the basis of mutual reciprocity within five years (that is, before the end of 1999).

Notes

Chapter One

1. For a review of the literature on the "convergence controversy" and the link to endogenous growth theory, see Paul M. Romer, "The Origins of Endogenous Growth," *Journal of Economic Perspectives* 8, no. 1 (Winter 1994): 3–22. See also M. Ishaq Nadiri and Ingmar R. Prucha, "Sources of Growth of Output and Convergence of Productivity in Major OECD Countries" (New York University, December 1992, mimeograph).

2. The term is used by the National Research Council in a report published in 1990 based on studies by the National Academy of Science and the National Academy of Engineering. See *Science, Technology and the Future of the U.S.-Japan Relationship* (Washington, D.C.: National Academy Press, 1990), 7–9.

3. OECD, *Gaps in Technology* (Paris: OECD, 1970). The "Gap" study was launched by science and technology ministers at their second meeting in January 1966.

4. This account is largely drawn from Sylvia Ostry and Richard Nelson, *Technonationalism and Technoglobalism: Conflict and Cooperation* (Washington, D.C.: Brookings Institution, 1995), chap. 1. See also Richard Nelson and Gavin Wright, "The Rise and Fall of American Technological Leadership: The Postwar Era in Historical Perspective," *Journal of Economic Literature* 30, no. 5 (December 1992): 1931–64.

5. For a fuller account and bibliography, see Richard Nelson and Gavin Wright, "The Rise and Fall of American Technological Leadership: The Postwar Era in Historical

Perspective," *Journal of Economic Literature* 30, no. 5 (December 1992).

6. Angus Maddison, "Growth and Slowdown in Advanced Capitalist Economies," *Journal of Economic Literature* 25, no. 2 (June 1987): 688.

7. See *The Work of the Organisation for European Economic Co-Operation: A Report of the Secretary-General* (Paris: OEEC, 1959), 85–90.

8. David Dollar and Edward N. Wolff, *Competitiveness, Convergence and International Specialization* (Cambridge: MIT Press, 1993), 83–88. These estimates, based on growth accounting, are challenged by some of the new growth theorists and others. For example, see Gene M. Grossman and Elhanan Helpman, "Endogenous Innovation in the Theory of Growth," *Journal of Economic Perspectives* 8, no. 1 (Winter 1994).

9. See Nadiri and Prucha, "Sources of Growth," for review of estimates.

10. Bart Van Ark and Dirk Pilat, "Productivity Levels in Germany, Japan, and the United States: Differences and Causes," *Brookings Papers: Microeconomics* (1993:2): table 5, p. 20.

11. David T. Coe and Elhanan Helpman, "International R&D Spillovers" (discussion paper no. 840, Centre for Economic Policy Research, London, October 1993), 6.

12. For a review of the case studies and other estimates, see Magnus Blomstron, "Host Country Benefits of Foreign Investment" (working paper no. 3615, National Bureau of Economic Research, Cambridge, Mass., February 1991).

13. Moses Abramovitz, "Catching Up, Forging Ahead, and Falling Behind," *Journal of Economic History* 46, no. 2 (June 1986). But he notes, "The trouble with absorbing so-

cial capability into the catch-up hypothesis is that no one knows just what it means or how to measure it" (388).

14. For a review of estimates and differing methodologies, see M. Ishaq Nadiri, "Innovations and Technological Spillovers" (working paper no. 4323, National Bureau of Economic Research, Cambridge, Mass., August 1993).

Chapter Two

1. Charles P. Kindleberger, *Marshall Plan Days* (Boston: Allen & Unwin, 1987), 100.

2. John Gerard Ruggie, "International Regimes, Transactions, and Change: Embedded Liberalism in the Postwar Economic Order," *International Organization* 36, no. 2 (Spring 1982): 379–415. This analysis also includes a review of the hegemonic literature. The term "consensual hegemony" is from Charles Maier, "The Politics of Productivity: Foundations of American International Economic Policy after World War I," in *Between Power and Plenty: Foreign Economic Policies of Advanced Industrial States,* ed. Peter J. Katzenstein (Madison: University of Wisconsin Press, 1977), 630–31.

3. For a full account of the formation of the institution established to administer the Marshall Plan, see Royal Institute of International Affairs, "The Organization for European Economic Cooperation (OEEC)" (memorandum, Chatham House, London, November 1958), 2.

4. Kindleberger, *Marshall Plan Days,* 99.

5. Richard Strout, *New Republic,* May 5, 1947, quoted in J. Bradford de Long and Barry Eichengreen, "The Marshall Plan: History's Most Successful Structural Adjustment Program" (working paper no. 91–184, Institute of Business

and Economic Research, University of California at Berkeley, November 1991), 10. But the alliance did not prevent serious debates over policy. As Charles Maier has argued, American policy was ambivalent. Treasury wanted tough stabilization measures and limited government. Many of the Marshall Plan administrators were more Keynesian in orientation. See Charles S. Maier, *In Search of Stability* (Cambridge: Cambridge University Press, 1987), 138–39.

6. J. J. Servan-Schreiber, *The American Challenge* (New York: Athenium, 1968), 8.

7. De Long and Eichengreen, "Marshall Plan," 37.

8. The role of American officials and union leaders in encouraging non-Communist unions is described in Maier, *In Search of Stability*, 142–44. See also Robert W. Cox, "Labour and Hegemony," *International Organisation* 31, no. 3 (Summer 1977). He documents in detail the role of the AFL and the CIA in their efforts to purge European labor organizations of communist sympathizers (394–99).

9. Barry Eichengreen, *Reconstructing Europe's Trade and Payments: The European Payments Union* (Manchester: Manchester University Press, 1993), 89–92. As the author also points out, the terms-of-trade gains were significant in moderating pressures for lowering real wages, thus contributing to modest wage demands (86).

10. For a full review of the history of the OECD stance on macroeconomic policy, see Sylvia Ostry, "From Fine-Tuning to Framework-Setting in Macro-Economic Management," in *Interdependence and Co-Operation in Tomorrow's World: A Symposium Marking the Twenty-Fifth Anniversary of the OECD* (Paris: OECD, 1987), 70–88.

11. Ostry, "From Fine-Tuning to Framework-Setting," 73. Angus Maddison also stresses this view and argues that

"the absence of downside risks in terms of output, and the buoyancy that continuous price increases gave to profits, nurtured a secular investment boom." *Phases of Capitalist Development* (Oxford: Oxford University Press, 1982), 130.

12. Angus Maddison, *The World Economy in the 20th Century* (Paris: Development Centre Studies, OECD, 1989), 69.

13. This account is taken from James M. Silberman, "The History of the Technical Assistance Program of the Marshall Plan and Successor Agencies, 1948–1961" (mimeograph, Global Technology Management for World Bank, Washington, D.C., November 1992), and James M. Silberman and Charles Weiss, Jr., "Restructuring for Productivity" (Industry Series working paper no. 64, World Bank Industry and Energy Department, Washington, D.C., November 1992).

14. Silberman, "Technical Assistance Program," 10–14.

15. Silberman and Weiss, "Restructuring for Productivity," viii.

16. Raymond Aron, *The Imperial Republic: The United States and the World, 1945–1973* (Englewood Cliffs, N.J.: Prentice-Hall, 1974), 191.

17. Silberman, "Technical Assistance Program," 63.

18. J. J. Servan-Schreiber, *The American Challenge* (New York: Athenium, 1968), 23.

19. Ibid.

20. Eichengreen, *Reconstructing Europe's Trade and Payments,* 115–16. But private firms remained cautious because of memories of the 1930s.

21. Sherman Gee, *Technology Transfer, Innovation, and International Competitiveness* (New York: Wiley, 1981), 71.

22. John Dunning, "United States Foreign Investment

and the Technological Gap," in *North American and Western European Economic Policies,* ed. Charles Kindleberger and Andrew Shonfield (London: Macmillan, 1971), 398–403.

23. Gee, *Technology Transfer,* 42–43.

24. Aron, *Imperial Republic,* 217–18.

25. Shigeto Tsuru, *Japan's Capitalism: Creative Defeat and Beyond* (Cambridge: Cambridge University Press, 1993), 11.

26. Ibid.

27. Jon Halliday, *A Political History of Japanese Capitalism* (New York: Pantheon, 1975), 176.

28. Ibid., 169.

29. Nazli Choucri, Robert C. North, Susumu Yamakage, *The Challenge of Japan before World War II and After* (London: Routledge, 1992), 228.

30. Ibid.

31. G. C. Allen, *A Short Economic History of Modern Japan* (London: Macmillan, 1981), 215.

32. Sakae Tsunoyama, *A Concise Economic History of Modern Japan* (Bombay: Vora, 1965), 105–6.

33. Ibid.

34. Halliday, *Political History,* 194.

35. Ibid., 168.

36. Ibid., 163.

37. Jon Choy, "Uncertain Impact of Administrative Reform Law," *Japan Economic Institute Report,* no. 40B, (Oct. 21, 1994): 3–6.

38. Tsuru, *Japan's Capitalism,* 56.

39. Ibid.

40. Michu Morishima, *Why Has Japan "Succeeded"?* (Cambridge: Cambridge University Press, 1982), 164.

41. Tsuru, *Japan's Capitalism,* 57–59.

42. Choucri et al., *Challenge of Japan*, 228.

43. Ibid.

44. A particularly interesting example of rapid reconversion was the Toyota Cotton Company. Spurred by Korean War demand, production surged. When a Japanese parliamentary delegation received an extremely hostile reception on a visit to Manchester, Toyota converted to car production at the government's instruction. See Andrew Graham with Jay Nish, "Japan" in *Government and Economies in the Postwar World*, ed. Anthony Seldon (London: Routledge, 1990), 258.

45. A. E. Safarian, *Multinational Enterprise and Public Policy: A Study of the Industrial Countries* (Aldershot, U.K.: E. Elgar, 1993), 272–76.

46. For a comprehensive account of Japan's foreign investment policy, see Safarian, *Multinational Enterprise*, 236–82. For an analysis of the broader strategy of financial policy see Kent E. Calder, *Strategic Capitalism* (Princeton: Princeton University Press, 1993).

47. Safarian, *Multinational Enterprise*, 244. An exception to these entry requirements were the so-called yen-based companies, wholly owned subsidiaries allowed in from 1956 to 1963, but which did not enjoy an unconditional guarantee of repatriation of profits and principal.

48. Boston Consulting Group K. K., "Trade between Japan and the United States: The Setting, the Current U.S. Position, and U.S. Prospects" (Boston Consulting Group K. K., 3–6, Ohtemachi 2-chome, Chiyoda-ku, Tokyo, April 1978, mimeograph), 26.

49. Ibid., 27. Also at that time, U.S. antitrust policy forced high-tech companies to make patents available at a reasonable price, providing a windfall gain from American

R&D. This policy was no longer in play during the 1980s, when patent protection became a highly contentious trade issue.

50. Calder, *Strategic Capitalism,* 42–44.

51. Ibid.

52. Morishima, *Why Has Japan "Succeeded"?* 162.

53. This account of the productivity movement is taken from *Seisansei Undou Sanju Nen Shi* (Thirty Years of the Productivity Movement) (Japan Productivity Centre, 3–1–1 Shibuya, Shibuyaku, Tokyo, March 1985).

54. Japan Productivity Centre, *The Productivity Movement in Japan* (Tokyo: Japan Productivity Centre, May 1993), 4–5.

Chapter Three

1. John A. C. Conybeare, *Trade Wars: The Theory and Practice of International Commercial Rivalry* (New York: Columbia University Press, 1987), 251. He argues that the U.S. role is better described as "hegemonic predation."

2. The "macromyopia," which permits a "see no evil" approach to microconsequences persists today. For example, in many of the articles and essays written on the fiftieth anniversary of Bretton Woods, fulsome praise has been accorded Dodge. The great postwar "rescue" in Japan was "engineered" by the 1949 Dodge Plan and the "virtual elimination of inflation" was followed by twenty years of "stable—exchange rates." Ronald McKinnon, "Recapturing a lost spirit," *Financial Times,* June 21, 1994, 16. The two solitudes, treasuries and trade ministries, prevent meaningful coordination in national capitals and international institutions.

3. Jay Culbert, "War-time Anglo-American Talks and the Making of the GATT," *World Economy* 10, no. 4 (December 1987): 387.

4. Karin Kock, *International Trade and Policy and the GATT, 1947–1967* (Stockholm: Almquist & Wiksell, 1969), 9.

5. Jacob Viner, "Conflicts of Principle in Drafting a Trade Charter," *Foreign Affairs* 25, no. 4 (July 1947): 621–22.

6. Viner, "Conflicts," 628.

7. Kock, *International Trade and Policy*, 58.

8. Ibid., 60.

9. William Diebold, Jr., "The End of the I.T.O.," *Essays in International Finance* no. 16 (Princeton: Department of Economic and Social Institutions, Princeton University, 1952), 14.

10. Ibid., 20–21.

11. Ibid., 22.

12. Because GATT was expected to be replaced by the ITO, and for various other legal reasons, the countries that signed it adopted a Protocol of Provisional Application (PPA). This legal device in effect ensured that the tariff negotiations would be implemented but did not require that other substantive obligations be ratified by domestic legislation. The PPA called for implementation of Part II (which includes a wide range of obligations such as quotas, subsidies, antidumping duties, etc.) "to the fullest extent not inconsistent with existing legislation." For a comprehensive account of these aspects of the GATT, see John H. Jackson, *The World Trading System: Law and Policy of International Economic Relations* (Cambridge: MIT Press, 1989), chap. 2, pp. 27–58.

13. David Henderson, *1992: The External Dimension* (New York and London: Group of Thirty, 1989), 14.

14. Gerald Curzon, "Crisis in the International Trading System," *In Search of a New World Economic Order* (London: Croom Helm, 1947), 39.

15. For a different view, but the same conclusion, see Patrick Low, *Trading Free: The GATT and U.S. Trade Policy* (New York: Twentieth Century Fund, 1993), 42–50. Low places primary emphasis on the problems arising from the legal status of GATT under U.S. law. Never approved by Congress as a treaty, this legal arrangement weakened the power of the executive (to whom Congress can delegate trade policy under the Constitution) and also weakened the impact of international negotiations in constraining noncompliance with agreed rules.

16. For a detailed account of the August 15 decision-making process and the subsequent negotiations, see Paul A. Volcker and Toyoo Gyohten, *Changing Fortunes: The World's Money and the Threat to American Leadership* (New York: Times Books, 1992).

17. *Positive Adjustment Policies: Managing Structural Change* (Paris: OECD, 1983).

18. Ibid., 7–8.

19. Sylvia Ostry, "Interdependence: Vulnerability and Opportunity" (Per Jacobsson Lecture, George Washington University, Sept. 27, 1987), 4–5.

20. See Marina V. N. Whitman, "Flexible Markets, Flexible Firms," *American Enterprise* 5, no. 3 (May/June 1994): 27–37.

21. See, for example, Stephen D. Krasner, "The Tokyo Round: Particularistic Interests and Prospects for Stability in the Global Trading System," *International Studies Quarterly* 23, no. 4 (December 1979): 502–7, and Charles Lipson, "The Transformation of Trade: The Sources and Effects of

Regime Change," in *International Regimes*, ed. Stephen D. Krasner (Ithaca: Cornell University Press, 1983), 258–62.

22. For review of studies on this point see Lipson, "Transformation of Trade," 261–62.

23. OECD, *Costs and Benefits of Protection* (Paris: OECD, 1985), 38–39. See also Low, *Trading Free*, 75–76.

24. Gary Clyde Hufbauer and Joanna Shelton Erb, *Subsidies in International Trade* (Washington, D.C.: Institute for International Economics, 1984), 2.

25. O. Hirschman, *Exit, Voice and Loyalty* (Cambridge: Harvard University Press, 1971. This comparison is amplified in Alexis Jacquemin and David Wright, "Corporate Strategies and European Challenges Post–1992," *Journal of Common Market Studies* 31, no. 4 (December 1993): 535–36 and in Sylvia Ostry and Val Koromzay, "The United States and Europe: Coping with Change," *OECD Observer*, May 1992, 9–13.

26. Gilbert K. Winham, *International Trade and the Tokyo Round Negotiation* (Princeton: Princeton University Press, 1986), 60.

27. C. Fred Bergsten, *Toward a New International Economic Order: Selected Papers of C. Fred Bergsten, 1972–1974* (Lexington, Mass.: Lexington Books, 1975), 98–99.

28. This preference reflected the complex internal political dynamics of decision-making in the EU. See Gardner Patterson, "European Community as Systemic Threat," in *Trade Policy in the 1980's*, ed. William R. Cline (Washington, D.C.: Institute for International Economics, 1983), pp. 223–42, and Sylvia Ostry, *Governments and Corporations in a Shrinking World* (New York: Council on Foreign Relations, 1990), 30–350.

29. Of the eleven international agreements produced by

the Tokyo Round, only two (the tariff protocols and the framework agreements) were incorporated into GATT. The remaining nine, which covered the codes on procurement, standards, trade remedies, and so forth were all separate treaties. This decision reflected a desire on the part of the major trading powers to avoid the application of the consensus rule, which would have allowed any country to veto or amend the codes. For a full description of the meaning of conditional MFN in the codes, see Winham, *International Trade*, 354–56.

30. Rodney de C. Grey, "The General Agreement after the Tokyo Round," in *Non-Tariff Barriers After the Tokyo Round*, ed. John Quinn and Philip Slayton (Montreal: Institute for Research on Public Policy, 1982), 8.

31. Ibid., 11.

32. Senator John Danforth, cited in William R. Cline, *"Reciprocity": A New Approach to World Trade Policy?* (Washington, D.C.: Institute for International Economics, 1982), 8–9.

Chapter Four

1. See, for example, Lipson, "Transformation of Trade." See also Gilbert R. Winham, *International Trade and the Tokyo Round Negotiations* (Princeton: Princeton University Press, 1986), 50–54. Winham argues that growing intra-industry and intrafirm trade would create "a bias toward trade liberalism" (54).

2. Lipson, "Transformation of Trade," 269.

3. Robert O. Keohane, *After Hegemony: Cooperation and Discord in the World Political Economy* (Princeton: Princeton University Press, 1984), 189.

4. Grey, "General Agreement," 8, 17.

5. See, for quantitative analysis, J. Michael Finger and Tracy Murray, "Policing Unfair Imports: The United States Example," *Journal of World Trade* 24, no. 4 (August 1990): 39–54.

6. Ibid., 45.

7. Sylvia Ostry, *Governments and Corporations in a Shrinking World* (New York: Council on Foreign Relations, 1990), 39–46.

8. Gary N. Horlick, "The United States Antidumping System," in *Antidumping Law and Practice: A Comparative Study,* ed. John H. Jackson and Edwin A. Vermulst (Ann Arbor: University of Michigan Press, 1989), 102.

9. Geza Feketekuty, "U.S. Policy on 301 and Super 301," in *Aggressive Unilateralism: America's 301 Trade Policy and the World Trading System,* ed. Jagdish Bhagwati and Hugh T. Patrick (Ann Arbor: University of Michigan Press, 1990), 92.

10. Ostry, *Governments and Corporations,* 28.

11. For a full historical account of the evolution of 301, see Robert E. Hudec, "Thinking about the New Section 301: Beyond Good and Evil," in *Aggressive Unilateralism,* ed. Bhagwati and Patrick, 113–59. The president had the authority under the 1974 act to initiate action without receiving a private complaint but had not used it before. A 1984 amendment to 301 expanded the scope of "unreasonable" practices—that is, those that do not clearly violate established GATT rules—and included the right of self-initiation for the United States Trade Representative (USTR) in an effort to further prod the administration to aggressive use.

12. For a fuller exposition of the two sides of increasing interdependence, see Sylvia Ostry, "The World Economy: Marking Time," *Foreign Affairs* 62, no. 3 (February 1984),

and "Interdependence: Vulnerability and Opportunity" (Per Jacobsson Lecture, George Washington University, Sept. 27, 1987).

13. The linkage of macropolicy coordination and trade policy in the context of summitry is detailed in Michael Artis and Sylvia Ostry, "International Economic Policy Coordination" (Chatham House Papers 30, Royal Institute of International Affairs, London, 1986), 55–73.

14. I. M. Destler, *American Trade Politics: System Under Stress* (Washington, D.C.: Institute for International Economics and Twentieth Century Fund, 1986), 3. Cited in Ostry, *Corporations and Governments*, 20.

15. *Chairmen's Report on a New Round of Multilateral Trade Negotiations*, Submitted to the United States Trade Representative, May 15, 1985, Advisory Committee for Trade Negotiations, et al., p. 3.

16. *Ibid.*, p. 5. Cited in Ostry, *Governments and Corporations*, 28.

17. *Annual Report of the President of the United States on the Trade Agreements Program 1984–85* (Washington, D.C.: GPO, 1986), Appendix B, pp. 114–15, cited in Ostry, *Governments and Corporations*, 28.

18. Hudec, "Thinking about the New Section 301," 125–31. The Export Enhancement Program (EEP) of the 1985 U.S. Farm Act, which launched the transatlantic subsidy was in grain products, but technically violated the weak and ambiguous GATT Subsidy Code, is another example of "justified disobedience" to bring the EU to the negotiating table on agriculture.

19. Ostry, *Governments and Corporations*, 21–25.

20. On American declinism, see, for example, Robert Gilpin, *The Political Economy of International Relations* (Princeton: Princeton University Press, 1987); Paul M. Ken-

nedy, *The Rise and Fall of the Great Powers: Economic Change and Military Conflict from 1500 to 2000* (New York: Random House, 1987); David P. Calleo, *Beyond American Hegemony: The Future of the Western Alliance* (New York: Basic Books, 1987), and on the uniqueness of Japan, Chalmers Johnson, *MITI and the Japanese Miracle: The Growth of Industrial Policy, 1925–75* (Stanford, Calif.: Stanford University Press, 1982); Clyde V. Prestowitz, Jr., *Trading Places: How We Allowed Japan to Take the Lead* (New York: Basic Books, 1988); Stephen D. Cohen, *Uneasy Partnership: Competition and Conflict in U.S.-Japanese Trade Relations* (Cambridge, Mass.: Ballinger, 1985).

21. Ostry and Nelson, *Technonationalism and Technoglobalism*, pp. 23–27.

22. For a review of the many studies on the current account developments in the 1980s, see Stephen S. Golub, "The United States–Japan Current Account Imbalance: A Review" (paper on policy analysis and assessment, International Monetary Fund, Washington, D.C., March 1994). For data on U.S. net savings since the 1950s, see Masaru Yoshitomi, "Main Issues of Macroeconomic Coordination: The Peso, Dollar and Yen Problems" in *The Halifax G-7 Summit: Issues on the Table*, ed. Sylvia Ostry and Gilbert R. Winham (Halifax, N.S.: Centre for Foreign Policy Studies, Dalhousie University, 1995), 45.

23. There has been an unresolved and continuing debate among economists about Japanese import behavior. See, for example, Robert Z. Lawrence, "Imports in Japan: Closed Markets?" and "Efficient for Exclusionist? The Import Behavior of Japanese Corporate Groups," *Brookings Papers on Economic Activity* 2 (1987): 517–54, and 1 (1991): 311–41, and Gary R. Saxonhouse, "What Does Japanese Trade Structure Tell Us about Japanese Trade Policy?" *Jour-*

nal of Economic Perspectives 7, no. 3 (Summer 1993): 21–43, and references cited therein.

24. Thomas O. Bayard and Kimberly Ann Elliott, *Reciprocity and Retaliation in U.S. Trade Policy, Institute for International Economies* (Washington, D.C.: Institute for International Economies, 1994), 37.

25. See, for example, ibid., the most recent and comprehensive review.

26. Conybeare, *Trade Wars*, 261.

27. For a fuller exposition, see Kenneth A. Oye, *Economic Discrimination and Political Exchange: World Political Economy in the 1930s and 1980s* (Princeton, N.J.: Princeton University Press, 1992).

28. For a more comprehensive analysis, see Ostry and Nelson, *Techno-Nationalism and Techno-Globalism.*

29. This issue of the "law of unintended consequences" of innovation policies is explored at length in ibid., especially chaps. 2 and 4.

30. See Stephen Woolcock, *Trading Partners or Trading Blows? Market Access Issues in EC-US Relations.* (New York: Royal Institute of International Affairs and Council on Foreign Relations, 1992), 85–91.

31. For further discussion of the use of Article 23:1(b), see Sylvia Ostry, "New Dimensions of Market Access: Overview from a Trade Policy Perspective," *OECD Roundtable on the New Dimensions of Market Access in a Globalizing World Economy* (Paris: OECD, 1995). Indeed, at Punta del Este, in the final hours of negotiating the declaration to launch the Uruguay Round, a long and contentious debate ensued over an EU proposal to add a reference to "balance of benefits," or BOB as it came to be called. A Japanese journalist explained to the author that BOB was known in the Japanese press corps as "bash the oriental bastards." (The reference

was not added to the Punta Declaration.) For an account of the Second Banking Directive of the EU, see Bayard and Elliott, *Reciprocity and Retaliation*, 286–94. The acting U.S. treasury secretary, Peter McPherson, objected to the reciprocity provisions by asserting that "the danger of this approach is that legitimate differences in national regulatory regimes could be used to justify discrimination against foreign firms" (290).

32. International Trade Reporter, *Current Reports*, Mar. 18, 1992, 494–95.

33. Ostry and Nelson, *Technonationalism and Technoglobalism*.

34. See "Joint Statement on the U.S.-Japan Framework for a New Economic Partnership, July 10, 1993," *Japan Economic Institute*, no. 26B (July 16, 1993), 7–9.

35. "U.S. Tables 'Comprehensive' Proposal for Deregulations in Japan," *Inside U.S. Trade*, special report, Nov. 18, 1994, pp. S-2, S-3. The basic principles were: A. Broad and Continuous Review; B. Freedom from Regulation in Principle, with Regulation as the Exception; C. Enhanced Transparency and Accountability; D. Prohibition of Informal Delegation of Government Authority; E. Non-burdensome Local Regulation; F. Inclusion of Sunset Provision; G. Promotion of Market Mechanism. The "chapeau" of the four elements of the Deregulation Process states: "The five-year action plan should be developed and implemented based on the recognition that deregulation needs to be an ongoing process responsive to the ever-changing marketplace. The United States Government believes that the Government of Japan should develop the five-year action plan with full participation by interested private parties, both domestic and foreign. The United States Government urges the Government of Japan not to deem the drafting of the five-year ac-

tion plan in March 1995 as the completion of the deregulation process itself. Instead, the Government of Japan should continuously review the implementation of, and where appropriate annually revise on the basis of public comments and other information, the five-year action plan. In this connection, the United States Government urges the Government of Japan to consider the following specific recommendations." A request by the EU proposed a week earlier includes mainly sector-specific suggestions to increase transparency and the greater use of international standards and conformity testing. See *Inside U.S. Trade*, Nov. 11, 1994, 8–12.

36. Office of Technology Assessment, Congress of the United States, *Multinationals and the U.S. Technology Base: Summary of the Multinationals Final Report* (Washington, D.C.: Office of Technology Assessment, September 1994), 28–30.

Chapter Five

1. World Bank, *The East Asian Miracle*, Policy Research Report (New York: Oxford University Press, 1993).

2. Dollar and Wolff, *Competitiveness*, chap. 8, pp. 152–70. See also Dani Rodrik, "Getting Interventions Right: How South Korea and Taiwan Grew Rich" (working paper no. 4964, National Bureau of Economic Research, Washington, D.C., December 1994), and Alwyn Young, "The Tyranny of Numbers: Confronting the Statistical Realities of the East Asian Growth Experience" (working paper no. 4680, National Bureau of Economic Research, Washington, D.C., March 1994) and Paul Krugman, "The Myth of Asia's Miracle," *Foreign Affairs* 73, no. 6 (November/December 1994): 62–78. Rodrik, Young, and others dispute the growth analy-

sis of the World Bank. But there is no dispute that the role of TFP was not a predominant force for rapid growth in East Asia over the past two decades. The World Bank estimates that between 60 and 90 percent of the East Asian output growth derives from investment in physical and human capital (ibid., 58).

3. See Maddison, "Growth and Slowdown," table 19, p. 678. For comparison of structural change in the NIEs and other countries, see Alwyn Young, "A Tale of Two Cities: Factor Accumulation and Technical Change in Hong Kong and Singapore," in *NBER Macroeconomics Annual, 1992* (Cambridge, Mass.: NBER, 1993), 29.

4. See Stephen Marglin and Juliet Schor, *The Golden Age of Capitalism: Reinterpreting the Postwar Experience* (Oxford: Clarendon, 1990), 135, 212, 243. In Japan real-wage growth also accelerated in the first half of the 1970s but significantly moderated after the first oil shock. Ibid., 287.

5. This summit was preceded by other actions. The European Commission as well as individual member governments are promoting a "New Asia Strategy" designed to catch up with the United States and Japan. See Commission of the European Communities, "Towards a New Asia Strategy" (mimeograph, Brussels, Commission of the European Communities, July 27, 1994). A new "global policy" for China was announced in July 1995 (see *International Trade Reporter,* July 12, 1995, p. 1184).

6. Some of the inflow into China might be "round tripping" whereby domestic Chinese investors channel their transaction through foreign intermediaries to benefit from preferential treatment. See Peter Petri, "Corporate Links and Direct Foreign Investment in Asia and the Pacific" (mimeograph, PAFTAD, Hong Kong, June 1–3, 1994), 18, and Department of Foreign Affairs and Trade, Australia,

Overseas Chinese Business Networks in Asia (Canberra: AGPS, 1995), esp. 197–98.

7. See, for example, Mark Z. Taylor, "Dominance through Technology: Is Japan Creating a Yen Bloc in Southeast Asia?" *Foreign Affairs* 74, no. 6 (November–December 1995): 14–20. See also a summary of the concerns by B. Anne Craib, "Japan and the United States in Southeast Asia in the 1990s," *J.E.I. Report*, no. 32A, Washington, D.C., Aug. 19, 1994. For an analysis of the developments in the region, see Masaru Yoshitomi, "Building a New United States–Pacific Area Economic Relationship for the Post Uruguay Round Era," in *Economic Cooperation and Challenges in the Pacific*, Joint U.S.-Korea Academic Studies, vol. 5 (Berkeley: Korean Economic Institute of America, 1995), 15–46. The trade issue—that is, a pattern of triangular trade is developing that involves limited imports to Japan, increasing exports of technology intensive goods from Japan, and exports of finished goods to the United States and Europe—is explored and documented in Stephen S. Cohen and Paolo Guerrieri, "The Variable Geometry of Asian Trade" (mimeograph, Berkeley Roundtable on the International Economy, University of California, Berkeley, 1994.

8. JETRO, *White Paper on Foreign Direct Investment, 1994* (Tokyo: Japan External Trade Organization, March 1994), 19. Interviews of all the major Japanese electronic firms in November 1993 undertaken by the author in Tokyo did, however, suggest that plans to expand in East Asia were under way but not yet completed. Sylvia Ostry and Farid Harianto, "The Changing Pattern of Japanese Investment in the Electronics Industry in East Asia, 1958–1993" in *Transnational Corporations* (Geneva: UNCTAD, Division on Transnational Corporations and Investment, June 1995).

9. For a review of productivity by sector, see A. Steven

Englander and Andrew Gurney, "Medium-Term Determinants of OECD Productivity," *OECD Economic Studies*, no. 22 (Spring 1994): 49–129.

10. K. Akamatsu, "A Historical Pattern of Economic Growth in Developing Countries," *Developing Economies*, no. 1 (March–April 1962): 3–25. Updated in E. K. Y. Chen, "The future direction of industrial development in the Asian NIE's," in *Strategies for Industrial Development*, ed. J. W. Suh (Seoul: Korea Development Institute, 1989). The "flying geese" analysis is allied to that of the "product cycle," which was explicated in R. Vernon, "International Investment and International Trade in the Product Cycle," *Quarterly Journal of Economics* 80, no. 2 (1966): 190–207. For a comprehensive critique of the flying geese model, see Mitchell Bernard and John Ravenhill, "Beyond Product Cycles and Flying Geese: Regionalization, Hierarchy and Industrialization of East Asia," *World Politics* 47, no. 2 (January 1995): 171–209.

11. For a number of examples of such changes, see Fumio Kodama and Takao Kiba, *Emerging Trajectory of International Technology Transfer* (Stanford: Asia Pacific Research Center, Stanford University, June 1994), and Yun Yongwook and Denis Fred Simon, "Technological Change and its Impact on the Foreign Investment Behaviour of Firms in Asia and Pacific: The Evolving Role of Strategic Posture of Japanese Corporations" (mimeograph, PAFTAD Conference, Hong Kong, June 1–3, 1994).

12. See Shigeki Tejima and Hiroyuki Nakashima, "The Outlook of Japanese Foreign Direct Investment in the 1990's based on the EXIM Japan 1994 Survey," *EXIM Review* 15, no. 1 (1995): 1–108, and JETRO, *White Paper on International Trade, 1995: Survey on the Effects of Yen Appreciation, May 1995* (Tokyo: Japan External Trade Organization, 1996), 43–52.

13. JETRO, *White Paper on International Trade*, 46–47, 51.

14. Tejima and Makashima, "Outlook," 94. Similar results with respect to East Asian "localization" are shown in a survey by the Nikkei Research Institute of Industry and Market as reported in *Nikkei Weekly*, March 25, 1996, p. 23.

15. Asia Productivity Programmes, 1994–1998, Asia Productivity Organization, Tokyo, July 1993, and Ostry and Harianto, "Changing Pattern," for details on Japanese training and technology upgrading initiatives financed by development aid funds.

16. John P. Stern, "Japan: The Philosophy of Government Support for Information Technology" (mimeograph, Symposium on International Access to National Technology Development Programs, National Academy, Washington, D.C., Jan. 19, 1995), 6.

17. "Asian Production More than Just Flight from Yen," *Nikkei Weekly*, Aug. 15, 1994, p. 2.

18. B. Anne Craib, "Tokyo Proposes Using APEC as Technology Transfer Platform," *J.E.I. Report*, no. 36B (Oct. 1, 1993): 5–6, and "Asian Companies Setting Up Shop in Japan," *Nikkei Weekly*, Oct. 16, 1995, p. 1.

19. Dennis J. Encarnation, "Bringing East Asia into the U.S.-Japan Rivalry: The Regional Evolution of American and Japanese Multinationals," in *Japanese Investment in Asia*, ed. Eileen M. Doherty (San Francisco: Asia Foundation and BRIE, 1994), 60–61. Unfortunately very little information exists about these networks, indeed far less than is the case for Japan.

20. This point is emphasized by Encarnation, "Bringing East Asia," and also in his *Rivals Beyond Trade: America Versus Japan in Global Competition* (Ithaca: Cornell University Press, 1992), 212–18.

21. See JETRO, *White Paper on International Trade*, 18–19.

22. Examples are TI Taiwan and Acer; AT&T and Lucky Goldstar. Some of these alliances include government participation in Singapore and also Japanese MNEs; see James C. Abegglen, *Sea Change: Pacific Asia as the New World Industrial Center* (New York: Free Press, 1994), 42.

23. See for analysis of Japan's concerns, *J.E.I. Report* on telecommunications (no. 45A, Dec. 10, 1993); personal computers (no. 6A, Feb. 11, 1994), computer software (no. 13A, Apr. 1, 1994). And for some examples of new alliances, see J.E.I., no. 13A, Apr. 1, 1994, 8–9); "Microsoft in Video Game Link with Sega," *Financial Times*, Mar. 8, 1994, p. 1; "Microsoft Joins Sony in Deal," *Wall Street Journal*, Jan. 24, 1995, p. C2; and "Microsoft Plans Japanese Games Joint Venture," *Financial Times*, June 16, 1995, p. 18.

24. *Overseas Chinese Business Networks in Asia* (Canberra: AGPS, 1995), 2. See also Louis Kraar, "The Overseas Chinese: Lessons from the World's Most Dynamic Capitalists," *Fortune*, Oct. 31, 1994, pp. 91–114.

25. Paul S. P. Hsu, "Taiwan–Hong Kong–China: The Chinese Productivity Triangle" (paper presented to International Conference on the Asian Regional Economy: Growing Linkages, Global Implications, National Taiwan University, Taipei, May 7–9, 1992), 5.

26. Kraar, "Overseas Chinese," 104.

27. *Overseas Chinese Business Networks*, 245–47.

28. Ibid., 240; and Louis Kraar, "Need a Friend in Asia? Try the Singapore Connection," *Fortune*, Mar. 4, 1996, pp. 171–80.

29. Ryuji Sato, "China High-Tech Spree Pays Dividends," *Nikkei Weekly*, Nov. 7, 1994, p. 24.

30. Masaru Yoshitomi, "The Comparative Advantage of

China's Manufacturing in the 21st Century" (mimeograph, Forum for the Future Conference on China in the 21st Century, OECD, Paris, January 1996).

31. For Malaysia, see *International Trade Reporter*, Washington, D.C., Jan. 31, 1996, pp. 170–71. For Korea and Taiwan, see Richard G. Lipsey and Russel M. Wills, "Science and Technology Policies in Asia Pacific Countries: Challenges and Opportunities for Canada" (mimeograph, Industry Canada, Ottawa, December 1995).

32. Bernard and Ravenhill, "Beyond Product Cycles," 176–77.

33. See, for example, the discussions of national innovation systems in Korea and Taiwan in Richard R. Nelson, ed., *National Innovation Systems* (New York: Oxford University Press, 1993), chaps. 11 (by Linsu Kim) and 12 (by Chi-Ming Hou and San Gee).

34. Samuel P. Huntington, "The Clash of Civilization?" *Foreign Affairs* 72, no. 3 (Summer 1993): 22–49.

Chapter Six

1. For a review of estimates of computable general equilibrium models of the impact of the Uruguay Round agreements on income and trade, see Jeffrey J. Schott, *The Uruguay Round* (Washington, D.C.: Institute for International Economics, 1994), table 2, p. 17; and Ernest H. Preeg, *Traders in a Brave New World: The Uruguay Round and the Future of the International Trading System* (Chicago: University of Chicago Press, 1995), 201–7.

2. Ostry and Nelson, *Technonationalism and Technoglobalism*, 71–72.

3. Brian Hindley, "Two Cheers for the Uruguay Round,"

Trade Policy Review, Centre for Policy Studies, London, September 1994, p. 27.

4. Ostry and Nelson, *Technonationalism and Technoglobalism,* 83–87. See also Sylvia Ostry, *Technology Issues in the International Trading System* (Paris: OECD Trade Committee, 1995).

5. Ostry and Nelson, *Technonationalism and Technoglobalism;* Ostry, *Technology Issues.*

6. GATT articles include only one reference to IPRs. In Article XX(d) it is recognized that the nondiscriminatory enforcement of IPRs to protect domestic IP would not ordinarily be considered a proscribed nontariff barrier to trade.

7. Geza Feketekuty, "General Agreement on Trade in Services" (mimeograph, Seminar on the Uruguay Round Agreements from an Asia-Pacific Perspective, Gaston Sigur Center for East Asian Studies, George Washington University, Aug. 1–3, 1994), 4.

8. For a full account of the financial services negotiations, see Bureau of National Affairs, *International Trade Reporter,* July 19 and 26 and Aug. 2, 1995. For a defense of the American position, see Jeffrey Shafer and Jeffrey Lang, *Financial Times,* July 25, 1995, p. 11.

9. Actually the GATS approach is a hybrid. A positive list may be modified by a negative list of restrictions that apply to each of the four modes of entry.

10. United States International Trade Commission, *Foreign Protection of Intellectual Property Rights and the Effect on U.S. Industry and Trade,* Publication 2065 (Washington, D.C.: USITC, February 1988).

11. Keith Maskus, "Uruguay Round Agreement on Intellectual Property Rights" (mimeograph, Seminar on the Uruguay Round Agreements from an Asia-Pacific Perspec-

tive, Gaston Sigur Centre for East Asian Studies, George Washington University, Aug. 1–3, 1994), 10.

12. The only exceptions that still allow "conditional MFN" are the civil aircraft agreement, the government procurement agreement, and the meat and dairy arrangements, which apply only to their signatories.

13. The issue of the WTO and U.S. sovereignty was first raised by Newt Gingrich, then the House Republican whip, in an Apr. 24, 1994, interview broadcast on NBC's *Meet the Press*. The link with the UN was made explicit. Mr. Gingrich cited the United Nations' failure to resolve the war in Bosnia as an example: "If you look at the mess in Bosnia and the U.N.'s incompetence, this World Trade Organization will have 117 member nations with one vote each. So in effect, we could be outvoted by Antigua, by Botswana or by Venezuela." A paper prepared for Duncan Hunter, then chairman of the Republican Research Committee, states that the WTO would act as an "economic United Nations" and that two-thirds of (prospective) WTO member states voted against the United States in the UN General Assembly on at least half of the votes taken during the past year. *Inside U.S. Trade*, special report of the Republican Research Committee (Apr. 29, 1994), S1–S3.

14. *Inside U.S. Trade.*

15. Robert L. Paarlberg, *Leadership Abroad Begins at Home: U.S. Foreign Economic Policy after the Cold War* (Washington, D.C.: Brookings Institution, 1995), 23–26.

16. Ibid., 25.

17. For details see Schott, *Uruguay Round*, 138–39.

18. For a full analysis of this and other aspects of this dispute settlement procedure, see John Jackson, "Dispute Settlement Procedures," *The New World Trading System:*

Readings (Paris: OECD, 1994), 117–24; and Robert E. Hudec, "Strengthening of the Dispute-settlement Procedures" (mimeograph, Seminar on the Uruguay Round Agreements from an Asia-Pacific Perspective, Gaston Sigur Centre for East Asian Studies, George Washington University, Aug. 1–3, 1994).

19. Section 301(a), the mandatory provision, should, however, be amended or clarified to provide more discretion to the president (Jackson, "Dispute Settlement Procedures," 120–21).

20. Hudec, "Strengthening of the Dispute-settlement Procedures," 12–13.

21. "U.S. Official Admits Constraints on Section 301 Retaliation under WTO," *Inside U.S. Trade,* Jan. 20, 1995, pp. 10–11.

22. Hudec, "Strengthening of the Dispute-settlement Procedures," 16.

Chapter Seven

1. See Renato Ruggiero, "The Road Ahead: International Trade Policy in the Era of the WTO" (Fourth Annual Sylvia Ostry Lecture, May 28, 1996, Geneva, World Trade Organization, May 29, 1996).

2. See Ostry, "New Dimensions," 25–33.

3. Ostry and Nelson, *Technonationalism and Technoglobalism,* 95–110. See also F. M. Scherer, *Competition Policies for an Integrated World Economy* (Washington, D.C.: Brookings Institution, 1994), 70–76.

4. The relevant articles cover national treatment on internal taxation and regulation and technical regulations and standards.

5. Scherer, *Competition Policies*, 75.

6. See "A Bad Design for Parts," *Financial Times*, July 31, 1995, p. 13.

7. For other examples related to high-tech and competition policy, see Sylvia Ostry, "Technology Issues in the International Trading System" (OECD Trade Committee, Paris, September 1995, mimeographed).

8. See Fan Gang, "Incremental Changes and Dual-track Transition: Understanding the Case of China," *Economic Policy*, supplement, December 1994, pp. 100–122, for a useful review of the economics literature comparing the Chinese model with the European experience.

9. Susan L. Shirk, *How China Opened its Door: The Political Success of the PRC's Foreign Trade and Investment Reforms* (Washington, D.C.: Brookings Institution, 1995).

10. While the term "dynamic rent-seeking" is not used, the rationale for incorporating corruption as an integral part of the Chinese growth model is presented in Randall Jones, Robert King, and Michael Klein, "The Chinese Economic Area: Economic Integration Without a Free Trade Agreement" (Economics Department working paper no. 124, OECD, Paris, 1992), 17–18.

11. See, for other examples, James X. Zhen, "The Role of Foreign Direct Investment in Market-oriented Reforms and Economic Development: The Case of China," *Transnational Corporations* 2, no. 3 (December 1993): 121–48.

12. For a comprehensive analysis of the interrelationship between external and internal conditions under differing scenarios, see W. Michalski, R. Miller, B. Stevens, *China in the 21st Century: Long-term Global Implications, an Overview of the Issues* (Paris: OECD, 1996).

13. For a review of many of these proposals, see OECD, "Trade and Competition Policies in the Global Market

Place," *New Dimensions of Market Access in a Globalizing World Economy* (Paris: OECD, 1995), 105–218. See also a comprehensive proposal, to be phased in over seven years, by Scherer, *Competition Policies*, 91–96; on the environment, see for a bibliography of current studies in Richard N. Cooper, *Environmental and Resource Policies for the World Economy* (Washington, D.C.: Brookings Institution, 1995); see also C. Ford Runge, *Freer Trade, Protected Environment* (New York: Council on Foreign Relations, 1994).

14. WTO Negotiating Group on Basic Telecommunications Services: Submission by the United States.